Rick Gekoski, a former senior lecturer in English at the University of Warwick, is now a dealer in rare books and manuscripts, a publisher and the proprietor of a small art gallery in London. An American who came to England in 1966, he has written a critical book on Joseph Conrad, was co-author of *The Bibliography of William Golding*, and has contributed articles and reviews to various magazines and newspapers.

A lifetime sports fan, he has supported Coventry City since 1971. He lives in London and has two children, both of them Coventry supporters.

'Rick Gekoski explains one of the great mysteries in the heart of the British male. His book tells me more about my favourite football team than the thousands of column inches I have ever read on the subject'

Donald Trelford

'The author triumphantly manages to gain a fair degree of insight into the collective psyche of a Premiership club'

Total Football

'Unusually informative . . . It actually tells us things we don't already know about how football clubs are run. *Staying Up* is a richly comic report . . . an intelligent, well-written effort.'

Ian Hamilton, *Sunday Telegraph*

'An engaging and thoughtful outsider account of Premier League life. The tone is personal, permitting insights drawn from Gekoski's fascination with the differences between players' and fan's relationship to their club'

Huw Richards, *The Financial Times*

STAYING UP

A FAN BEHIND THE SCENES
IN THE PREMIERSHIP

RICK GEKOSKI

WARNER BOOKS

A *Warner* Book

First published in Great Britain in 1998
by Little, Brown and Company
This edition published in 1999
by Warner Books

A CIP catalogue record for this book
is available from the British Library.

ISBN 0 7515 2859 5

Typeset by Palimpsest Book Production Limited,
Polmont, Stirlingshire
Printed and bound in Great Britain by
Clays Ltd, St Ives plc.

Warner Books
A Division of
Little, Brown and Company (UK)
Brettenham House
Lancaster Place
London WC2E 7EN

To Bertie
This souvenir of so many happy days together
and to Barbara and Anna
with love

Contents

Foreword

Gordon Strachan was kind enough to read this book before it went off to the printer for hardback publication in 1998. Even after a year of my company in the inner sanctum of Coventry City – observing at practice sessions, on the team coach, during meals at hotels before matches, early in the mornings in his office – he still had little idea of what to expect. The book that finally emerged surprised and somewhat distressed him.

'If I had known that you were going to write this sort of book,' he told me, 'I would never have allowed you access to myself or to the team. I suppose I should have thought about it more. I'm a very private person, and it gets too close.'

'Having said that,' he added, generously and disinterestedly, 'I think it's one of the best books about football ever written. The closest anybody could get to what it's really like. I enjoyed reading it a lot. I just wish it was about some other team.'

I have not altered the text for the paperback edition. Gordon Strachan did ask me to remove one anecdote about Dion Dublin from the original text, which I declined to do. I would certainly have done so had I foreseen the reactions the story would cause. I have allowed it to be reprinted because it seems to me an empty gesture to omit it once it has entered the public domain.

However, I have omitted the Postscript which appeared in the hardback, since the updates to individual careers that it provides becomes less relevant as time passes.

Rick Gekoski
November 1999

Acknowledgements

This book could not have been written without the permission, counsel, enthusiasm and encouragement of Bryan Richardson, chairman of Coventry City Football Club, and I am extremely grateful for his support.

Gordon Strachan, Alex Miller, Garry Pendrey, Jim Blyth, George Dalton and Trevor Peake have borne my presence and constant questioning with good grace, and the Coventry City players have put up with me with remarkable forbearance. Whatever I have learned about football during the course of the year has been largely thanks to them.

Mike McGinnity, John Reason, Graham Hover, Neil Bryson, Mark Jones and Val Wright have been consistently friendly and helpful, as have the following members of staff at Highfield Road and Ryton: Raj Athwal, Lesley Brooks, Michelle Cleaver, Suzanne Crawley, Julie Grimmett, Jenny Poole and Avantika Tailor. Innumerable further members of the staff at Highfield Road have been exceptionally courteous, and I would like to express my appreciation, en bloc, to all of them. I am also grateful for the interest and assistance provided by Geoff Foster, Rob Gurney and Andy Turner. Bertie's gang of pals – Guy Voce, James Pendred, Sam Cleary, Birdie Worthy, Rich

(East Brompton) Allen and Stef Passantino have provided a useful sounding-board throughout the season.

My literary agent, Giles Gordon, has managed, against his inclinations, to develop a genuine interest in Coventry City, which seems to me beyond the call of duty; my publisher, Alan Samson, though an Arsenal supporter, has shown an admirable and disinterested enthusiasm, and I am deeply grateful to both of them. Steve Broome, Adam Dent, Peter Grogan, Jim Irvine, Caroline North, George O'Brien, Anna Shelley, John Simpson and Max Smith read various versions of the text, in part or in its entirety, and the book has profited from their suggestions, corrections, and encouragement.

My major thanks, though, go to my family: to Barbara, for wise counsel, understanding beyond any reasonable expectation and a deft editorial touch; to my daughter Anna, who was writing a book of her own during the same period (and so understood so many of my problems and worries) for her support and sharp critical eye; and to my son (whose real name is Aaron, but whose family nickname is Bertie), who has not only intelligently read along, but been along, and to whom I am profoundly grateful. My sister Ruthie and her husband Roy, and their sons Matthew and Jesse Greenberg, have been a source of constant love and support.

Jonathan Strange has been a remarkable source of information about Coventry City Football Club, as well as an enthusiastic and critical reader of various drafts of this book. He has checked the text lovingly and assiduously for errors. Any that remain are certainly my fault. I am exceptionally indebted to him.

1

Popping the Question

ATKY IN £3m MAC RAID

The reader will be excused if he thinks this is gibberish, an obscure advert for McDonald's, or some sort of impenetrable code. In fact it was a headline in the sports section of the *Sun*, on 10 July 1996. I was rather proud of my ability instantly to understand it, as if I were a member of a cipher-breaking outfit. But my capacity to unravel the mystery was attributable, to be frank, to the fact that I am a Coventry City supporter. When I admit this in company, it is usually greeted with a laugh, or a sneer. Coventry are widely regarded as the barnacles on the hull of the Premiership: clinging to the bottom, ugly, useless, abrasive and impossible to scrape off. In thirty seasons in the top flight, between 1967 and 1997, Coventry have ten times gone into the final game facing the possibility of relegation, and ten times have stayed up. We supporters are a proud lot, if a little defensive, and we live out our seasons in a mixture of irrational hope and reasonable dread.

And here, at last, was a real cause for hope: Ron Atkinson, our manager, had made an attempt at a major signing – Gary McAllister, of Leeds and Scotland. The story read:

Gary McAllister is lined up for a shock £3 million transfer from Leeds to Coventry. Coventry boss Ron Atkinson has agreed to splash out the asking price for Scotland's skipper, even though the player is now 31. The midfield star is due back from holiday this weekend, when Atkinson will aim to persuade him that a switch to Highfield Road can keep his Premiership career flying high. Leeds sounded out clubs about McAllister's availability during Euro '96, until he hinted he felt the time was right for him to move on. And Big Ron made his move while others have hesitated. Arsenal and Rangers have backed off because of the valuation. Sheffield Wednesday boss David Pleat, McAllister's manager at Leicester, remains in the hunt but has yet to offer the money Leeds want. Barcelona boss Bobby Robson has also asked to be kept informed, though even with the wealth of the Spanish giants behind him he may be reluctant to blow £3m on a player of McAllister's age.

Stripped of the amiable bullshit that passes for style in the *Sun*, what this really implied was that those profligate idiots Coventry had made a rash offer for an over-the-hill player who as yet knew nothing about it.

I was still excited. McAllister, who had looked the best player on the pitch in the Euro '96 game between Scotland and England, has that unmistakable attribute of the class athlete, time to play, and what seems a genuine footballing brain. Why Gary McAllister would have wished to come to Coventry is another story. If Big Ron – or more likely assistant manager Gordon Strachan, who had played with McAllister at Leeds – could have assured him, in the words of the *Sun*, that Coventry was the right place to keep his Premiership career 'flying high', then McAllister must be stupider even than your average footballer is reputed to be. You can't fly any lower than Coventry and still be in the Premiership. Indeed, it was the fear (no, historically the likelihood) of sustained low flying at Highfield Road that had recently prevented the possible signing of Crystal Palace's Chris Coleman, who went to Blackburn instead.

And, sure enough, by the evening's Radio 5 *Sports Desk*, reports were that the putative deal was off: McAllister wouldn't be coming to Highfield Road after all. I was disappointed, but not surprised: after all, most football supporters spend the off-season like this, anxiously listening to rumours and gossip, scouring the newspapers for stories about their clubs, calculating how many days are left until the season opens and what needs to be done to strengthen the squad. And for every rumour that turns out to be true, myriads drift away into nothingness, leaving us puzzled as to where they came from, and why. So my capacity to understand the *Sun*'s headline merely seduced me into the illusion of insiderness. I knew nothing, but I was prompted to believe that I was privy to the secrets of the trade.

Where did the story in the *Sun* – which was repeated in more literate form in a number of the more serious papers – come from? Had it been planted by Leeds, to indicate to other possible buyers that there was some club prepared to fork out a large, if not outlandish, sum for the services of a thirty-one-year-old? By Coventry, to reassure fans that the club was indeed trying to make a major signing? By McAllister's agent, to suggest that if you wanted him, you'd better move fast? What was going on?

It's a football supporter's constant cry and lament. Beyond all things we crave reliable information, some sense of the inside workings of our clubs on which we can rely, and which acknowledges that our passionate and committed support of the team is met, in its own way, by the club's commitment to us. We are the children of neglectful parents; even repeated doses of callousness will never overcome our yearning for closeness and trust.

Was it true that McAllister might have come to Coventry?

Were any other signings in the offing? I'd been a passionate supporter of the club since 1971, and a season-ticket
holder for many years, and I didn't have any idea what
the answers were. It is hard to think of any other form
of life in which enthusiasm and exposure produce so
little in the way of knowledge. Even students of that
other deeply impenetrable game, politics, are granted a
clearer and deeper insight into the inside story than are
football supporters. Compared to a football club, the Tory
Party are paragons of open government. What incessantly
irritates me about supporting the Sky Blues is not unique;
it would be reiterated by fans at other clubs. I do not have
the fantasy that while Coventry remain utterly opaque
to me, the supporters at, say, Everton are constantly
aware of the inner workings of their club. They don't
know much either. They're asking, 'What's going on?'
as anxiously and hopelessly as I am.

And we're persistent, we fans are, and we never learn
from the past. The next day I got on the phone and
called, first, the Sky Blues ClubCall number, the hotline
run expressly for the fans, giving rise to the hope, until
you've made the first few calls, that this is where the
inside dope is dished out. But it's all 50p-a-minute stuff,
not unlike those other hotlines ('Strict Madam Will Tame
Bad Boys'), full of teasing innuendo, promising a lot and
delivering nothing, feeding off excitement but leading
only to anticlimax.

ClubCall told me that, yes, there was a rumour about
McAllister – I already knew that – and that perhaps it
was true. Whoever the guy on the other end of the
phone was, he not only talked profitably slowly, he
didn't know anything, either. He was no more use than
any other supporter. He was in the dark, too. In fact,
he'd been in the dark for the whole of the close season.
I called him regularly, and each recording mirrored my
questions, rather than answering them. The ClubCall
guy was worried too: when would Big Ron make his
move? Were any signings on the way? Would the secret

talks that were known to be going on result in transfer activity? His favourite phrase, designed to make me call back, was: 'We'll have to wait and see.' The information not only didn't get me inside, it actually reconfirmed my outsiderness.

I should have known better. I hung up before the recording ended, saving another few 50p's worth of banality and useless information, and called my friend, the violinist Jonathan Strange. A lifetime City supporter who contracted the virus in some peculiar way during a childhood in Dorset, he is now a mainstay of the Coventry City London Supporters Club – all 250 of them – and a knowledgeable student of the history of the club. He can tell you against whom Cyrille Regis scored his first City goal (indeed, the security code on his mobile phone is 'REGIS'), how we did in the Cup in 1964, how many times Tommy Hutchison played for Scotland, how many children Peter Ndlovu fathered in Coventry (and by how many women), which pub Kevin Drinkell used to frequent.

He didn't know anything, either. We discussed where McAllister would have fitted in, who would have been left out, why Macca might have solved some of our problems, and (perhaps) created others – the endless hypotheses that most fans, in their ignorance, have to fall back on. He wanted to know if I could find anything out. I said I'd call Max, and ring him back.

I live, some of the time, in Leamington Spa, to which I moved in 1971, when it might appropriately have been called shabby but genteel. Now it is neither, having grown into a pretty and prosperous, if anodyne, amalgamation of chain stores and wine bars. In this sleepy, unsophisticated setting, my pal Max Smith rather stands out. Holder, with his stepson Guy, of the two season tickets next to my son Bertie and me, Cambridge graduate in English, copywriter and advertising whizz, he spent some time doing promotional work for City under the previous chairman, Peter Robins, and could usually be counted on for something approaching accurate information about the club. I asked him: 'Heard anything from Highfield Road about the McAllister signing? Or anything else?'

'Ah, Ricky,' he replied, 'if only I had.'

I rang Jonathan back with the news.

I don't know what it was about the McAllister incident – perhaps that this was our chance, as a club, to move up a gear, or perhaps, after so many years in the darkness that every fan inhabits, I simply cracked. Like most cracks, this one didn't happen all at once: a little fissure opened, and slowly expanded and widened. I brooded on the incident, even past the time when it all worked out, and McAllister eventually signed for Coventry. Though I was delighted by the news, my problem was unaffected. I cared about Coventry City – a lot, probably too much – and, again and again, I was confronted with the fact that I didn't know much about them. Trying to figure out how the club worked was like trying to understand the principles of locomotion by watching a train pass by.

I wanted two things: first, I wanted to get a look behind the scenes, to be exposed to what really went on, to go everywhere, and to talk to everyone. I wanted to call Gordon Gordon, and for him to call me Rick. Second, and just as important, I wanted to be able to tell everything that I found out to my friends, to everybody. If not right away, at least as soon as possible. What's the sense of being there if you don't get to talk about it?

So I had an interest, and an audience: the perfect set of conditions, you may observe, in which you write a book. Some time in early August, I got on the phone and called Coventry City, and requested a meeting with the chairman, Bryan Richardson.

'What is it regarding, sir?' I was asked by a secretary used to shielding her boss from time-wasters.

'Well,' I said, 'my name is Gekoski, and I am a season-ticket holder. I know Mr Richardson personally' – I had in fact met him once, briefly, at a club function – 'and I have a proposal to put to him.'

'And what would that be, Mr Gekoski?'

'I want to write something about the club, and I need to discuss it directly with Mr Richardson. I only need five minutes with him, if that is possible.'

She didn't sound enthusiastic, but promised that she would speak to him to arrange an appointment and ring me back.

I had anticipated this. Bryan Richardson is well known among supporters for his willingness to respond to questions. If you ring him, he'll ring you back. If you fax, or even e-mail him, he'll fax or even e-mail you back. He not only has very good manners, but a career in marketing and public relations has taught him the importance of the relationship between a business and its customers. Educated at Malvern, Richardson went on to play cricket for Warwickshire, scoring both of his hundreds in one match, against Cambridge University. His brother Peter had opened the batting in thirty-four Tests for England, appearing in one of them with another brother, Derek. In his two years at the helm, Richardson had seemed uncommonly intelligent and approachable for a chairman of a football club. He was the sort of person, I was guessing, who might think it an interesting proposal that a fan be allowed behind the scenes in order to write a book.

Such a thing had never been done before. Even Hunter Davies's excellent book *The Glory Game*, which gives a memorable account of a season with Bill Nicholson's Spurs side of 1971–2, was confined in its focus to the players and manager, because Davies never had access to the administrative side of the club. Football clubs are notoriously secretive places. I presume that if you were a supporter of Manchester United or Spurs, and approached Martin Edwards or Alan Sugar with a request to be given access behind the scenes for a full season, you would be laughed at, if you got any answer at all.

Why should they? Football people keep themselves to themselves, because they are under siege from within and without. The supporters of a club are voracious for

information, acknowledgement, and, above all, contact.
They don't so much want to talk to the players as to touch
them, to imbibe them. And the newspapers, radio and
television have an unassuageable appetite for football
news, trivia, gossip. Because the game, like all games,
is fundamentally simple and intrinsically uninteresting,
it is a constant challenge to the media to find something
striking to say about it, to spice it up a little. Premiership
football, particularly the behaviour both on and off the
pitch of its players and management, is a subject of
constant, and frequently unsympathetic, media attention. We may recall, for instance, the unconscionable
treatment of England manager Graham Taylor, a decent
and competent man, pilloried as a turnip by the *Sun*, and
made to look a fool by a slanted television documentary.
So Richardson, if he was at all typical, was surely going
to say no. The only way in which he was unusual, I
presumed, was that he would say it in person. He lets
people get a foot in his door. That part, at least, was easy
enough: a few days later I was on my way to his office.

Though it is called Highfield Road, the Coventry ground
faces on to Thackhall Street, a depressing inner-city street
with a run-down pub and a rutted car park sprinkled
liberally with bits of debris, old programmes and broken
glass. It is not, as English stadia go, remarkable in this
respect. They are almost all built in depressed parts of
town, surrounded by modest terraced houses, corner
shops, and an air of time having passed them by. A
football ground wouldn't have been built there if it was
prime property. And they are all isolated among their
surroundings. The Highfield Road ground itself is well
kept and prosperous looking, from the inside; but it is
as separate from its environment as it is from its fans.
A yearly sum that wouldn't buy you a one-legged full-
back from Grimsby could easily be spent on landscaping
and paving the car parks and surrounding areas, making a happy contribution to the urban sprawl that is
Coventry.

I have been going up to Highfield Road for some twenty-odd years, but I had never been inside the club offices. Indeed, I'd never really noticed them: they have nothing to do with the supporters. Located through an unassuming entrance a little way past the club shop, the door opened on to a small reception area where Michelle, the pleasantly throaty-voiced woman whom one hears on the club phone line, offered me coffee while I waited for Richardson to see me.

At the back of this modest area was a closed door, which apparently led to the offices of the club's staff and officers. It didn't look intimidating – quite the opposite, it had the shabby homeliness of your average National Health dentist's waiting room – but as I sat waiting for the chairman, I was uncomforted by the ordinariness of it all. I was shortly, after all, to ask him an extraordinary question, and I already felt apprehensive, and not a little silly. It's one thing to fantasise about talking the chairman of a Premiership club into letting you in on all of its secrets, quite another to be about to do it.

The inner sanctum disclosed by the opening of the inner door led to a narrow staircase before which a strategically placed sign read: 'NO SMOKING BY ORDER OF THE CHAIRMAN'. It was curiously intimidating, in a Maoist sort of way. Why didn't it just say 'NO SMOKING'? Would the smoking ban have been ignored unless the chairman said so? The subliminal message was clear: here was a fellow who paid attention to detail, had standards, wasn't afraid to issue orders: a hands-on sort of guy.

At the top of the staircase, an enormously long corridor ran most of the length of the building: that is, almost the length of the football pitch. A makeshift structure, the corridor was narrow, with a sharply sloping ceiling on its right-hand side and a warren of tiny offices along the left, testimony to an ill-designed renovation at some time in the past. It would be easy to knock yourself out if you veered to the right, so the corridor was liberally peppered with signs that read: 'BEWARE PLEASE MIND

YOUR HEAD', which seemed appropriate for a club with Coventry's history of relegation crises.

Bryan Richardson greeted me warmly, and ushered me into his modest office, somewhat larger than the others along the corridor, but without pretensions of any kind. On a table by the door rested an architect's model of the proposed new Coventry stadium; the walls carried photographs of current players, and a small settee, a couple of chairs and a desk completed the furnishing of a space no larger than your average double bedroom. Richardson returned to his desk, which had two phones and a mobile on it, and a lot of apparently unsorted papers, offered me a chair, and said it was nice to see me again. I rather doubt that he remembered me at all, but it had the effect of making me a little less anxious.

'So, what can I do for you?' He made it sound as if he were interested. Poised and well dressed, though without foppishness, he had that indefinable polish that one often observes in people of wealth or celebrity. By polish I do not mean good manners, though that frequently accompanies it, but something more tangible: a kind of glow, as if the rich and famous applied some mysterious ointment (available only to themselves) every morning, and then buffed their faces to a healthy sheen.

I want to talk to you about an idea I have,' I said. 'I have supported this club since the seventies, and I'm starting to get frustrated by watching so much and knowing so little.' He gazed at me with a degree of interest mixed with incomprehension. 'What I mean,' I added, 'is that every football fan is dying to know what it is really like, what's actually going on, yet all we get to see is what happens on the field.'

He considered this for a moment. 'Well,' he said, 'there is the ClubCall line, the match-day programmes, and the articles in the local and national papers. And the fanzines, though they get most things wrong. There's lots of information about.' He sounded like a politician trying to claim for his party the moral authority of open government, while at the same time giving nothing away. And I didn't wish to be fobbed off.

'They all make it worse, not better. They all purvey gossip and rumours, and most of what they say turns out to be either uninteresting or incorrect. Your average supporter ends up in the dark most of the time.'

As I was speaking, the mobile phone rang, and he answered it with an apologetic shrug. A brief and cryptic one-sided conversation ensued, with obscure references to hotels and phone numbers. When he hung up, he explained: 'We're trying to sign a Belgian full-back from Standard Liège, name of Régis Genaux. He's played for Belgium. Good player. But there are three agents involved, and two continental sides want to sign him, so we've got him hidden in a hotel. If we can keep them away from him for another couple of days, he'll sign.'

'Now that,' I said, 'is just the sort of thing I want to know about. I'd like to write a book about the club this coming season, to know about the deals, the comings and goings, all the factors involved. To get to know how a Premiership football club actually works.' As I said this I feared that it was a futile request, but I'd drawn a little hope from the fact that he had been so open about Genaux, as if he had already decided to consider the project. 'I want to know about buying and selling players, how the finances work, to go down to the training ground, travel with the team, talk to the players and Gordon Strachan.'

There, I'd done it. The worst that he could do was to tell me to bugger off. Part of me, to tell the truth, would have been just a little relieved. But he didn't do anything. He sat quite still, listening, letting me make my pitch.

'Let me tell you a little about myself.'

He leaned back to make himself comfortable, sensing that this might take a while.

'By training I'm an academic. I came here from America in the sixties, got a doctorate in English at Oxford, then taught in the English Department at Warwick University for fifteen years. Now I run my own business, dealing in rare books and manuscripts in London, and do some freelance writing. But I'm not a journalist.'

He nodded gently. 'Good,' he said firmly.

'That's part of the point. I want to write about the club from the point of view of the supporters, a sort of fan's eye view. Getting behind the scenes is every fan's dream – whether it's here or somewhere else. I've never written anything like this, although I have written a couple of books.' I decided not to mention that they were about the novelists Joseph Conrad and William Golding. 'And I am trained, as an academic, in habits of analysis, in trying to figure out how things work – whether those things are novels, or even football clubs. And I'm a supporter of the club, so I don't think there is anything to fear.'

I was starting to babble, and as I spoke I was aware of how foolish all this must be sounding to him. At one point he put his hands quietly in his lap, under the desk, and I had the distinct, if paranoid, impression that he was ringing some sort of hidden alarm, and that three orange-shirted stewards would shortly come in and escort me from the ground (By Order of the Chairman).

Not at all. 'It's funny you should ask,' he said, 'because you're the second person this week who has come in with a request to write a book about the club. And I've just been approached by the BBC with a proposal to do a six-part documentary about Coventry City. I think that they see us as an ambitious club, in a process of transition, at what is a very interesting time in the development of the game as a whole.'

'Are you going to let them do it?'

'I don't think,' he said wryly, 'that a six-part series on what a nice club Coventry City is would make good television. But a book is certainly a good idea. I came to all this relatively late in my career, and it's a fascinating business. I find it more so all the time, and I don't have any doubt that people would be interested to read an account of it. The other chap who wants to do a book is someone who works for Sky Sports – not one of the presenters – very knowledgeable about football, and he's also a supporter.'

That was that, then. This other guy – I hated him already – would certainly know more about football than I do, and had an inside track. The disappointment must have registered on my face, because Richardson quickly added: 'Let me think it over, and I'll get back to you. There's something to be said for such a book being written by an outsider.'

He stood up and we shook hands. 'I'll be in touch,' he said. And a few weeks later, in mid-August, he was. It was too late, he felt, to do the book for the forthcoming season – he hoped I didn't mind – but if I could pop into his office, perhaps we could discuss doing it for the 1997–8 season?

And that was it. 'There's a great story here,' he said. 'Go ahead and do it next season. I like the idea of the book being written by someone outside the game: you're a university lecturer, and an American. I'll introduce you to the people up here at the club, and to Gordon.' (Gordon!) 'Go everywhere, talk to everybody, you'll find it fascinating.'

I was surprised, and delighted, but tried not to gush. 'Thank you,' I said. 'It's very open-minded of you.'

'We've got nothing to hide. But you'll be surprised by what you learn. It's an amazingly emotional business.'

'It must be,' I said. 'The supporters can see that. So many of the games are like an emotional rollercoaster. Sometimes the whole season is.'

'Yes, sure. But I mean something more than that, something more complicated.'

'What's that?' I asked.

He smiled. 'You'll see.'

2

Big Ron and I at Oxford

When I came to England from America in September 1966, to do postgraduate work in English at Oxford, the question I was most frequently asked by new college acquaintances was, 'What did you think of the World Cup, then?' The first time the question was put, in the Merton College bar during a tea that consisted, amazingly enough, of cucumber sandwiches, it was delivered with a kind of hearty pride which suggested to me that, obscure as the question was, something momentous was up. But there was no way to fake an answer, so I came clean: 'What's the World Cup?'

My new companion, a remarkably well-scrubbed public schoolboy recently arrived to read History, looked at me with astonishment. 'You're taking the piss,' he said.

'Sorry?' I said. (I'd already learned that English people are constantly saying 'sorry'. You walked down any crowded street brushing imperceptibly into people to a constant stream of sorries.) But taking his piss seemed even more alarmingly obscure than the previous reference to cups.

'The World Cup,' he reiterated crossly. 'What did you think in America?'

Of course it was obvious to any Englishman at the time

that Americans are a provincial lot – instantly recognisable by their twangy accents and button-down collars,
without the faintest gastronomic or intellectual sophistication, indefatigable observers of the historic and the
quaint: earnest, innocent, gullible. I had never felt so
incessantly patronised, though it was never clear what
I was being patronised for. It was only just beginning
to occur to me that part of the problem was linguistic:
we were all, erroneously, united in the belief that we
were speaking the same language. And the resultant
confusions were getting tiresome.

'OK,' I said, 'I give up. What's the World Cup?'

'Football,' he said slowly, already doubting my powers
of either hearing or of intellection, 'the world championship of football. Which England – this country, you know
– has just won.'

It was news to me. I was an avid reader of the sports
pages of the *New York Times*, and not a single allusion to
this alleged cup – not a story, not a mention, not even
a list of scores of the alleged games – had come to my
attention. As far as America was concerned, there was
no such thing as this so-called World Cup. And yet I
knew plenty about football, a brutal but compellingly
complex game, played by improbably gigantic men. The
great Jim Brown, full-back of the Cleveland Browns – still
the greatest player I've seen – weighed 235 pounds and
could run the 100-yard dash in 9.6 seconds. Not even
Sam Huff, ferocious centre linebacker of my team, the
New York Giants, could stop him unaided. I sure never
saw anybody like him in England.

I followed football, so how come I didn't know that
English people played it? In fact, I didn't even know
that a country could play it – there was no American
football team. Thinking fast, I decided that the likelihood was that other countries played some diminished
and inferior version of the game, which related to the
Giants in the same way that Little League baseball might
relate to the Yankees. Presumably this was fun for them,

and a cause for pride. I took a correspondingly benign attitude.

'That's nice,' I said. 'I'm glad for you. And I didn't even know that you people played football.'

My new friend mistook this for an ironic allusion (as I later learned) to the remarkable World Cup defeat once inflicted on the England team by those unregarded minnows, those pipsqueaks, the Americans. Of course I didn't know this, just as I didn't know about irony, which flourished at Oxford but was as yet undiscovered in America.

'1950 was a fluke,' he said, 'and it couldn't happen again.' At this point, a number of other undergraduates, having previously confined themselves to smirking on the edges of the conversation, joined in. 'Anyway,' said one large fellow who, I was told, rowed boats, 'we hit the post ever so many times. If the strikers had done their job, we'd have stuffed you. It was a one-off.'

It was impossible to respond; I'd never encountered, in the space of a few seconds, so many implausibilities. A man who thought that a whole year of our century was a fluke? A group of taxidermists who had gone on strike after attacking a Post (presumably a Post *office*? Not, I hoped, a Post *man*?). A one-off what? The old block? The wrist?

It turned out, of course, that they were talking about soccer. Why didn't they say so? Of course I'd heard of soccer: that game where you dribbled. It was what you played at school if you weren't good at games – it made the kids who were scrawny and couldn't catch or hit a ball feel better, because we were all newcomers to it, and anyway it didn't take any skill. We played it – its introduction a testimony to the sporting sophistication of Mr Lange, our PE teacher – on the baseball field, where, hoping the ball didn't hit a rock or bounce oddly off the pitcher's mound, we could use the football goalposts on the sides of the diamond. Tackles were unknown, and would in any case have resulted in serious injury from the rocks. Passing was unknown, too: you got hold of the ball, by chasing it until you could establish control, then you set out for goal, and toe-poked a shot. Defenders, so-called, tried to stop you by sticking their foot out – always the right one, so all you had to do was veer to their left. It seemed a pretty simple game, and it was surprising that my new friends were so excited about it.

In time, though, so was I. Feeling deprived of proper live sport, I decided to see what England had to offer: there was rugby, which was obviously inferior to real football, cricket, which was silly, and utterly impene-trable, and soccer. I took to watching *Match of the Day* – those Manchester Uniteds looked good – and it turned out there was even a local team to support, called Oxford United (clearly no relation to those Manchesters). The Manor Ground in Headington had a kind of rustic charm, like an Irish hovel, but unlike at Yankee Stadium you at least got close to the play. It wasn't much of a team, languishing somewhere in the middle of the Second Divi-sion, but it had some useful players. A curly-haired midfielder called Graham Atkinson was fast, displayed the occasional flashes of skill, and tended to account for most of the creative moves.

His brother, Ron, on the other hand, was a hope-less plodder, lumbering about trying to win the ball, and then rather inclined to keep it too long. He was large and full-hearted, appeared to know, but not to respect, his limitations, and was admired, if ironically, by the crowd. Whenever he got the ball cries of his nick-name would ring from the terraces: 'Tank!' we'd scream, 'Tank!' He seemed, somehow, to personify the whole team: modest of talent, with ideas above his station, unlikely to go very far. It was with some surprise that I later learned he'd gone into management at Kettering Town, and then, appropriately enough, with Cambridge United, themselves a team of no special merit, and pre-sumably a fitting, and final, home for the Ron Atkinsons of this world.

But Cambridge did well: promoted for the first time to the Third Division, they were on their way to promotion again when Ron departed to become manager of West Brom, and then, amazingly, of Manchester United. No longer Tank, but Big Ron, garrulous, affable, greatly successful, decked out in fancy suits and virtually plated in gold, always good for another drink or an amusing quote. He was famous for his training-ground routines, in which, having screamed for the ball, he would take on all defenders, pretending to be Maradona or Pelé, to the immense amusement of his players, who, if they hadn't seen him in his days as a player, could easily enough guess his standard. When he was fired from United in 1986 (despite their having won the Cup in 1983 and 1985), for failing to do what all of their post-Busby managers had failed to do (win the League), he drifted back to West Brom. There followed a few months at Atlético Madrid, and just over two years at Sheffield Wednesday, after which, in June 1991, he took over at Coventry's most-hated rivals, Aston Villa. (A favourite chant at Highfield Road – 'Shit on the Villa! We're gonna shit on the Villa!' – has no equivalent at Villa Park, where fans, if they think of Coventry at all, merely regard them as an easy six points a season.)

Having acquired a taste for the game at Oxford, and having got my lectureship in English at Warwick University in 1971, I became a Coventry City supporter – for football allegiances, like those of love, are often prompted by nothing more profound than local availability. As we marry girls from school or the office, and have affairs with our neighbours' spouses, so too we often engage with the nearest football team to hand. I ended up in Coventry, and have supported them ever since – save for a period after the sale of star striker Ian Wallace to Nottingham Forest in 1980, when I boycotted the club.

I stayed away for some six years, until my friend Jonathan Strange convinced me that it was time to introduce Bertie, then six years old, to the pleasures of football.

City, he said, had a good side, and he anticipated a Cup run (in the 1986–7 season); anyway, he thought it inhuman to have a young son and not take him to football matches. Jonathan and I, curiously, had known each other for two years before recognising that we both supported Coventry. He was a London musician and I an antiquarian bookseller: neither of us likely Sky Blues fans.

My memories of supporting Coventry were not unambiguously happy ones, but Jonathan urged me to see the club in an historical context. In years gone by promotion hopes had been destroyed by the war, as had so much else in Coventry. In the sixties, with the new cathedral and a prospering economy, the football club, under the dynamic leadership of Derrick Robins as chairman and Jimmy Hill as manager, helped give expression to a new optimism in the city. In the season after promotion in 1967, home League gates averaged nearly 35,000. Under Noel Cantwell, having struggled to avoid relegation in their first two seasons, City qualified for Europe, and had reason to hope to consolidate as one of the larger and more successful clubs at the top of the game.

But the Coventry dream diminished: for successive boards, it became a priority merely to survive in the First Division and to balance the books, in tacit acknowledgement of the fact that the Coventry Cities of this world do not belong, really, with the Arsenals and Manchester Uniteds. In those days, if no longer in these, it was possible by dint of imagination, hard work, faith, and charismatic leadership to build a team out of virtually nothing, and to win. Bobby Robson, like Alf Ramsey many years before, did it at Ipswich, and the incomparable Brian Clough and Peter Taylor made silk purses out of not one, but two sows' ears at Derby County and Nottingham Forest.

But Coventry, who once came close to appointing Clough as manager, and looked as if they might make it onto the big stage, gradually diminished in ambition and began to pride themselves on their longevity rather than on their achievements. After Arsenal, Everton and Liverpool,

Coventry are the longest continuous members of what is now, regrettably, called the Premiership. We have watched Manchester United go down, and Newcastle, Villa, Chelsea and Spurs. Improbably, in one year after another, Coventry, certain to be relegated, have pulled back from the brink of the abyss.

It is an unparalleled case of the survival of the unfittest. And if Coventry fans are used to seeing Darwin turned upside down, that is because it is how they have been trained to look at things. On viewing a new season's schedule, while your average supporter first looks at the opening fixtures, hoping his team will get off to a good start, the Coventry fan invariably looks at the last few, calculating in advance how hard the run-in will be, and what the chances are, yet again, of staying up.

The 1994–5 season, under Phil Neal, was, in this respect, typical. The Sky Blues had looked good intermittently, with an attack led by Peter Ndlovu and Dion Dublin (recently acquired from Manchester United for just under £2 million), but the team slowly drifted down the League table as the season progressed. If it came as no surprise when Neal was sacked after twenty-eight League games, it was astonishing when his successor arrived in the person of Ron Atkinson, recently fired by Doug Ellis at the Villa, a team beginning to fear relegation trouble. Big Ron at Coventry City? What would he want to do that for? Did he have an unconscious desire to return to his humble origins? And how could we afford him? What was going on?

From a supporter's point of view, it looked like a stab at the big time. Yes, we'd won the Cup in 1987, but as an unfashionable outsider. Indeed, until the arrival of Big Ron, it was a choice between Coventry, Southampton and Wimbledon as to which was the least regarded (and most neglected in the media) regular member of the top division. Year after year there was no disputing the fact that, when the Sky Blues came to your town, attendances fell; when they were featured on *Match of the Day* or Sky

Sports, viewing figures declined perceptibly. And since Atkinson's arrival you could almost graph a quickening of interest: attendances at Highfield Road went up by an average of 4,000, away fixtures were better attended by City supporters, and the press seemed to pay more attention.

And the magic worked, just: after the not unexpected burst of good results that greets virtually any change of manager, as players fight extra hard to make a favourable impression, and a surge of adrenaline shoots through the club, Coventry went into something of a decline, but ensured survival with a 3–1 away win at Spurs. It was only the penultimate game of the season, and we were already safe. All thoughts turned to next year: what would Big Ron have up his sleeve? He'd already brought over his captain from Aston Villa, Kevin Richardson, and signed a new left back, David Burrows, whom Big Ron characteristically announced should be playing for England. He soon recruited Gordon Strachan from Leeds as heir apparent (and an occasional if reluctant player still, at the age of thirty-eight). Given his reputation as a wheeler-dealer, surely the fun was only just beginning?

Within the next year, Coventry, those legendary misers and skinflints, the club that seemed more interested in its standing at the bank than in the League, seemed to have lots of money. Where did it come from? And at this point, of course – the very point at which the fan is most engaged, because money means good new players, and such players bring better results – the view from the terraces is most obscured. Something was happening. Was Richardson richer than we thought? Did he discover a bank manager with more generosity than (footballing) sense? Had he attracted someone new and rich – and presumably foolish – on to the board, somebody whose ego would be flattered by being at the centre of a Premiership club, and who could afford a few millions to indulge himself? It must have been the case, surely, that a compulsive spender like Big Ron wouldn't have come without the assurance of funds to buy players.

Wherever the money came from, in the close season Big Ron was spending it. The Brazilian Isaias, scorer of two goals at Highbury to put Arsenal out of the European Cup in 1991, was signed from Benfica for £500,000; winger John Salako arrived from Crystal Palace for £1.5 million; Paul Williams, who can play in both defence and midfield, came from Derby County for £1 million; Paul Telfer, a useful midfield player, moved for £1.15 million from Luton. In the space of a few months, Atkinson had practically created a new team: the only players from the side taken over from Phil Neal who were still likely to command a place were striker Dion Dublin, keeper Steve Ogrizovic, right back Brian Borrows and the Zimbabwean winger Peter Ndlovu: a distinctly useful quartet.

And so the 1995–6 season started with an unprecedented wave of optimism: the new East Stand, with its swish members' clubs, had attracted a lot of new revenue, season-ticket sales were booming, and a team widely perceived as having potential, with pace in the forwards, and a solid midfield, was confident of a bright start. That the defence looked pedestrian was something of a worry, but Big Ron's teams traditionally looked better going forward. It was certainly the most exciting squad put together at Coventry since the Cup-winning team; indeed, man for man, it looked even better.

Though early results were indifferent, some exciting football was being played, and during a home fixture against Manchester City I kept jumping up and shouting 'Olé!' – an exclamation previously never heard at Highfield Road, which unsurprisingly failed to catch on – as Isaias initiated one sweet passing movement after another. Or perhaps conducted is the more appropriate verb, as he was so unfit he didn't actually move about much. At one point, in early mid-season, we beat Blackburn 5–0 in a ravishing display of creative football, and no one could have been confused as to which team had genuine class.

'Just a one-off,' sniffed a Blackburn supporter to me on the way out. But we at Highfield Road were convinced that all of the other games had been the one-offs. This was the real City.

We were wrong. Despite repeated infusions of cash and good players – centre-back Richard Shaw from Crystal Palace for £1 million; striker Noel Whelan from Leeds for £2 million; Liam Daish, to shore up the centre of the defence, from Birmingham for £1.5 million; Eoin Jess, the Aberdeen forward, for £1.6 million – the squad, the best ever assembled at Coventry, resolutely failed to become a team. Defensively, aside from the reliable Oggy, the side was a shambles (until the last six games, in which only one goal was conceded). As soon as Whelan arrived, scoring regularly, Dublin seemed to get the sulks, and ceased scoring at all. Typically, we went into the last game of the season needing a result, and typically, we got it. Manchester City, QPR and Bolton were relegated.

Coventry had spent well over £13 million since Ron's appointment, most of it on players of quality, and had won only eight games during the season – not only the (equal) lowest number of wins in the Premiership, but Coventry's worst since joining the Football League in 1919. In such circumstances, there are often cries from the stands for the resignation of the board or the sacking of the manager, so it was interesting to observe what happened before the start of the final game against Leeds at Highfield Road. At about five minutes to three, Bryan Richardson came on to the field (bravely, you might have thought), to wave to the fans. And he was given, from all parts of the ground, a standing ovation. And when Big Ron came out with the team two minutes later, he was too. Nor did it occur to most of the crowd, as they applauded, how curious this was. After all, weren't they the best chairman and the best manager we'd ever had?

We had stayed up, just. But it had been a dreadful season, and all of us in the crowd had our theories as to why. Theories are what you have in the absence of facts.

With the foolish optimism that can occasionally affect even the most seasoned of City supporters, I had believed things would come right in 1996–7, as the new players finally turned into a team. And McAllister had joined us: the final piece of the jigsaw. I was wrong. The season started disastrously, and went downhill from there. A pre-season friendly with Benfica at Highfield Road was lost by 7–2, and had it been a boxing match the referee would have stopped it. A few days later, the opening-day match was lost 3–0 at home to a Nottingham Forest side that was eventually to finish bottom of the League. Coventry looked hopeless, tactically at sea, lacking in confidence: doomed.

It was hard to foresee anything other than relegation. It had to come some time, and this, surely, was going to be the year. After twelve games, from which only 9 points had been laboriously gathered, something not entirely unexpected, but still surprising, happened: Big Ron resigned. On 5 November, looking grim, he gave a press conference in which he announced that he would be moving up to become director of football, and that Gordon would be manager henceforth.

Although this transition had, in any case, been planned for the close of the season, Ron was clearly deeply unhappy about it, and declined entirely to give the reasons for his resignation. It was widely rumoured that he had been sacked, but both he and the chairman denied it, without explanation. They had just decided, they both maintained, that it would be wise to push the date of Ron's move upstairs forward a little.

A lot of us reckoned they'd got rid of the wrong man. Not that we knew a lot about it, but one of the stewards had heard that the players found Gordon's methods abrasive. (Not that he knew a lot about it, either.) After gathering only one point from the first four games, results picked up under Strachan, particularly in a marvellous December run in which the team won four consecutive games, and Strachan was named Manager of the Month. Inexorably, though, the side began to slip back towards the bottom three. The November signing of striker Darren Huckerby (from Newcastle for £1 million), to give added weight to the attack, and the addition of central defender Gary Breen for £2.5 million from Birmingham, did little to halt the slide. Results failed to improve and the team went into the final fixture of the season needing a win (and for Middlesbrough and Sunderland to fail to win their away matches) to ensure survival. Fortunately, that final game was to be away at Spurs: Coventry play better at White Hart Lane than Tottenham do.

In an unbearably tense atmosphere, with Gary McAllister leading the side superbly, Coventry went ahead 2–0, and after Spurs got one back, spent the last fifteen minutes defending frantically, at one point keeping Spurs out only by the width (pretty wide, to be fair) of Oggy's right foot. The game had kicked off fifteen minutes late, so once we knew that neither Sunderland nor Middlesbrough had won, all the team had to do was protect their lead. It was impossible to watch, or to breathe. The crowd whistled longingly for the ref to end it all. At the final whistle, Strachan rushed over to hug McAllister, who collapsed in his arms, weeping. (Recovering, a few minutes later, McAllister gave his shirt to one of the disabled children in the crowd.) Richardson later observed, wearily but accurately, that 'some people will go through their whole lives without experiencing the sort of excitement we did at the end of last season'. Lucky them.

At Liverpool, they sing 'You'll Never Walk Alone', and have hope in their hearts. They can afford to. But for the Sky Blues supporter, there is only one song that really matters, and it rang round White Hart Lane at the close of play:

Staying up! Staying up!
City are staying up!

thunderously allied to the chant:

> We are Premier League!
> Yes, we are Premier League!

Not much of a boast, that: like getting up in the morning and rejoicing merely because you are still alive, though I suppose that it is theologically proper that we should thank God for our continued survival. Consider the alternative to still being alive. Worse still, consider the alternative to Staying Up: Going Down. If the grave is no happy prospect, one is presumably at peace there. Who could be at peace at an away fixture at Tranmere or Crewe? 'I am a Premiership player,' said Oggy. 'I'm not sure how I would have coped.'

At the start of the game, William Hill were offering 9–1 on that Coventry would go down. But I was feeling curiously confident: this was the sort of position that we are good at. Now, any philosopher will tell you that it is an unsafe assumption that the future will resemble the past – that there is no logical necessity for Coventry City to stay up, or indeed for the sun to rise tomorrow. But I've never met a philosopher who would bet that it won't. So I bet £20 (at a miserly 5–1) that Coventry would do it. We always do. After the game I pocketed my £100 and set off to spend it, in the exultant company of Jonathan Strange and my sixteen-year-old son Bertie, who, I was determined, ought to develop a taste for champagne. We'd done it again.

Outside the Premiership, there are many clubs, seeking to emulate former glories, who have reason to look a little jealously and disapprovingly at Coventry City, who, having taken eighty-four years to reach the big time, have so often seemed content merely to hang on to their top-flight status. Implicit in this attitude is the belief that Coventry are parvenus, moving in fancier company than they really deserve.

Yet people ought to admire the capacity to thrive in a

situation that is challenging, and a little above one's perceived station. So why the animus against Coventry? Is there not something quintessentially English in this prejudice against those who, defying the odds, make something of themselves? In America, the triumph of the underdog is a triumph for the common man; in England almost everybody rather resents those who rise above their station. 'Who does he think he is?' they say knowingly. 'I knew his family.'

That's how Coventry are regularly treated in the media. A nice example occurred on 13 February 1995, in a match report on the 2–0 away win at Crystal Palace, by Jasper Rees in the *Daily Telegraph*, which began:

> What, ultimately, is the point of Coventry City? . . . In 28 seasons they have failed to imprint themselves in the nation's consciousness, let alone its affections . . . No one even notices them for most of the calendar, but by an odd coincidence, you vaguely begin to notice them around Valentine's Day, when they begin their annual worm-like wriggle away from danger.

Similar things are said all the time about Coventry. A writer in *The Times* once began his match report with the line: 'Coventry City, like the poor, are always with us,' which, if sardonic, at least had some lurking respect. But the *Telegraph* piece had the facetiousness without the admiration, and it infuriated Bryan Richardson. He wrote immediately to the sports editor of the *Telegraph*, and to Jasper Rees himself. When he got no reply to his complaints, he made a statement to the *Coventry Evening Telegraph*:

> There is this attitude about Coventry City and it makes me bloody angry . . . I don't know where the writer comes from . . . They were facetious remarks.

I can think of 85 other clubs who have a less consist-
ent record than ours . . . People should be proud of
what we've done.

Richardson's was neither the only complaint sent to
Jasper Rees, nor the mildest. One Coventry City supporter, whose letter to the *Telegraph*'s sports editor also
went unanswered, found a different way to express the
fact that he, too, was 'bloody angry'. Cutting Rees's article
neatly from the *Telegraph*, he sparingly wiped his bottom
with it, sealed the besmirched paper in a plastic folder,
and sent it to the journalist with an affixed note which
read: 'What, ultimately, is the point of Jasper Rees?'

Now, I don't know Jasper Rees, but, as it happens, I do
know his wife Jenny, who writes for the London *Evening
Standard*. Some time later she told me that Jasper had
received 'an utterly disgusting' response to his Coventry
piece, and was so upset and revolted that he quit sports-
writing entirely. He has continued to write, intelligently,
about the arts.

I made no response to this, because it put me in rather
a difficult position. I knew who wrote the shit-smeared
riposte. When I reported to its author the story of Rees's
response to his missive, expecting him to be a little contrite, he just smiled and said, 'Good.'

As I walked arm-in-arm with Bertie to buy our bottles
of champagne, I felt proud that we supported Coventry
City. The club and its players are good models for him
– not too successful, and only likely to stay up by dint
of toughness and hard work, and a little luck. Professional sport may be all about winning, but life isn't.
Most of us lose, most of the time – which partially
explains, I suppose, why so many folk choose to support
winning teams, even when they aren't their local ones.
Their children grow up wanting to be like Ryan Giggs. I
rather regret this: it is not merely absurd, but positively
wicked, for a society to promote top-class sportsmen as
role models.

Americans are particularly keen on this: a whole generation of American children – however unco-ordinated, short, ugly, and ordinary – have been raised to want to be like Michael Jordan. Even the girls. Can you imagine anything more likely to lead to a life of disappointment? In the old days, all a kid wanted, when he grew up, was to become the President, which (if you weren't black, a woman or a Jew) was at least possible if you had a little luck, and hyperactively cultivated the qualities of ambition, hard work and veniality. It wasn't easygoing, and not a lot of people managed it, but at least you didn't have to be as tall as a giraffe, as fast as a gazelle, able to jump four feet in the air and hang there magically, fake three ways, and nail a 20 ft jump shot.

In this sense Michael Jordan, like the Chicago Bulls – like Manchester United – is bad for you. But you might base a life on what you learned by watching the Sky Blues. A life informed by realism and gratitude, in which you win occasionally and struggle most of the time; in which achieving the goal of holding on to what you've got, of simply staying up, will be something for which to feel grateful. Anything more than that is a treat, not an entitlement.

3

Buying and Selling

They take a lot out of you, these annual fights to escape relegation, and you need the summer to recuperate. Nobody supports Coventry City because it's fun. Max Smith heads off for Edgbaston, where he gets to watch a successful side in a relatively peaceful setting, and let his blood pressure come down; Jonathan Strange is often found at Lord's, watching cricket benignly; I head for the golf course, with an occasional stop-off at my office to help keep staff morale high.

Encountering Bryan Richardson again, a couple of months after the climactic win at White Hart Lane, I thought I could still perceive a look of relief on his face. He was still the chairman of a Premiership football team. There was, I suspect, some relief on mine as well. Compared to my last anxious visit to his office, the atmosphere this time was friendly and personal, and he greeted me in a tone that acknowledged that I was to have, now, some role in his life, and in that of the club. Having agreed to sanction the project, he was immediately frank and engaged: if he decided to do something, I could see, he would do it wholeheartedly.

He'd been working hard. Richardson hadn't had a holiday in several years, since that period to which his wife refers as BCCFC (the 'B' stands for Before): he is that relatively new phenomenon, the full-time chairman, and the close season is one of his busiest times of the year. We had stayed up only in the last game, and the sustained uncertainty, he observed, meant that it was virtually impossible to plan for the 1997-8 season: 'In the morning we didn't know: first the odds were one way, then the other. So you're looking at a totally different scenario, and all of a sudden your ability to hold on to players, or to attract players, is totally different. There's no doubt at all that we would not have got two or three of the players that we've signed if we had been in the First Division. And one or two of them we already have might have said, "I don't want to play in the First Division, even though I am contracted to play in the First Division." And, rightly or wrongly, I'd say: you've got us in the fucking First Division, you can get us out of it.'

He joined the club, under then chairman Peter Robins, in 1991, and is still shaking his head in astonishment at how enormously, and how quickly, things have changed. 'The week I arrived, our bank [Lloyds] bounced a cheque for £20 we'd written to get a fence mended. The situation was dire. When I went to see the bank manager, in the hope that we could arrange some new terms, the club didn't even have a cashflow analysis to give him. The figures were done on the proverbial back of an envelope, and even they were wrong. So the major thing we had to do was get the right financing in shape, and that meant a lot of changes: in the boardroom, officers of the club, with the banks. It was a tough period.'

What Coventry were experiencing, of course, was being duplicated throughout the football world: the swift transition from a club culture to a new, harsher business climate. Most football clubs had been cosy venues in which local people found jobs, local businessmen found places on the board and for which local banks and building societies did the financing. They were not public companies, and thus were often the playthings of their owners.

But no one could have predicted, or planned, for the effects of the influx of new money from Sky Television, and the European Court's Bosman ruling, which would lead to players being able to transfer between clubs in the European Union, without a fee, once they were out of contract. Since no transfer fee would be involved in these cases, it followed that the money previously spent on buying players would increasingly go towards paying them. ('I don't really mind that,' said Richardson, 'because in some ways it makes financial planning easier: I can just tell the manager how much he can have in salaries, and go forward from there. Whereas if you have to find capital for transfer fees it can be more difficult.') Further, under the new EU arrangements, players with EU citizenship would soon no longer need work permits, and no limits could be imposed on how many such players a British team could sign, or field.

All this occurred within a few years: there was a lot of new money about, and a lot of desirable players were now available. And the people in charge of the clubs were, in a great many cases, ill equipped to respond to the change. 'I think,' said Coventry director of sales and marketing, Mark Jones, 'that football people were used to a club atmosphere, and only felt comfortable in it – many of them are still like that – and they found it hard to adapt to modern business practices.' All of a sudden Coventry – which seems in retrospect to have been like a cottage industry, with an income of £3 million a year in 1991, and a team in which the highest-paid player was David Speedie on £1,200 a week – was now a decent-sized business. Five years later, the club had a turnover of £15 million, a number of players on long-term contracts at substantial salaries – and one (Gary McAllister) widely reported to be on £15,000 a week – with plans well advanced to build a new stadium and have a share flotation some time round the turn of the century.

'I remember,' said club secretary Graham Hover, shaking his head wryly, 'the day we had our first overdraft of

£1 million, and how nervous it made me. And that was only a few years ago. Now we owe something like £20 million. I'm still nervous, but I've got used to it, and we have the situation under control.' General manager Neil Bryson agreed: 'The thing is that Bryan is so optimistic that Graham and I have to try to rein him in occasionally. But it's almost impossible: he just says "Let's have a go!" And that's what we're doing. It's very exciting, but . . .'

The problem, of course, is that increased revenues are in danger of being used up on increased costs: the new wage bill, for instance, now accounted for 57 per cent of all expenditure, which, Richardson said, 'is too high. The problem is you're fighting just to keep up with the game, and you have to find a way to get ahead of it, and generate new revenue. Look at Manchester United – they only pay a small percentage of their income on salaries [26 percent], the smallest in the Premiership, because their other income is so high. And that's what we have to do – not that we can be like Manchester United, but we have to find new or alternative means of raising money, and keep income rising ahead of wages. We're now achieving this.'

It is easier for a football club to get a decent overdraft these days, but it has been Richardson's particular genius to find new sources of revenue to fund the purchase of players. These have come in the form of long-term loans from a few wealthy backers whom Richardson was able to introduce, the first of whom, Derek Higgs, put up £2.5 million from a family trust, on advantageous terms, to help fund the acquisitions of players. But the major financial input, from local Labour MP Geoffrey Robinson, a long-time supporter of the club and a man of substantial means, came out of the blue. 'About eighteen months ago,' said Richardson, 'Graham Hover got an unexpected phone call from Geoffrey, who said he would like to help.' The offer consisted of a long-term loan of a first tranche of money – some £5 million – to help purchase players, with another such sum on offer if necessary.

The signings of both Noel Whelan and Gary McAllister were thus made possible, though it took some time to work out the legal implications: 'Cost us £50,000, just in lawyer's fees,' said Richardson. 'The problem was that if a football club goes bankrupt, the contracts of the players, which guarantee the loan, revert to the PFA, so we had to find a way to safeguard the investments of our backers. We've done that now, and it has given us the money to strengthen the squad in ways we couldn't have dreamed of only a couple of years ago.'

Richardson took over the club from Peter Robins in 1994, and has adapted swiftly to the new trading conditions, though they are not always congenial to him. 'The major problem is that nobody minds paying big money to the really good player – if you want to have Sinatra at your birthday party you'll have to pay a million dollars to get him to sing, because he's the best. But some other singer will ask half a million dollars, and he should really only get five thousand. The really good players deserve what they get: they're the ones who put bums on seats, and win you matches. But people are determining how good they are not by how much they can perform, but how much they earn: an ordinary player who is paid too much will think he's fucking good, because it's a money system of quality, not a quality system of quality.'

You can't resist the process, and Richardson has reconciled himself to paying three times as much money to ordinary players as star ones were getting only a few years ago. But, he feels, if there are new rewards, there should be new responsibilities. This attitude was being brought to bear at Coventry for the first time in the 1997–8 contracts. 'We will,' said Richardson, 'be going on to a system based more on incentives and performance-related payments. There's no sense paying out huge salaries to a team that gets relegated. Perhaps we might give an extra £250,000 to the players for every position they achieve ahead of a set target – so that I can imagine that if they finished, say tenth, they would get an extra million plus.'

This new system of bonuses is unprecedented in the Premiership, according to Graham Hover, who has been at Highfield Road for fourteen years, and is an immense source of information about the club. Possessed of an engaging grin, he reminds one a little of Tom Hanks, and is the conduit for most club business. According to Hover, the new contract was first presented to the players in May, when Oggy, Gary McAllister and Dion, the senior players, were invited to the chairman's office to meet him and Hover. The new system of bonuses was explained to them, and they then left the meeting to present the package to the rest of the players. There was, said Hover, some feeling among the rest that they would have preferred the usual game-by-game bonus structure, but the principle was accepted by most. 'There was some debate about it all,' Oggy was later to tell me, 'but it doesn't actually come to that big a difference financially, and it wasn't worth fighting about. Anyway, the principle seems fair.'

The new agreement now ensconced, most of the team quickly agreed contracts, which is an essential safeguard to their value. Once they are free agents, under the Bosman ruling, players can go abroad without any transfer fee – an arrangement that Richardson believes will pertain between English teams (perhaps with the exception of players under the age of twenty-four) by 1999. David Burrows was late signing his contract, as was midfield player Willie Boland, but only Kevin Richardson failed to do so at all. 'I don't have any complaint with the gaffer,' he told me, 'but I want to be in the first team, and Gordon has told me that he can't guarantee it.' Though the chairman respected Kevin greatly – 'I thought he was magnificent in a lot of games last year, but he isn't the sort of player who can direct and change the course of a game' – he accepted that he, like Brian

Borrows (who was not offered a new contract), was likely to leave.

It is Gordon Strachan's job to decide who he wants to sign, and who will be extraneous; Richardson makes the financial decisions about what can be afforded. And after the heavy spending of the past two years, money was tight, though Richardson said that there was still cash in the kitty 'for the right players'. In June he was negotiating for two players in essential positions: a goalkeeper and a midfield player. Steve Ogrizovic had had yet another excellent season in goal, but he was almost forty now, and his back-up, the Australian John Filan – 'not quite good enough, we thought' – was soon to be sold to Blackburn for £750,000. So Richardson was delighted with the signing of Magnus Hedman, the current Swedish international reserve goalkeeper, who was acquired through his agents, IMG. 'It was a pleasure to deal with them. They're professional, and the quality of detail and advice they give is first class, unlike a lot of agents, who aren't fit to sell used cars.'

I wondered why Hedman would wish to join a side as an understudy to a goalkeeper as established as Oggy? Richardson smiled quietly and shook his head. 'Who said he would be an understudy? If he has a good pre-season, I would expect him to be in goal for our opening game against Chelsea.' I immediately felt a pang of regret and sympathy for Oggy, the most reliable and stable of keepers, and a man constantly regarded within the club as an example of the old-style virtues of loyalty and professionalism. What a cruel game it seems, in which you can lose your position without having done anything wrong, simply because someone better shows up. If a man treated his wife like that, he would be regarded as a hound.

Among the influx of foreign players into the Premiership there are a great number of Scandinavians. They like coming to England. English football is on television in all the Scandinavian countries, the players speak

English, and a nasty English winter must seem balmy to them. Richardson likes signing them, believing 'they're stable characters, not like your emotional Latins'. To combat the perceived weakness in midfield, the major acquisition was Trond Soltvedt, for £500,000 from the Norwegian club Rosenborg, who had recently scored goals against both Milan and Juventus in their European Cup campaign. A thrusting and powerful runner, he was intended to be the answer to Gordon's perception that the problem last year was that the midfield didn't link properly with the forwards due to a lack of athleticism, of power and pace.

Though Kevin Richardson and Gary McAllister, and occasionally Eoin Jess, gave class and experience to the midfield, none was a natural goalscorer, and none had the stamina or pace to play up and down the field for a full game, joining the attack and then shoring up the defence. It is the hardest job in football, and last season Coventry singularly lacked a man to do it. This absence, in turn, partly explained McAllister's disappointing year, since, in trying to fulfil the role, he simply didn't have time to settle in midfield, let someone else win the ball – as David Batty had done for him so successfully at Leeds – look about and find the telling pass, or the opportune moment to go forward. Put simply, the available manpower was insufficient to prise the best out of McAllister.

During the winter break in the Norwegian season, Soltvedt had accompanied Coventry on their trip to Liverpool, which City won in a fixture that was crucial to their survival. It was a happy time, and according to Richardson, 'He loved it – the boys liked him and he was magic with them. And he said he'd never felt it anywhere, but he immediately felt part of the situation. When the opportunity came at the end of the season he wanted to come.'

While having tea in the hotel lounge, one of the players had admired Soltvedt's new Rolex watch, and asked to have a look at it. Trond took it off, and passed it over.

On the back was engraved 'Trond Soltvedt: Man of the Match. European Champions' Cup, Rosenborg v. AC Milan, 1997.' Four of the Coventry players admiringly passed it around, and then solemnly took off their own watches and dropped them in a nearby bin.

Coventry had already signed free agent Martin Johansen, from FC Copenhagen, who had won a cap for Denmark and was described by Richardson as a 'bright and chirpy sort of player, who can play as either a striker or in midfield, and is a little like Alan Ball'. His boyhood hero, according to the chairman, had been Strachan himself. Two further signings went relatively unnoticed. Kyle Lightbourne, a Bermudan, a regular goalscorer for Walsall for a few seasons, was picked up for £500,000; a second, younger striker, Simon Haworth, had already been signed for £300,000 from Cardiff, and seemed a possible long-term bet. But it is impossible to buy a high-quality striker from a League club at a bargain price. So Lightbourne and Haworth looked like squad players rather than potential challengers for a place. Who were they meant to replace, after all, Dublin or Huckerby?

None of the three signings was likely to set the place alight. Negotiations were advanced, however, with Roland Nilsson, the Swedish full-back who played for some time for Sheffield Wednesday, and who was still, at the age of thirty-three, an international player. 'I'm keeping my fingers crossed,' said Richardson, 'because we need a right back to replace Brian Borrows, who's a lovely player, but finding it difficult to keep up with the game.

'That's the sort of player we want. There is no point in collecting players. What you don't want is quantity, you want quality. And Gordon, like all managers, likes keeping players, and doesn't like selling them, so you have to nudge it a bit and say, this player or that player, is he going to be there, or do you realise he's got one year left of his contract and costs us £400,000 a year? Couldn't you use the money better?' There is only, he maintains, one criterion to use when contemplating a new signing: 'Is he better than what we've fucking got?'

He was enthusiastic about the signings, but I had my doubts. Lightbourne and Haworth, entirely unproven at the highest level, had come in, and Peter Ndlovu had been sold: not, on the face of it, an attractive swap. The transfer of Ndlovu, to Birmingham City, was a particularly interesting story. With only a year left on his contract, the talented but physically fragile forward had not entirely fulfilled the extraordinary promise of his first years at the club. Perhaps, Richardson believed, it was time to take a bird in the hand: 'Otherwise you have to offer him a new contract, when you're thinking we're only offering him a contract to protect ourselves. What happens if nobody comes in and we aren't able to sell him? We've still got him on hundreds of thousands a year. We'll be buggered both ways.'

Though he was a great favourite at Highfield Road, Ndlovu's career faltered with the coming of Big Ron, who clearly felt – and rightly – that he was too bad a crosser of the ball to be reliable on the wing, while, when played as a striker, he was too snatchy in front of goal, and missed too many good chances. The obvious answer was to try him directly behind the front two, where he could run at the defence, which, given his lifelong commitment to adventurous football, Atkinson was curiously unwilling to try. Under Strachan, Ndlovu was even less certain of his place, and scored only one goal.

So Ndlovu was made available for sale – an obscure process, and by no means as obvious in its methods as sticking up an estate agent's 'for sale' sign in front of a property. Richardson was vague about how the process actually works. You let one or two agents know, perhaps leak a story to the press (the *Sun* is practically a trade *Exchange and Mart* in this respect), inform an agent on the continent, and see what happens. It seemed, from the outside, a haphazard method when one considers the money at stake, but perhaps the grapevines in football are more reliable than one might suppose. The Ndlovu case makes one rather doubt this, because no one but Birmingham City came up with a substantial offer, against the asking price of £2 million. A deal was finally agreed at £1.7 million, with another £200,000 if Birmingham gained promotion, a deal which was made more attractive because Birmingham were prepared to put the money up front – relatively uncommon in big-money transfers, which are often paid in instalments.

The fact that only Birmingham came up with an offer, according to Richardson, 'is quite enlightening in its own way about the way that other people perceived Nuddy', though he added that a deal was almost made with Genoa, who withdrew at the last moment, thus necessitating the acceptance of the Birmingham bid. And then the deal fell through. Though Ndlovu's history of knee problems was well known, Birmingham, at the last minute, wanted to renegotiate on the basis of the player's medical condition. Richardson, normally the most urbane of men, was apoplectic.

An unusual club, even in a league which has its fair share of unusual characters, Birmingham were owned by porn-king David Sullivan, and in Karren Brady had the only woman managing director in the League. They had done business with Coventry before, in the transfers of central defenders Liam Daish and Gary Breen, and Richardson had expected difficulties. 'They weren't a public company at the time, and the negotiations with them over Breen could be loosely – no, accurately – termed a nightmare. Normally we don't encounter so many problems. Both players were having serious problems with their signing-on fees. It seemed the club were trying to hike up the transfer fee, and cover themselves. It proved to be one of the most difficult negotiations to deal with.'

Knowing that they were the only bidders for Ndlovu, Birmingham struck a hard bargain, which involved paying only £200,000 up front, the remainder of the fee to come in game-by-game instalments based on Ndlovu making up to eighty appearances, at which point the full £1.7 million would be realised by Coventry. Not a bad bit of business by Birmingham, one might say. It seemed as if, having decided to unload Ndlovu, Coventry were simply determined to take the first decent offer, however unattractive it turned out to be, and to get on with other business. But, of course, such sales have to be concluded quickly, and given that negotiations can often lead to nothing, you sometimes have to do a deal when it's on the table, even if it isn't quite what you had envisioned.

Football players, especially when still on longish contracts, are the major capital of a football club, and one cannot escape the feeling that they are bought and sold, if not on the wing, at least on a prayer. The resale of Eoin Jess also seemed to point to this conclusion. Signed from Aberdeen in 1996 for £1.6 million, little more than a year later he returned to that club for £750,000 – a loss of nearly a million pounds on a player who is an established Scottish international, and whose training-ground skills, according to Richardson, were the most impressive of the whole squad. With transfer fees escalating almost by the hour, it seemed hard to believe that a player of such quality wasn't worth more than he eventually fetched.

But I have no experience of such things, and was rather inclined to doubt my own judgement. Presumably, as the season progressed, this was likely to happen more and more often. Football supporters are overladen with opinions, most of them based on flimsy evidence and even less experience. That's part of the fun of being a football fan. But I could already see that, as I learned more, I was going to have to rethink a number of my own prejudices. I resolved to keep my mouth shut. When I told Bertie this, he laughed.

It would be hard to argue that the club had strengthened its resources in this package of deals. But one possible transaction, widely rumoured in the press during July, linked Chelsea midfield player Craig Burley with Coventry City. It was the deal that might have swung the balance in favour of the new players, finally providing McAllister with the high-quality midfield partner who would allow him the space to realise his proper role in the side. Once again, though, Richardson met with business practice – 'all too common these days, I'm afraid' – that left him feeling bruised. Over a weekend, he believed he had agreed transfer terms of £2 million with Colin Hutchinson, managing director of Chelsea, and been given permission to negotiate personal terms with Burley. 'What then happens is I ring Colin on the Monday, and he says, "Well, no, I've spoken to Ruud, and he's not too sure he wants him to leave. And, anyway, I've got a bigger bid." I said, "I don't care whether you've got a bigger bid or not, I thought you and I reached an agreement, and as far as I'm concerned that's the end of it." He said, "Oh, no, it's not as simple as that."' Richardson was furious. But Hutchinson said, "Well, that's it. You put up the money again. I've got a bigger offer."'

The offer – £2.5 million 'plus some bits and pieces' – had come from Celtic, and Hutchinson was adamant that Coventry couldn't talk to the player until they matched it. Richardson wouldn't budge. 'I don't doubt,' he said, 'that it was a real offer from Celtic, because it's through the player's agent, and the agent has no desire to make the transfer fee higher. He's not on a percentage of the transfer fee – he makes his money negotiating the player's personal terms.'

So Burley went to Celtic. Would it have helped if Richardson had unbent a little, and gone up to £2.5 million? It might – although Celtic are a huge club, and represented a homecoming for the Scottish Burley, the player was known to want to stay in England. But Richardson was entirely unrepentant, if inwardly chagrined at being gazumped. 'I'm not paying any more than what I agreed.'

For every potential purchase that fell through, there were rumours of a potential sale. Dion Dublin, particularly, had been linked in the press to Spurs – 'never any money on the table', said Richardson dismissively, which was also true of a rumoured move by the out-of-contract Kevin Richardson to West Brom. The chairman was severely realistic with regard to any potential sales: 'Everyone has a price, even at Man United or Arsenal. But what is the sense of selling, say, Dion Dublin, unless you can replace him? And once they know that you have some money in your pocket, prices go over the moon. That's why, if you've negotiated a major sale, you try to delay announcing it for three or four days, so you can try to buy someone at a fair price.'

In any case, there wasn't much money available, and Strachan had said as much to the press over the summer. Richardson, however optimistic he is by nature, was clear about the dangers. 'We're having a bit of a punt here. We're £20 million in debt and the effects of relegation would have been catastrophic. And last year it was very, very close. I always knew we'd beat Spurs, but I was afraid one of the other results might have gone against us, and we'd be down. And relegation affects everything: the money, the whole culture of the club. Gordon says that once a player has experienced relegation you can always smell it on him.'

So he was anxious to buy further players. 'We're always looking to add to the squad, but not just anybody. What we want is twenty quality players competing for places. We're not going to sign someone just as a useful squad player, or for the reserves.' But his analysis of the failure of the last season was not based on the belief that the squad wasn't good enough. He thought Coventry had better players than those at five or six other clubs. What concerned him, though, was 'that there would be games when we fought like tigers, and others when we didn't play. It's very much a question of confidence, of being able to do it on the training ground, then on the pitch, then carry it over week to week. Gordon has been working on this. He says it comes from work, work, work, and trust in each other and the team. You'll have to talk to him about it.'

Leaving the chairman's office, I got Gordon's phone number from his secretary, and resolved to do just that.

4

A Trip to Torquay

It was a hot summer, and I'd had the top down a lot. Why drive a convertible otherwise? In the centre of Warwick, stuck behind a bus, I inhaled five minutes' worth of point-blank poisonous fumes (why drive a convertible at all?) while watching the folks ambling round Warwick's modest antique shops and tacky arcades. I was feeling apprehensive, and the tourists' boredom and lethargy made me envy them a little. All they had to do was slope about in the sun. I had to go talk to Gordon Strachan.

This having been my purpose all along, I was surprised to find myself dreading it slightly. But I had, after thirty years of supporting football sides, never met a football player, much less a Premiership manager. Not to talk to, anyway. This is not to say that I had no idea what to expect. We see managers on television all the time, and we have images of them: Kenny Dalglish is dour, mordant and charmless; George Graham is well dressed because he had a black (Armani) bag full of cash which he bought the clothes with; Kevin Keegan is a little media darling. That sort of nonsense. And Gordon Strachan? Gordon Strachan is a fiery little Scottish person who lives on adrenaline and seaweed.

My head spinning with these risible stereotypes, I was trying to calm myself down as I left Warwick and headed into the surrounding countryside. The radio, on Classic FM, was playing something soothing, but I couldn't concentrate on it. I was producing my own inner music – 'One Gordon Strachan! There's only one Gordon Strachan!' – which, once having taken up residence in my mind, was proving impossible to displace.

Gordon's directions were impeccable, and I arrived with ten minutes to spare. As I drove by, observing the spacious and well-tended gardens, the sweep of the drive, and a pleasant, decent-sized house 100 metres away, it all had the prosperous look of the residence of a well-off local farmer, or, more likely, a retired merchant banker from the City. I continued down the road for a minute, stopped the car, got out to smoke a cigar – I wouldn't do it in his presence, he was sure to hate smoking – in a copse of trees, and composed myself. With a final wrenching act of will, I got 'One Gordon Strachan!' out of my head, climbed back into the car and drove back to the house.

Wearing a casual bright blue shirt and khaki trousers, Gordon was perched on a tractor, mowing the lawn. He looked like a kid at an agricultural fair, having fun driving one of those large farm machines that are too big for him. Behind him, a long drive ended at the front of the house, where an enormous blue bubble covered an outdoor swimming pool, sitting just outside a long room which housed a snooker table, a lot of framed football memorabilia and a lounge area arranged round a fireplace. To his left was a small paddock with two tiny, hairy ponies eating grass by the fence; at his feet gambolled a couple of small, ugly dogs. He paused to stroke the ponies fondly – 'You all right, girl?' he said to each in turn – before coming over to shake my hand.

I was tempted to think that the miniature scale of the animals must be some unconscious mimicry of his own stature, but the odd thing was that he seemed larger than he ought: larger, in fact, than he actually is. It was hard to believe that it was him at all: just as we fail to recognise our bank managers when we see them shopping at Sainsbury's, out of context, it was hard to believe that this relaxed fellow was actually the Coventry manager. He looked like somebody who looks like Gordon Strachan. All of my previous sightings of him had been from the stands, where his distinctive, slight appearance, with that shock of red hair, made him seem like a hyperactive tot among men. But in person he had a quiet confidence about him, clear-eyed and still, and as he walked with me up to the picnic table in the garden he revealed himself, in his tone and carriage, as a person of substance. I was curiously impressed, and immediately ashamed that I should find this curious. Why shouldn't he be?

Not that he was particularly keen to see me, though he was polite. He had better things to do with his time: players had arrived back from the summer carrying various sorts of injuries, five pre-season friendly games were coming up in the next ten days, five new players were yet to be assimilated into the squad. The season was to begin in three weeks, against Chelsea on 9 August. The last thing he needed was the further obligation to talk to me, not merely now but throughout the season, with no tangible gain to himself or to the team. But I had been passed on to him by the chairman, and he seemed prepared to make the best of it.

'When you want to talk,' he said, 'come up and see me at the house. I'm only ever really relaxed here.' He reflected for a moment. 'Except,' he added thoughtfully, 'sometimes on a Sunday. But I always recover by Monday.' I told him that the same thing was true of me: that if Coventry lost I could be speechless with depression on Saturday, and pretty glum on Sunday, but then I recovered. He looked at me, puzzled: I must be a pretty sad case.

Assuming that he would want to know something about me, I began to fill him in on some details about myself, and the nature of the book I wanted to write:

the sort of stuff I'd told Bryan Richardson. But it was immediately obvious that, unlike Richardson, he wasn't interested. He fidgeted a little and looked round the garden. As far as he was concerned, I realised, I had come to interview him. It didn't matter who I was. Why didn't I just get on with it?

When Strachan and his wife Lesley moved down from Leeds in 1996, they bought the first available place, a show house on a new estate in Leamington Spa. 'It was too small,' he remembered. 'We were just crammed in. We were used to a big house in the country in Leeds, a bit like this.' Lesley, a friendly, blonde Scotswoman in her late thirties, dressed in a white tennis dress and pumps, came out with a beer for me and joined us. 'It was all right,' she said, 'and I liked it in Leamington, but we bought the house with all the furniture and everything: it was like living in a holiday home. As soon as we found this house I knew it would be better for us, and for the kids.' Gordon agreed. 'The house in Leamington was so small, Lesley would have it clean by ten in the morning, and there wouldn't be enough left for her to do.'

A teenage daughter, playing with a recently acquired floppy brown puppy that looked like it came from the stuffed-animal section at Hamley's, was sitting on the grass near us, close to a greenhouse filled by an enormous grapevine, but no grapes. ('We ate them,' she said.) The puppy flopped off towards the house, and made it up two steps before its rear end collapsed, and it fell back down again. Lesley grinned. 'The thing about this house' – she pointed at the rambling stone building, constructed round the remains of an old barn – 'is that there's plenty to do. And the local people have been wonderful – there's a lovely local pub, farmers and all, none of them football fans, and they've been ever so good to us.'

She reflected for a moment, clearly satisfied with her new surroundings. 'The good thing, too, is that while you have to take the kids everywhere – we left them in school in Leamington because it didn't seem fair to move them:

Gordon just pops them off in the morning – at least this way you always know where they are. Off riding, or at the golf course. You know they're safe.'

Gordon was equally at ease. 'I'm not obsessed by football; I love the game, and I love to talk about it, but I'm only really relaxed at home, when I can let go of it. But some of them that are obsessed by football, it's really pathological, there's nothing else. They may get to be successful, some of them, but they aren't happy. I'm not like that. I don't like being interviewed. You won't see me on the telly much. If I haven't got anything to say on a subject then I say nothing. But I do love to talk about the game.'

His main priority, clearly, was to build a team in his own image, to make it Strachanish. It distresses him not so much to be outplayed – 'We'll never compete with the Manchester Uniteds in terms of ball skills' – but to be outfought. In crucial home losses at the end of last season, to West Ham and Derby, this was what had occurred. 'Whereas in the Chelsea game we chased them, and harried them, got a foot in, won a couple of fifty-fifty balls in their half, made chances out of those. It's not like on the training pitch. You don't get a goal, you see, with Oggy rolling out the ball, then five or six passes, then a chance comes. It's not like that. You work hard, harder than they do, and sometimes the ball falls right for you, and a chance comes. You have to make it come.'

He acknowledged the need for new players, and rue-fully accepted the difficulty in persuading them to join the club. 'The hard thing about getting players to come to Coventry City is we're just not fashionable. You talk to foreign players, and they want to play in the Premier League, but not in Coventry. And it's my job over the next few years to change that, to produce the kind of results that make players want to come here.' Mark Jones had made the same point to me earlier, from a marketing point of view: 'Coventry is a hard sell.'

Strachan, meanwhile, is determined that the legacy of

the mere hunt for survival has to end. What went wrong last season? He paused, and then told a story: 'When I first played for Scotland, they used to tell us that you had to pace yourself in international games, so I would take it a little easy – not chase a ball here, not make a run there – and then I found I could never catch up with the game, and I'd end up getting taken off. I finally decided that I had to go out and give it a hundred per cent, and if after seventy minutes I was knackered, I'd go on anyway. It's a bit like training to run a marathon: first you can go seventy minutes, then eighty, then ninety: you just keep pushing yourself.

'And last season we never really got started. We'd only just stayed up, on goal difference, and everybody thought that couldn't happen again, now Gary's here. And by the time sixteen games had gone, and we only had ten points, it was all uphill. It's all about getting a good start: after ten or twelve games we'll know how the season is going to go.' Though aware of deficiencies in manpower, his major focus was on attitude and commitment. After all, teams with less impressive squads – most notably Leicester, who finished ninth, had a run in the FA Cup and won the Coca-Cola Cup – finished well ahead of Coventry, and worked harder and more coherently.

Of course, the team that began the 1996–7 season had been assembled and managed by Big Ron, and had many of the infuriating hallmarks of Atkinson teams, playing exciting football one week, ineffective stuff the next. It is hard to imagine that the conjunction of the two men, despite their friendship, could have been entirely comfortable. Atkinson, large and generous-natured, played the kind of football that reflected his own expansiveness. Although the champagne-swilling, cigar-smoking media image was something of a role that he liked to play (he hasn't, in fact, smoked a cigar in twenty-five years), he was nevertheless the kind of manager whose instincts were to attack. He is reported to have told Noel Whelan, on the latter's arrival from Leeds, that he wanted to play 'the sort of games that we'll win 4–3'.

That is a philosophy contrary to Strachan's nature. Associated more with the intake of seaweed and bananas (though I was never to see him eat either) than caviar and champagne, Gordon has always been known for the fierceness of his dedication, his fitness and drive, and his non-stop competitiveness. Strachan won twenty-eight of his fifty Scotland caps at Aberdeen, the club which, under the managership of Alex Ferguson, managed to challenge the dominance of Celtic and Rangers. They won the Championship in 1980, the Cup in '82 and '83, beat Real Madrid in the Cup-Winners' Cup final in 1983 and did the double in 1984. As a youngster Strachan modelled himself on Billy Bremner, but as he matured he came to realise that there was more to the game – his game – than tigerish combativeness. He was a fine reader of the play, a canny passer of the ball, a decent goalscorer: a complete player.

Rumours of discord between the fiery Strachan and the steely Ferguson were widespread, and were substantiated when the 'wee man', as he was called, was transferred to Manchester United (managed by Ron Atkinson) in 1984. United won the FA Cup in 1985, but seemed to lack the qualities needed for the long haul of the Championship. Strachan's analysis of this failure is revealing: 'If the pitch was right and the occasion right we could beat anybody, but over the long slog of a season we lacked physique', which seems an oblique way of saying that it was an Atkinson sort of team, not a Strachan sort.

Certainly it was an Atkinson sort of team, built round attacking players, that Gordon inherited when Big Ron resigned as manager after the disastrous start in 1996–7. So the 1997–8 season was the first in which Strachan's distinctive qualities as a manager could be tested. Sadly, Big Ron had already spent most of the money, and Gordon was left with a side which had proven, as comprehensively as possible (short of being relegated), that it was not good enough. In any case, his sense of what needed improving did not focus on the hunt for new star players, though he was still trying to strengthen the squad.

'What your average fan sees, when he watches a game, is individual performances. How Huckerby played, what Dublin did. What I'm looking at is a pattern, a group of players playing as a team. And our problems were in the middle of the pitch, and on the right side of defence. Yesterday we signed Roland Nilsson, so that's one problem solved. I just need one more midfield player.'

By the end of this first meeting, which I drew to a close after about forty-five minutes, he had warmed a little. 'You'll need to talk to the players, too,' he said, 'especially some of the senior ones. Try Oggy, Gary Mac, Dion, David Burrows. The ones who've been around, and can be a bit thoughtful, and have that little bit of loyalty to the club. The rest of them,' he said quietly and a little sadly, 'I'm not sure you'll get much out of them. Most of the younger ones are just in it for what they can get.'

'Who,' I asked, 'should I talk to of the younger ones?' He thought for a moment, and a shadow of frustration clouded his face. 'You might try Huckerby, I guess . . .No, Whelan, you might try Whelan . . .' He seemed to have been considering whether either of them could speak English. He gave the impression, somewhat, that he was immersed in an uncongenial new culture where the old values of work and loyalty have been superseded by those of getting what you could for yourself, and moving on. 'Hired guns' is what Richardson calls the players, with a philosophical smile. Strachan clearly agreed, without the smile.

'I guess,' he said, as I rose to leave, 'there's no sense you just hanging round the training ground. We have a friendly at Torquay a week on Friday. Why not come on the team coach? Then you can chat to the players, hang out, let them get used to you. The coach leaves from the training ground at Ryton at about nine-thirty – see you then.'

It had been a satisfying experience, a little heady, even. I'd learned a lot, and I was going – that was so cool – with the team to Torquay. But, as I left, there was an underlay of disappointment in my mood as well. It had gone well, and I couldn't have asked for more. There I was, after all, basking on the lawn with Gordon Strachan, drinking a beer, talking football. Or, more exactly, he was talking football, and I was asking questions and then listening. He had constructed the experience along the lines he was used to and was comfortable with: I was an anonymous interviewer, and he was responding carefully to questions. If the exchange didn't have the give and take of genuine conversation, that was only to be expected.

But it wasn't satisfying. There was an odd sort of deadness about it all, and I had no doubt that Gordon would have said exactly the same things to anyone else. Fair enough: he neither knew me, nor wished to know me. But I made a little resolution to myself, all the same: in the future I'd try to avoid that sort of format if I could. I'd try to find ways of seeing him that were more spontaneous, less easy to manipulate into something safe and anodyne. How to do so? I hadn't the foggiest idea. But it would sort itself out. There was a long season ahead of us. We could start with a good chat on the way to Torquay.

It was 1 August, the first day of the new R-reg season. John Salako drove up to the Ryton training-ground car park in his spanking new red Isuzu Trooper – one of those half-car, half-Jeep macho runabouts so beloved of Americans – and parked it proudly near the team coach. We were off to play Torquay in a testimonial match for John Uzzell. (Fans always call their side 'we', but all of a sudden 'we' was literally right.) Garry Pendrey, the reserve-team coach, bullet-headed and moustachioed like a drill sergeant, and a member of Gordon's touchline squad (the others were Alex Miller, the assistant manager, and George Dalton, the club physiotherapist), walked over to the window of Salako's car. 'You know what they say about people with red cars,' he said, groping his crotch, 'a bit lacking in the masculinity department.'

Salako smiled happily, and got out into a car park chock-full of other new Isuzus and Subarus. Subaru were the new team sponsors, having just taken over from Talbot Peugeot, paying £400,000 (rising by 10 per cent a year) for the privilege (Peugeot paid only £160,000). Mark Jones was extremely pleased with the new relationship. 'Football is absolutely taking off in Japan, and they have just signed a deal for Premiership football on the telly, so we reckon – and they do – that Japan is the new growth market.' Certainly Subaru had offered particularly attractive deals on the cars. Almost everyone had one. Salako, Ogrizovic and Paul Williams wandered from car to car, comparing models and specifications: which had four-wheel drive, metallic paint, air-conditioning.

A few of the youth team ambled out, happy to get away from their boot-polishing for a moment, quietly on the fringe of things, unacknowledged by the senior players. One of them looked disdainfully at a compact Subaru. 'It's shit, that,' he said. 'Slow as a pig.' He wasn't old enough to drive. He sauntered over to my car, an old-model Saab convertible, and looked at it with a mixture of respect and bemusement. It was smart, and interesting in its way, but it didn't fit.

Neither did I. As I watched from the car-park equivalent of the sideline, further Subaru-clad players arrived: Gary Breen, Kevin Richardson and a clutch of barely recognisable Scandinavians, two large, one small. On a corner of the driveway Paul Telfer and Richard Shaw were testing a new bubble-burner Taylor Made driver. Shaw took a comfortable, wide-arced practice swing. Telfer then gripped the club, and lazily executed a more tucked-up swing with a collapsed left arm. 'It feels pretty good,' he said. (It turned out he has a handicap of 1.) Garry looked on. 'It should for £388,' he said. 'You could go on a whole golfing holiday and rent clubs for the same price.' Shaw and Telfer shrugged.

At exactly 9.30, yet another Subaru, driven by Lesley Strachan, pulled up, and Gordon popped out. She gave a cheerful wave to everyone and drove off. He greeted the players with a nod, saw me, and walked over. I was ever so grateful. I could, I suppose, have gone up to one of the players and introduced myself, but I felt rooted to my spot on the sidelines, as out of place here as one of them might be sitting in on a seminar on Keats. 'Come and sit with us at the front of the coach,' Gordon said to me. The players piled on. A few had injuries and weren't making the trip: Roland Nilsson, who was still in Sweden, Liam Daish, still recovering from an operation, and Noel Whelan and Darren Huckerby, who had picked up minor knocks. Steve Ogrizovic was having a last-minute cigarette and joking with the coach-driver. He pointed disdainfully at the coach: 'It's at least three years old. I thought we were a big-cheese team now. Time we got a big-cheese coach.' I waited for him to get on, and followed him, the last person aboard.

Gordon and I sat opposite each other in the second row, separated by a table. Across the aisle Alex Miller and Garry Pendrey settled in, while the players took seats at the rear of the coach, put on their Walkmans, got the newspapers out. A couple of card schools formed, with Marcus Hall, Dion and Gary McAllister together at one table.

'Alex, Garry,' said Gordon, 'meet Rick – he's going to be with us most of the season, doing a book about the club. A sort of behind-the-scenes thing.' Garry looked over, smiled, said, 'Nice to meet you.' Alex looked at me directly with cool, who-the-fuck-are-you eyes, and nodded briefly. He wasn't merely unfriendly, but positively hostile. Either he had some serious personality problem, or he hated the look of me. I presume you don't get a lot of long-haired, bearded, overweight people on Premiership team coaches. He looked outraged by my presence.

Distinctly uncomfortable, I reached into my bag, got out my copy of the *Sun* (the *Independent* could come later, when I had established a little credibility) and turned to the sports pages. Just a normal sort of guy, that's me. Alex resumed work on his charts – mapping out defensive positions for corners, set pieces, walls, free kicks – which would be posted in the dressing room before the game. Garry read his copy of the *Sun*.

Within a few minutes, Gordon, who was much more subdued than he had been out at his house, had moved a row forward and stretched himself across a couple of seats – he seemed smaller in this context. In front of him, but recessed somewhat, and invisible from the rest of the coach, was our driver. Above his head, nicely visible from all points, was a sign that read: 'YOUR DRIVER GORDON' which seemed cosy, and appropriate.

It's a long trip down to Torquay – Gordon (the driver) estimated three and a half hours – and the coach was surprisingly silent and peaceful. Perhaps it was because of the early start, but I had imagined something more noisy, laddish. But we could, if you substituted the *Financial Times* for the ubiquitous copies of the *Sun*, and suits for tracksuits, have been an outing of chartered accountants on our way to a seaside convention.

By now I had read the *Sun* from cover to cover and perused every ad for Tarot readings, used cars and marital aids. There didn't seem to be any columns of advice on how to break the ice with football players. Alex had finished his diagrams, and Garry was snoozing happily. Gordon, awake now, had rejoined me. Desperate for human contact, I asked him how the recent series of three friendly games in Scotland had gone. 'Good,' he said, and picked up the *Sun*. You might have supposed that he'd never met me before. Or perhaps Miller's disdain was infectious?

Garry, awake now, walked over to the food-provision counter situated discreetly behind my seat – fridge, microwave, coffee, tea. 'Cuppa tea, mate?' he asked me as he went by. 'Gordon?' The manager nodded his assent. Having taken a few sips from his mug (the rest of us got plastic cups), Gordon settled down with the paper. Suddenly, through the front window, I saw a blue Ford Escort cut in sharply, dangerously, ahead of us. Braking quickly, our driver averted an accident, only for the jolt to send Gordon's mug flying across the table and over the edge, depositing most of its contents directly between his legs.

His reactions were so quick – a tackle from Vinnie Jones couldn't have been avoided more adroitly – that almost all the tea hit either the seat or the floor, a few drops catching the seat of his beige trousers. Alex and Garry were on their feet immediately to begin the mopping up, while Gordon peered intently at his behind to assess the damage and I swabbed down the tabletop. 'I remember once,' I said to Alex, 'I was on a train, and a lady spilled a cup of scalding coffee directly on my lap. My balls were red for a week.' He met my eye briefly, seemed to stifle the response 'Good!', went back to his seat, and worked some more on his charts. I decided to shut up.

It was a surprisingly quiet business altogether. Lunch at our hotel in Torquay was taken very largely in silence, interrupted by the scraping of chairs and the occasional *sotto voce* conversation. At the tables, the players and managers were eating with the kind of sustained inward attention that an intelligent jet plane might exhibit if considering the act of taking on fuel. Or perhaps it was merely vacancy. Tureens of scrambled eggs, baked beans, spaghetti bolognese and greasy chicken pieces were laid out in a buffet. Feeling particularly peckish after the isolation of my coach trip, I helped myself, after some thought about my options, to a large plateful of spaghetti.

Heading back to our table, I had a look to see which meal the players had chosen. They hadn't. They'd all had large amounts of everything, with the exception of team chow-hound Brian Borrows, who'd had an enormous portion of everything. No white showed from his plate at all: chicken and spaghetti flopped out over the sides. There was enough food to sustain the whole Israeli army. He looked pretty happy.

Gordon stood up. 'Can I have a quick word, lads?' The players looked up expectantly, munching away. 'I'd like to introduce you all to Rick,' he said, nodding at me. 'He's going to be writing a book about us this season – inside story sort of thing – so you'll all see him round a lot. I'm sure he'll be grateful for your co-operation.' He sat down again.

He hadn't warned me he was going to do this. Swallowing a last mouthful of spaghetti, slurping a little in my haste, I stood up. The players looked at me expectantly. It was a crucial moment. Either I would interest them in the project or, with a wrong tone or phrase, alienate – or just plain bore – them completely. I composed myself, thinking: this is, after all, what I am good at. They can kick footballs, I can talk. I've taught, acted, lectured to large audiences. I like talking impromptu, chatting away off the top of my head. No worries.

I looked round the room. To my left, through the picture windows, boats cruised gently in the bay and the sun shone; it was a perfect moment, but I could feel myself starting to panic. After so many years of supporting this side, these anonymous, mythical beings, these heroes, I had to keep their attention. Dion Dublin was smiling at me! Steve Ogrizovic was waiting for me to talk! Gary McAllister was going to listen!

'Thank you, Gordon,' I said, feeling like Gareth Southgate stepping up to take that penalty, in a voice that bore no relation to my own, curiously squeaky and out of tune, as if it needed oil. 'As Gordon says, I'm, um, going to be around a lot this year, and I'd sort of be grateful if I could talk to each of you.' The players nodded benignly. No one actually laughed. 'I promise,' I added, 'not to bother you too much. Just a little. And thanks in advance.' I collapsed back into my chair. My heart was palpitating and my hands were trembling and sweating. But the players gave me a nod or a smile, and someone clapped in a way that didn't sound entirely sardonic. They went back to their food. The room fell silent once again.

I felt stiff with humiliation. The moment was irretrievably lost. I ought to have told them about my long-term support for the team, the fascination that all fans feel about what is going on behind the scenes, to enlist their help in learning how properly to watch and assess a game of football; I ought to have told them of my talks with Bryan Richardson, and of his support for the project. Perhaps a little about myself as well. But what I had to stress was that I was not a journalist, that I was not looking for that quick fix of scandal so beloved of the readership of the tabloids. By failing to do so I had failed to dispel their initial suspicion, that wariness towards outsiders that any sportsman learns early in his career, when he sees what a little indiscreet behaviour, or an unchecked moment of candour, can lead to.

It was too late now. The players drifted off – it was almost two o'clock – to have an afternoon nap in their rooms. Gordon paused for a moment to have a word with John Uzzell, a pleasant, equine-faced man in his middle thirties, whose career had been ended in 1991 by an elbow thrown by a defender as they competed for a ball in the air. Uzzell's eye socket and cheekbone were crushed by the blow – you can spot a facial asymmetry round his nose – and, after prolonged hospitalisation, he emerged and sued the player. Though he was supported by his club, Torquay, and in possession of video evidence that seemed to suggest malicious intent, Uzzell's case eventually went against him. Now working as a postman, this testimonial game represented his last chance to get a little something back.

'Last season,' he told me, 'when I was trying to arrange a testimonial game, I wrote to the managers of all the clubs in the Premier League to ask if they might be able to come down here for a match. And I was really touched, and impressed – they all answered, even those, most of them, who said an outright no. I think they'd seen the incident on TV, and felt sympathetic. Footballers stick together at times like that. But the only manager to ring me personally was Gordon Strachan.'

With a couple of hours to kill, and no room to nap in, I contemplated a walk down the hill to the centre of Torquay. I like seaside towns, the sleepy 1950s feel of them, the gentlemen's haberdasheries full of tweed and corduroy, tea shoppes with slightly stale Madeira cake, fusty old bookshops, *Fawlty Towers*-ish bed-and-breakfasts. But my experience over lunch had stripped me of energy, and in an attempt at imaginative sympathy with the players, I tried to sleep in a comfy chair in the bar. Not unsurprisingly, I couldn't, and I was grateful when my mobile phone rang. It was my office. My associate, Jim Irvine (a Chelsea supporter), was calling to recommend that we pursue a cache of Ezra Pound letters, some 430 of them, which had recently failed to sell at Sotheby's and might be available at a reduced price. Perhaps, Jim thought, we could buy them cheaply, and break them up? But who could we sell them to? I wondered whether Dion Dublin was interested in Ezra Pound.

Alex Miller, sadly, was the first to reappear. Feeling refreshed by the interesting business news, I decided to see if he might thaw out a little. After all, he was the number two of the managerial team, and I would need his co-operation. Perhaps my bumbling over lunch might have endeared me to him? I certainly couldn't have alienated him by over-articulacy. Anyway, something was puzzling me.

'Excuse me, Alex?' He turned and gave me a kind of neutral attention. 'Why are the players upstairs having naps when we could have left three or four hours later and they could have had a lie-in at home?'

He perked up, willing to instruct me. 'You have to understand a footballer's life. It's not like other people's. Because they tend to have hard training sessions in the mornings, they often have a kip in the afternoon. That's why we get to a ground early, even for an evening kick-off, so as to eat the right sort of lunch, and then have a rest.'

'Do footballers eat differently than they used to?' (Not that I cared, but I was anxious to keep the conversation alive.)

'I guess so,' he said. 'In my day it was mostly steak – lots of protein – whereas today it's big on carbohydrates. Supposed to burn off, give extra energy.'

'Would you say that players are fitter now than they used to be?'

He considered this for a moment, inwardly comparing past and present. 'I think so,' he said. 'These days, we give them all targets for fitness to be maintained over the summer – weight, speed, endurance, and so forth – so that when we get back to training in July they are still pretty fit. And fitness can be the difference between going down and staying up. I think that last year we were still fresh in the last games, and that saved us. Some teams are fitter than others, no doubt about it.'

'Which teams in the Premiership,' I wondered, 'would you say are the fittest? Leicester City? Is that why they did so well?'

'I don't think so. I think that what they had was a system of playing that they all worked to. Like Wimbledon. It wasn't down to fitness.' But, he added, shrugging, 'I've only been here for six months, since I came down from Scotland, so I don't really know yet.'

We walked into the dining room together, where most of the players, looking slightly bleary, were consuming large amounts of toast, marmalade and tea. David Burrows, a chirpy, friendly Black Country fellow, burbled on happily about golf. He plays off 18, and wondered if he should buy one of the new Taylor Made drivers. 'Why add fifteen yards when you can only hit it a hundred anyway?' said Garry, who had just finished asking our waitress, a Dutch girl studying in Torquay to perfect her English, whether she had ever had her finger in a dyke. He seemed totally unaware of any double entendre. She wasn't, and looked at him quizzically. Perhaps this was an example of that famous English sense of humour?

Garry likes national stereotypes. He was soon to be heard inquiring of Martin Johansen whether he was a relative of the famous boxer of the same name. Johansen pointed out that he was Danish, and that Johansson was Swedish. 'Johansen, Svenson, Danish, Swedish, same thing,' remarked Pendrey happily.

Gordon, Alex and Brian Borrows were having a discussion about the available computer programmes, like the Carling–OPTA Index, which analyse football games: the sort of thing to which Sky Sports is addicted, and which generate statistics about 'passes completed' and other quantifications of performance. I hate these, regarding them as part of the Americanisation of the game, incapable of distinguishing between a significant pass and a conservative sideways push, and giving a false sense of mastery of a complex process. Surely no computer will locate the fact that a player has delivered two great balls in a game, which led to goalscoring opportunities, while another has simply played it safe, afraid to use the ball creatively? I made this point forcibly.

'Not at all,' said Gordon. 'It all depends on how good the programme is. I've seen some programmes that can distinguish between positive and negative passing. And the statistics on tackles, or shots, or corners, are all helpful.'

'So you really think that a computer description of a game, and of individual players' performances, can accurately reflect what has actually happened?'

'Sure,' he said. 'I wish we had one at Coventry.'

I was surprised. I had expected a kind of old-fashioned mockery of the new technologies, but the only person who seemed to feel that way was me. Kevin Richardson and Oggy both thought the information was helpful and accurate. Alex and Garry concurred. The general view was that what one needs is good and reliable information, and that there are no reasons not to look for it anywhere you can.

On the coach down to the ground, which left at 5.00 p.m. (kick-off was at seven), a discussion ensued about the opening fixtures of the season. Gordon, surprisingly – perhaps disingenuously – claimed to have looked at no more than the first five of the thirty-eight matches. 'I don't know what there is after that,' he said. 'You have to look at games in clumps, five or so at a time, and set yourself a target for those. Then you look at the next clump, and set a target for them. Otherwise you just end up playing game to game. You have to clump 'em.' Garry, though he agreed with this psychological strategy, had clearly studied the fixture list in depth. 'The first dozen games aren't too bad,' he said, 'after the first two.' (Chelsea at Coventry on 9 August, followed by an away match at Arsenal two days later.) 'And the League is pretty much in position after the first twelve games. So we have to get off to a better start than last year.'

It was a thought – this need to get off to a good start in order to avoid a protracted relegation dogfight – that I'd heard before, from Bryan Richardson and Graham Hover. And yet I wondered, as the season began, if it didn't have built into it an acknowledgement of inferiority, some tacit assumption that the only real item on the Coventry agenda was to stay up. Of course, if you take only a handful of points from your first dozen fixtures you will be in trouble; but it is equally essential for Liverpool or Manchester United to get off to a decent start. Is there a kind of fatalism involved when you keep saying, 'We must start well!' that either reflects, or might even cause, a failure of confidence in the squad?

Perhaps it was only realism. After all, it would be hard to argue that the squad with which Coventry were starting the season was any substantial improvement on the one with which they ended the last. That team won only nine games, and stayed up as a result of the three-point deduction levied on Middlesbrough, so why not assume that a similarly fraught year is, at least, likely? The only grounds for hope, then, were that the newcomers, especially the Scandinavians, settled in, and that Gordon would have time to make the squad more, well, Strachanish. And even that hope – for a tigerish, never-say-die quality which the team manifested the previous season, if only occasionally, under Gordon – might have been unrealistic. Gordon's career was a very successful one (though he was relegated with Dundee in 1975–6), and it wasn't yet clear if he could lower his sights sufficiently.

I don't know if pre-season friendly matches give much of an indication of how a team is going to perform, but the results had been good so far: three wins in Scotland, three clean sheets. Alex Miller told me this as I followed the team into the dressing room. I had decided to go wherever I wanted until somebody told me not to, a policy that proved remarkably successful as I accompanied the team on to the pitch for the pre-match warm-up. Airily announcing to two amiable Torquay stewards, 'I'm with the Coventry lads,' I ambled through the barrier and on to the pitch with Dion Dublin, only to hear one of the stewards say to the other 'Who's he, the chairman?' The other considered: 'Nah, probably the owner.' I was exultant. Life was different on the other side of the barrier.

You met a nice class of person there, too. I wandered over to watch from close range as Oggy and Magnus Hedman, the recently signed keeper, practised together, kicking balls at high velocity directly at each other from about twelve feet. Oggy was his usual efficient self, fielding almost everything authoritatively. Magnus, on the other hand, was astonishing. Every ball stuck to his fingers as a fly to flypaper; his hands and arms registered no reaction from the speed at which the ball was travelling. So quick were his movements that you had the illusion that he hadn't moved at all. If the rest of his keeping was on a par with this, it was hard to imagine that he wouldn't be in goal when the season began.

Oggy turned to me with a brief smile. 'So tell us about this book, then. Are you some sort of a reporter or what?'

'Not at all. Just a long-term supporter of the club who wants to know more, and got lucky.'

'How do you mean, lucky?' He continued kicking and catching, the conversation no distraction to him.

'I guess lucky because the chairman let me go ahead with the idea, and has been really supportive.'

'Why not?' he asked, plucking another ball out of the air. 'He's a good chairman, and it should make an interesting book. It's a good idea.'

Behind the goal, watching us, were a clutch of City supporters in sky-blue kits. One or two pointed towards me. I certainly didn't look like a new goalkeeping coach. So who the hell was I?

It was a good question, and I was starting to ask it, too. One thing I was not, any more, was one of them. I was on the other side of the barrier, chatting to Oggy, as I would later be chatting, I presumed, to Gary and Dion and the others. And it momentarily occurred to me that, as the process went on, what I would cease to be was yet another Coventry City supporter watching his heroes from afar. As I talked to Oggy, he started to become (as he'd been all the time, of course) just another person. Nice guy, Oggy.

One's attitudes to people one knows are richer and more complex, more understanding, more forgiving, than they are to mythologised members of a team. But in order to be a proper supporter some distance has to exist, a kind of compassion gap. Many a time I have sat at City games screaming for one player to be taken off, or yelling at another for making a bad mistake. We can only maintain that kind of fanaticism when the players are faceless functions of our own desires and fantasies. And I could already see that the next time Oggy made a terrible mistake and let a goal in, what I would mostly feel was sorry for him.

The point was reinforced in a long conversation with John

Salako after the game (which Coventry won 4–1, having trailed at half-time, before a disappointingly meagre crowd of 1,268). Over the post-match tea – nobody told me to keep out, so I tucked in – the players showed some interest in my project. Paul Telfer reckoned that it would be nice to have a book about the club during his time there. Hearing that I lived in Leamington Spa, he immediately, and somewhat puckishly, asked if I'd met Snowy (Noel Whelan). I admitted that I'd heard one or two stories emanating from the Leamington pubs and clubs. 'You've got to do something about Snowy,' said Telfer.

Salako wanted to know what sort of book this was going to be. 'Can we talk to you? Is it off the record, or what?' After my brief explanation, he was immediately frank and responsive. We sat in a corner of the room, eating chicken legs and drinking tea. A sensitive and intelligent man, he was clearly engaged by the process of thinking about the game. His analysis of what went wrong the previous season was revealing. 'Life was fun under Big Ron, he's a player's sort of manager. He assumes if you are a professional player he doesn't have to tell you much. But you know, I wonder if the days for that sort of approach aren't over. If you look at some of the teams that did well last year – better than you would have guessed they'd do, like Leicester – what they did was play to a plan. Everyone knew what his role was in that plan, and everyone did it.'

Surely that was now true under Gordon? He looked slightly doubtful. 'I'm not sure, yet,' Salako said, clearly choosing his words carefully, 'that we're all clear about our roles, that we're getting one plan and sticking to it.' This feeling was no doubt enhanced by the fact that, in the second half, Gordon and Garry had been constantly shouting at him, telling him to push forward, or to get out wider, or to drop back into defence. Standing next to them in the dugout – nobody told me not to – I was most struck by the fact that what I was watching was a football game. This may sound pathetically obvious – what did I expect, a ballet? – but what I mean is that it wasn't unlike watching one of Bertie's games when he played in a kids' league: players milling about chasing a football, with lots of people on the sidelines shouting much the same kinds of advice. These guys were better at it, but it was still a football game, played with a football.

It doesn't seem merely this from the stands. The distance adds glamour. Watch what happens when a ball is kicked into the stand during a Premiership game: everyone is desperate to get a hand to it. Whatever it is they are clutching after, and drawing energy from, it isn't just a football. It's a talisman, a grail, an object of such magical properties that merely to touch it is to gain some of its power. Alan Shearer kicks it, and imbues it with his essence; it goes into the crowd; a fan touches it, and Essence of Shearer magically passes into his body. He is brushed with magic: he too is a hero. But from up close, all of that mysterious nonsense dissolves: a football is just a football; a football game, whatever the level, is just people playing football. It was a mildly disappointing discovery.

Salako was interested in the investment that supporters make both in the game and in the performances of individual players. 'At Coventry,' he said, 'we have to be sure to lift the crowd, to get them into the game in the first five or six minutes. If we play well then, the crowd are behind us. But if we don't begin well, then they tend to get on our backs. And you can hear them – there's five or six I can hear who like having a go at me.'

'It's funny, that,' I said. 'I bet you don't hear the ones who are supporting you. You know, the ones chanting "Super John Salako!" I remember publishing a book once that got some good reviews, but I can only remember the one bad one.'

He nodded, recognising common ground. 'I suppose, if you're good enough, like world class, then it doesn't bother you. Maybe some players get bothered more than others. But there is a certain kind of player who needs to feel the crowd behind him, not on his back.'

He was clearly talking about himself, and I immediately felt ashamed. I could remember occasions when I, believing him to have failed to take on a man, or to have shied out of a tackle, had screamed criticism at him. Fortunately, I sit high up in the East Stand, so I couldn't have been one of the voices he remembered. Could I?

'It's a lot about confidence,' he said. 'When you're feeling confident, and the crowd is with you, you feel free to express yourself, not afraid of making a mistake.' He reflected for a moment. 'I've had two careers, really. First at Palace, when we came up, finished third, did well in the Cup. I played for England at twenty-two. Then came the injuries, and this time at Coventry is like a whole new career to get established. Sometimes I think I'm as good as I was, haven't lost any pace, but it's easy for you to fool yourself. Perhaps you can never tell if you are as quick as you were – it's up to others to judge that.'

Of course he had lost pace. I remembered watching him six years ago when he was really quick and confident. I think he knew this, but the very admitting of it would have been a kind of concession, a form of giving in. But he had had some serious injuries. Why shouldn't he have lost pace? And why should he admit it? I've lost hair, and memory, and libido, and I don't like to admit it, either – and my career isn't based on the possession of any of them.

He wished me luck with the book. 'Are you coming to all the games with us, then?' he asked. I said that I hoped to be as present as I might be allowed to be. He looked a little doubtful. 'Is there a problem with that?' I wondered.

'Oh,' he said, 'it'll be fine if things are going well. But when things get tight and tense, it's easy to look for someone to get mad at and blame. And you'll be there . . .'

The notion that I could be blamed for Coventry having

a bad season had a perverse appeal. I'd rarely felt so important.

It was a quiet ride home. We watched a Richard Pryor video, and then the players decided to make up a compilation of songs to play on the coach during the season. Garry Pendrey started us off by requesting 'My Way', Gordon sang a passable version of 'Help Me, Rhonda', and a series of other ballads and classics were put forward. Catching the drift, I suggested 'Bridge Over Troubled Water'. 'Great song,' said Gordon. It went on the list, and even Miller didn't object. I was beginning to make an impact already.

As we arrived back at Ryton at about 1.15 in the morning, I offered Oggy a ride home – he lives just down the road. He was a little cross about the disappointing attendance at the match, which would net Uzzell something like £10,000. In contrast, David Busst (whose career was ended after a terrible injury at Old Trafford) was given the proceeds of a full-house testimonial held at Highfield Road against Manchester United. A career as a football player is a precarious thing, and can be over in a moment, by accident or malice. The Uzzell incident had been given some television coverage, and Oggy thought 'it looked like he did him, but sometimes it's hard to tell. It happens, though.' He may well have been thinking of the previous year's match at Arsenal, when Ian Wright's injudicious tackle had flattened Oggy and broken his nose.

'Did Ian Wright do you, then?'

'I think so, yes. The ball was fifteen yards past when he hit me, but there was no camera well placed enough to show it. But I felt sure of it at the time.'

'How do you feel about it now?'

'I don't think about it. You have to let that sort of thing go, forget it. Some of the lads know him, say he's OK. Anyway, it was just a broken nose.'

Oggy's nose is legendary. Not only of nice size, it has so often been twisted, broken, misaligned, or displaced, that it looks a veritable refugee on his face, drawn first in one direction, then another. Or maybe it's just like a goalkeeper: battered, peripatetic, vulnerable. He got out as we pulled up outside his house – like Gordon's, a restored barn – and wished me goodnight.

5

Clump 1

Coventry v. Chelsea, 9 August
Arsenal v. Coventry, 11 August
Coventry v. Bolton, 23 August
Coventry v. West Ham, 27 August

It was 9 August, opening day of the new season. The day I became a vice-president. Bertie did, too, only he was in Spain, so my daughter Anna got to be one instead. We arrived for lunch at one o'clock. She was wearing one of those little black linen dresses that look so perfect if you're gorgeous and twenty-three, and I had on a black silk blazer and rather a nice tie. It was boiling hot. Coventry were to play Chelsea in a couple of hours.

During the course of the afternoon the catering department would serve some 865 lunches in a variety of venues and dining rooms, a figure that dwarfs the capacities of the mega-restaurants of Terence Conran. A team of nineteen chefs and assistants had been preparing vegetables and sauces for twenty-four hours, and that did not include the food that would be eaten round the ground by your non-executive sorts of supporters. The range of catering and viewing facilities at Highfield Road is organised according to a kind of class system. At the bottom is the lumpenproletariat, who are given hideous pies and chips, and coffee made out of powder; then there are the members of the various 'clubs', who have their own bars, dining facilities and seating areas; then the bored-looking company representatives who peer out from glass cages called executive boxes; then the directors' own dining rooms and suites.

The Ladbroke Club, situated in the East Stand, where Bertie and I were members the previous year, serves an edible, if expensive, fixed-price lunch, gives you free tea at half-time and has a badly understocked bar. At a slightly higher level, both geographically and socially, is the Premier Club, where the standard of catering is somewhat better, you can buy a small cigar and all the seats are behind glass. But the fanciest and most prestigious of these clubs – the one that shows that, in Highfield Road terms, you have made it – is the Vice-Presidents Club.

It was a stroke of marketing genius (initiated under Derrick Robins) that members be individually called vice-presidents, spuriously suggesting, to an outsider, an important role in the administration of the club. After all, members of the Ladbroke Club aren't called Ladbrokes. But all a vice-president is, really, is an upscale fee-payer. 'You'll enjoy it here very much,' I was told by Bill Hancock, the chairman of the Vice-Presidents. 'There are some very powerful and influential people here.'

I had joined on the advice of Bryan Richardson, who thought the Vice-Presidents 'closer to the action'. By this he meant something physical – the club is situated in the Main Stand, next to the directors' area, and near to the dressing rooms and players' bar – and also something metaphorical. More people in the know frequent the Vice-Presidents. The club's directors pop in from their private dining rooms down below for a drink; the chairman sometimes makes an appearance after the game. If the result is bad, he can take a bit of stick, but he's utterly imperturbable. 'I tell them I don't kick the fucking ball,' he says with a grin, 'and ask them if the roast beef was all right.'

Last year I was perfectly happy with the amiable folks in the Ladbroke Club: our friends Max Smith and Guy, who sat next to Bertie and me; a chap called John and his father, brother and son; the 'other' John Sillett (a spitting image of the former Coventry manager) and his friend, who once yelled at Bertie when he whistled too loudly; a fellow who was a Manchester City supporter but came anyway; and lots of people whose faces I knew and to whom I chatted animatedly without ever knowing their names. Names don't matter to football supporters. We have something better than names: a common pursuit, a shared passion.

The Ladbroke Club not only costs £400 a year less than the Vice-Presidents, it has a more relaxed dress code. No trainers or jeans, but otherwise you can wear what you like. People look casual, happy and relaxed. On a hot day they would dress in short-sleeved shirts, trying to keep cool. I, as a sign of my new status, was sweltering (jackets can come off, but the tie has to remain in place) as I tucked into my roast beef – the 'signature meal' of the Vice-Presidents, according to Val Wright, the club's catering manager – served direct from a trolley. It was good, though Anna thought it wasn't rare enough. What did she expect, carpaccio?

The clientele was largely middle-aged and white, but with a fair smattering of women – wives and daughters – stolidly dressed and coiffed, sporting suntans like fashion accoutrements. At the table next to us, two couples were enjoying their lunches – beef for the men, salmon for the ladies – while sharing stories of holiday pool-maintenance and golf in the south of Spain. They were a little loud, comfortable in their surroundings, proud to be there. It would have surprised me to hear them talk about football.

As we emerged into the open air, the ground looked fresh and cheerful, as if it had profited, like the rest of us, from the summer holidays. In the corner of the resplendently green pitch, the Coventry cheerleaders assembled in parallel lines to greet the teams. In 1994, in response to the occasional visits of the Sky Sports cameras to Highfield Road, someone at the club got the idea that what we needed was cheerleaders, and half-time entertainment. And so the Sky Blue Belles were born: a team of about fifteen adolescent girls, luridly dressed in sky-blue polyester and beige tights (which managed to suggest, from a distance, the absence of any underwear at all), undistinguished by talent or grace of form. This pom-pom-wielding, hapless group would twirl about in fixed routines, to an accompaniment of hideous rock music and to the general irritation of the supporters, who wanted to chat among themselves. Presumably the girls enjoyed it, though if there was any single adjective that could best have described them, it was joyless. For the most part they were lumpy, gum-chewing, rhythmless: it was astonishing that anyone could have believed this was entertainment. I suppose it had a sort of primitive authenticity, but any appreciation of that soon wore off.

It couldn't last, and it didn't. Within a couple of years, someone noticed that no one in the crowd gave a damn about the Sky Blue Belles. While they flopped about at half-time, life in the stands went on without so much as a glance in their direction. When they finished their routines and pranced off, pom-poms aloft, faces devoid of any expression other than relief, there would be a smattering of polite applause, led, I always suspected, by their families. With that acuity that characterises the sharpest marketing mind, it was decided that the Belles had to go. And what to replace them with? That was easy. They were replaced by the Sky Blue Crew, new cheerleaders who looked even younger – no longer adolescent, but many of them palpably pubescent. 'Don'tya get it?' I imagine my marketeer thinking. 'Now they're just kids. They don't have to be good, they're cute.'

I assume it was all intended to suggest that Highfield Road is a happening sort of place. The Sky Blue Crew are more professional than their predecessors: they train regularly, and give up to 140 performances a year, I was told by Sharyn, their manager and trainer, whose distinctly cute five-year-old daughter, the Crew mascot, regularly accompanies them in their routines. The Crew greet the team as it emerges from the tunnel at the start of the game and after half-time, wriggling about in their signature piece, which involves some unsynchronised shuffling with pom-poms, a great heaving and shaking of shoulders and wriggling of bosoms (by those of them who have them), followed by recurrent lascivious bottom-shaking and hip-thrusting. Most of them, I hope, are too young to have any clear idea of what it is that they are miming.

I don't know about the rest of the crowd, most of whom took no notice, but it made me uncomfortable. It seemed to me the kind of display that would appeal to a paedophile. I would call it pornographic, only that would be an insult to pornography: when a porn queen wiggles her arse at the camera, it's not cute, it's not family entertainment, and it's not thirteen years old.

Why do we have to have half-time 'entertainment' at all? Doubtless my bright marketeer has watched too many Super Bowls, and been beguiled by the fireworks, dance routines and cheerleaders. So we end up with our local version of the cheerleaders of the Dallas Cowboys, those amalgams of peroxide, enamel and silicone. Our girls, by virtue of their youth, are fresher and more appealing, if less adept.

It couldn't have been intentional, but part of the effect of having the team met by the Sky Blue Crew was that it made the players, when they came out of the tunnel, look terrific: bright, athletic, glowing with health. Subliminally it put hope in our hearts. Chelsea, on the other hand – can this have been wishful thinking? – seemed an odd assemblage of runts: Wise, Di Matteo, Zola and Petrescu looked like starving and deformed child extras from the cast of *Oliver!*

Sadly, they couldn't half play. Coventry spent most of the first half frantically scratching about for the ball, only to give it away upon occasional possession. Huckerby, still not entirely fit, took on the defence with abandon, and was relentlessly relieved of the ball; Gary Breen, playing on the right side of defence instead of in the centre as usual, made repeated adventurous forays upfield, only to give the ball away and end up caught out of position. Afterwards I asked David Burrows, the other full-back, what tactical idea had been behind these fruit-less upfield forays. 'If you find out,' he said quietly, 'you must tell me.'

Gordon was later to remark, acidly, that Breeny had 'a mental block' about playing anywhere other than his normal position. Which seemed quite a good reason not to make him do it. (Indeed, shortly after Gordon made this comment, Breen announced that he would rather play in the reserves than at right back.)

In spite of the marking of the dreadlocked Richard Shaw, so tough and adhesive, Zola seemed to have space and time, and looked a remarkable player. Shimmying about as if he has no bones, he is possessed not merely of great ball skills and passing ability, but of peripheral vision so acute that he actually seems to respond to the runs of players arriving from behind him. Most of the Chelsea attacks were directed through Mark Hughes, shielding the ball with his back to goal as if he were rooted to the turf, so that it became something of a mystery when he moved his feet and laid the ball off flawlessly. Chelsea looked dangerous, fluent, capable of generating chances at will, and they went ahead with a goal just before half-time. Hughes back-heeled a ball to Zola, who immediately located Sinclair arriving, unaccompanied by any Coventry defender. The well-struck goal was unsurprising, except that it had taken Chelsea so long to convert their obvious superiority into something tangible.

It was a bad time to concede a goal, but a great one, just a minute later, to get one back. Surrounded by defenders, Dion Dublin just got his head to a long throw-in and flicked it backwards over De Goey and into the far corner of the net. It was against the run of play, and a greatly relieved crowd rose to salute it. Except for most of the vice-presidents, who, true to those exalted ideas of their own decorum, did not stand, but instead applauded with the kind of mild disinterestedness that pertains at a cricket match. In marked contrast, Bryan Richardson, in the directors' area next door, leaped to his feet exultantly, a huge smile on his face. Gordon Strachan, seated next to him in the stands – as he often is in the first half, before going down to the dugout for the second – had a distinct look of relief on his face.

Anna, sitting next to me, had spent much of the half warding off the attentions of the guest of a vice-president next to her, a supporter of some team from Sheffield, apparently more interested in courtship than football. When the ball went into the net, Anna kept – rather primly, I thought – to her seat, though she applauded with some conviction. I whispered to her, 'You're acting like a goddamn vice-president! Why don't you stand up when we score?' Her answer was equally fierce. She hissed in my ear: 'Will you shut up! If I stand up quickly my dress will end up round my waist!' This being the end that her suitor had so ardently envisaged, she had decided on a policy of tranquillity and restraint.

It was a policy much taxed in the second half. Chelsea, constantly on the attack, scored again in the seventieth minute, when the substitute Flo nodded in a pass from Di Matteo. Twelve minutes later, though, after Wise, Flo, and even Zola had missed easy chances, Coventry went level again. In a set piece that had been success-ful the previous year, Dublin took up his position at the near post for a McAllister corner, then drifted four yards into the box and headed a perfectly flighted ball into the net, despite having two men in front of him to impede his movement, and one at the side to cut off the ball.

As I rose to applaud (Anna still sitting resolutely at my side), I felt a considerable degree of relief. Not just because we'd drawn even; what I was thinking about was a moment at Torquay the week before. During the first half, I had joined Gordon to watch the game from the directors' box. Knowing enough to keep still, I listened intently as he muttered his way through the forty-five minutes: 'Good ball . . . OK, OK . . . Close 'em down . . . bad shape, bad shape . . .' Late in the half, Dublin's header from a corner, as he drifted away from the near post, was nicely saved by the Torquay keeper. Turning to Gordon, I said, 'That's the corner we scored goals from last year, isn't it?' He looked at me coolly, and murmured quietly: 'Those two guys sitting next to you are Chelsea scouts.'

After the game, a vastly disappointed Ruud Gullit told the press that Chelsea had practised defending that particular corner for the whole of the previous week. But Strachan, reflecting later on the set piece, commented rightly enough: 'If you have the best header of a ball, and the best person at delivering it, it still isn't easy to stop it.'

The winning goal, with just two minutes left, came from open play: Paul Telfer, active as an escaped ferret, broke free down the right and crossed long for Dublin. Leboeuf seemed to misjudge his header, and when the ball dropped at Dion's feet, he had time to consider and to place his shot. This frequently means he will miss. On this occasion he didn't, and to the overall astonishment and joy of the crowd (except the Chelsea supporters and most of the vice-presidents), Coventry, entirely against the run of play, had won 3–2.

The decisive goal looked from the stands like a piece of good fortune, but according to Gordon it was the result of solid planning: 'We had scouted Chelsea five times, and noticed that Leboeuf always pushes forward too far when the ball is coming downfield from his left. So we thought he would be vulnerable to a diagonal ball behind him. There was nothing lucky about it.'

After the game, over a drink in the Vice-Presidents, while Anna perused a note from her suitor offering his phone number, I had a quick look through the match-day programme. Gordon's column assured us that the team were raring to go, and happily omitted any Big Ron-type posturing – could one really call it optimism? – about qualifying for Europe or the like. In further columns Bryan Richardson and Gary McAllister voiced thanks for previous support and hopes for the future. Also included was a delightful piece called 'At Home with Noel Whelan', which showed the club's acknowl-edged bad boy performing a variety of household duties (hoovering, doing the washing, drinking juice) while living happily – and, by implication, sedately – with his pregnant girlfriend, Joanne, in their converted barn. (That made almost as many converted barns as Subarus.)

A university graduate in media studies, Joanne is in many ways typical of the players' wives. I had rather expected brainless bimbos; instead, many of them are strong characters pursuing their own careers. Gary McAllister's wife works at the Warwick University Science Park; Oggy's is doing an OU course; Dion Dublin's wife, Louise, is doing a college course. Last year, when given the information that Dion was to serve a seven-match suspension for two sendings-off, Louise immediately profited from this bit of insider knowledge by selling him from her Fantasy League team while his price was still high and buying Gary McAllister instead. When asked if this was loyal (much less fair), her only comment was 'Business is business.'

Adam Dent, the chief football reporter of the *Coventry Evening Telegraph* and an amiable and intelligent jour-nalist, had an interesting explanation for the roles that players' wives play in their lives. 'When you think about it,' he said, 'most footballers are treated like children from the age of about fifteen onwards. They have everything done for them by their clubs: their clothes are laundered, many meals provided, housing picked out, mortgages applied for, cars laid on. They aren't used to making decisions about their own lives. They usually can't even choose what club they play for; they get bought and sold like commodities. They tend to marry and have children young, and to have strong and competent wives.' Acknowledging this, Gary McAllister added that players often have a hard time after they give up the game, because they are so used to having everything done for them.

Wandering down to the press room, I watched Gordon give a post-match verdict to the media: 'There was no luck about our win,' he insisted, with a straight face. 'It was down to hard work. We made it a bit scary for ourselves, but that's the way it goes. We can't expect to do too much – we only stayed up by one point last season – but we have improved a few things, and we know we can only get better.' Some time after the match, Alex Miller, an admirer of Chelsea when they are going forward, was to describe them to me as 'having good pictures in their heads', a lovely image, at once more literal and yet more suggestive than merely calling them 'imaginative'. The phrase helped to convey the clear fact that, as the game developed, Chelsea had more options, and saw more possibilities, than Coventry did. But they failed to convert the chances that they created.

Ruud Gullit, with exasperated inelegance, could only say: 'We must have had ninety-nine per cent of the game. It was the other three per cent that cost us the match.' When he came out of the dressing room to board the Chelsea team coach for the return trip to London, he was still shaking his head in bemusement, and muttering, 'Unbelievable.' He stopped to sign some autographs, hopped on to the coach, and Chelsea were away.

Only two days later, so were Coventry, at Arsenal. In recent years it had been a surprisingly profitable fixture, with a win and two draws at Highbury in our last four visits. But given the shaky defensive display against Chelsea, and the improvements in Arsène Wenger's side, there didn't seem much to hope for. Once it became apparent, in the opening minutes, that Dublin was not going to win much in the air, and that Huckerby was going to keep dribbling into blind alleys, all City could produce was a policy of containment. It worked pretty well for the first half-hour, but then a speculative shot from outside the box by the superb Vieira eluded Oggy, and was tapped in by Ian Wright. The game was over shortly after half-time when a mistimed back pass from Richard Shaw was happily seized upon by the predatory Wright, who coolly knocked in the second goal. In the eighty-sixth minute, Coventry managed their first shot on goal, which was easily saved by Seaman.

It had been a bad performance, devoid of ambition, quality or vision. The side hadn't lacked competitiveness, but it is no good winning a ball only to give it back through slack passing. Distribution from the back to midfield seemed haphazard, and the game was played almost entirely in Coventry's half of the field. Virtually the only consolation was that Arsenal hadn't created a single clear-cut chance, though one couldn't escape the conclusion that they could have done if they had needed to. They looked as sleek and dangerous as Chelsea, but much more solid at the back. Gordon was distinctly impressed: 'I thought Vieira was excellent. He does it all, tackling, everything. And they seemed to have another gear to go up if they needed, maybe two. But we were awful, never competed. I wonder if the lads were a little overawed, with the match live on television, and all?' Better teams than Coventry would lose at Highbury this year, and by bigger margins. Nothing boring about this Arsenal side. I'd quite enjoyed watching them.

Jonathan Strange, sitting with me, was appalled when I voiced this admiration. 'You can't admire them!' he admonished me, 'I hate fucking Arsenal. And as for

Ian Wright . . .' He paused for a moment, recollecting Wright's injury of Oggy in 1996–7, and trying to locate a suitable expression for his loathing. 'If you were to say that he had died I'd laugh.' A kindly and sensitive man, a violinist by profession, student of the poetry of Wallace Stevens, it is hard to imagine him swatting a fly. But he meant it, and with an intensity that would leave your average football hooligan looking pale and wan. He will not forgive what he perceives as the brutality, the sheer unfairness, of Wright's challenge on Oggy.

And this is, I suppose, the time to come clean about something: it was Jonathan who wrote that dirty letter (it gives something of a new twist to the meaning of the phrase) to Jasper Rees. I have asked him, of course, if I may say so. And he is not only unrepentant about the incident, he'd do it again. 'He deserved it,' he says. 'I think of it as the appropriate form of literary criticism. I sometimes read his other pieces, and they're quite good. He should stick to other topics.'

In midweek after the Chelsea game, Bertie and I had had a game of golf with Magnus Hedman, a friendly and approachable fellow, who had not, to his disappointment, started the season in goal. A relative newcomer to golf, he had a wide, ferocious swing, and hit the ball a long way, but didn't always know where it was going. Now and again it went into the trees, accompanied by the roar 'Fuck! Fuck! I hate this!' But having started only a couple of years ago, he was already down to a handicap of 18, and you could see he would get better. He's a professional sportsman, and he won't tolerate playing badly.

'Good thing you're a better goalkeeper than a golfer,' said Bertie chirpily as we searched for Magnus's ball. He could afford to be cheeky – he and Magnus had hit it off well, and, after all, he was playing off 12, and winning easily. As we strolled round, Magnus talked about the frustration of being a reserve keeper, playing occasional matches in largely empty grounds against second-rate opposition. 'There's no atmosphere in reserve matches.

It's dead. The thing is,' he said – and the implication was clear – 'it isn't going to be good enough to be a little better than Oggy. Oggy's a legend at the club. I could have signed elsewhere. I'll give it a year, and if I haven't got the job, I'm off.' By this time we'd got to the green, where Magnus studied a ten-foot putt intently and knocked it in. 'That's a five,' he said happily, looking over at Bertie. 'Four for me,' said Bert. 'That makes me four up.'

At the Ryton training ground, in the week following the Arsenal fixture, there was a sense of satisfaction at the yield of 3 points from two games, but I could sense the not very distant sound of whistling in the dark. The defensive performance against Chelsea had been poor, and the lack of ambition against Arsenal all too palpable. But Gordon was quick to observe that any points gained against the top five sides – a kind of league within a league – ought to count as a bonus. 'It's what we do against the rest, particularly at Highfield Road, that will matter.' This seemed a curious attitude in the light of the 1996–7 results against these five teams. Then we garnered 11 points from the ten fixtures (3 from Liverpool, 3 from Newcastle and Chelsea, 2 from Arsenal, none from Manchester United), a ratio of points per game about equal to our results against the rest of the League.

The key, most of the players agreed, was winning against the bottom sides at Highfield Road. The previous year we beat only Leeds and Middlesbrough of the bottom ten teams while compiling the second-worst home record in the League. So the next two games, at home to Bolton and West Ham, were going to be good indicators of what progress had been made. Though West Ham had had a good season the year before, it was hard to imagine that they would be far off the relegation places, while newly promoted Bolton looked likely to struggle, in spite of their impressive performance in winning the First Division championship in 1996–7 and the recent signing of Peter Beardsley, who was likely to make his debut at Highfield Road.

Coventry led by 2–0 at half-time, through goals by Telfer and Huckerby, and should have been four up. John Salako had a header turned on to the post, and Dion Dublin missed a couple of easy chances. With the midfield admirably controlled by Kevin Richardson, who still hadn't signed a new contract, Bolton had hardly been able to get the ball out of their own half. So when Beardsley came on with only thirty-eight minutes left, it seemed as if it was just for a run-out. Playing in midfield, he chuntered about easily, controlling the play, never making a bad pass or taking up an unintelligent position. And you could just see the pattern shifting. Bolton got upfield more quickly, and there Nathan Blake shielded the ball and brought an increasingly lively midfield into play behind him. Coventry looked distinctly uneasy, and were already starting to chase the game when a not very dangerous-looking through ball from Beardsley led to a moment of indecision between Oggy and Richard Shaw, of which Blake took immediate advantage.

It was at this point – or just prior to it – that, Alex Miller was later to tell me, we lost control of the game. 'What we needed,' he said, 'was for one of the senior players to ease the pressure on us, and go down with an injury. Then you get a minute or two to talk among yourselves and get it sorted out. The continentals are good at that sort of thing, and one of the more experienced players should have gone down. There's a lot of money at stake.'

But something more significant than the effect of Beardsley's intelligence and excellence could be observed: Coventry were being outrun and out-hustled. Richardson, playing his first match of the season, was chasing the game after about sixty minutes; Soltvedt, who was looking a little ponderous in the first half, now seemed to be plodding; Huckerby, such a happy chaser of fantasy in the first half, was again unable to keep it up for ninety minutes. Though Telfer ran about with his usual energy, there was no escaping the conclusion: this midfield was not fit enough to last ninety minutes.

Blake scored again, and we were lucky to preserve a 2–2 draw.

In the dressing room afterwards, the team were silent and utterly dejected. 'I think,' Kevin Richardson told me, 'that we simply couldn't believe how well we were playing – that we didn't have the confidence to go on. It's like we said to ourselves "Is this really us playing this well?" and simply got scared to keep it up.' Soltvedt put the point slightly differently: 'Perhaps we're not used to winning. In football there should be no history: you have to take each game, and each moment, as it comes.'

It surprised me that the team's confidence could be so fragile this early in the season. A couple of days later – leaving some cooling-off time – I asked Gordon whether Beardsley had made the difference. He bridled. 'I think it's a myth,' he said. 'You read it in all the newspapers: Beardsley the wonder-man. But we gave them the first goal, and without that, it would have been our game.' He was disposed to put the loss down, not to lack of effort, but to lack of fitness in the centre of the pitch. In his match report for the *Coventry Evening Telegraph*, Adam Dent had referred to the second-half display as 'spineless', and was duly carpeted, on Monday at Ryton, by an irate Strachan, who had circled the offending word. They agreed to disagree.

Everyone did agree, however, that the absence of Noel Whelan had been important. It was hard to believe that so much possession would have been conceded in the crucial areas of midfield had the tireless Whelan played. He had been healing nicely from the knock he collected in the pre-season Scottish game, when, in the previous week, he picked up another, more serious, injury. Having finished his day's hoovering and house-cleaning, and finding himself, drunk and belligerent, in Leamington one night after the pubs had closed, he made a fruitless attempt to batter in a shop window, before, remembering his football skills, he managed to kick it to smithereens. It didn't do his foot much good. Had the resulting wound been a quarter of an inch deeper it would have severed his Achilles' tendon and ended his career. He was going to be out for 'some months'.

After the requisite attentions of the casualty ward and the police, Whelan had to face the much more formidable duo of Strachan and Bryan Richardson. It wasn't the first time such an incident had occurred – he'd already been banned from driving – and the club had lost patience with him. A fine of £5,000 was immediately levied, along with a severe dressing-down. Whelan was contrite, but tried to offer some excuse. He had, he said, been goaded into behaving so stupidly. 'People do know who you are. I was just socialising when someone started chirping off at me and got me frustrated. We were out for a quiet drink and there was no reason for people to be like that. I know I have a high-profile job but I should be able to go out for a quiet drink. I know that is not the case now.' That sounds the sort of thing you hear, repeatedly, from Paul Gascoigne.

Privately, Strachan was unimpressed. 'When you get in that pattern you tend to stay in it. I need him, but nobody would criticise me if I decided he had to go.' Richardson was more direct: 'I could have killed him,' he told me. 'Gordon could, too.'

The effect of Whelan's absence was again apparent in the match against West Ham at Highfield Road four days later. The pattern was similar to that against Bolton: a half-time lead reflecting first-half dominance, loss of fitness and form in the second half, and an eventual draw (this time 1–1). Disgusted with the two draws against bottom sides, Richardson believed that 'Whelan cost us four points'. Perhaps the gap between the relatively modest 5 points from the first four games and Richardson's possible haul of 9 overestimates the difference Whelan might have made, but there were further areas of concern. Coventry had fielded a patently unfit side, through lack of quality replacements. McAllister being unfit, Strachan had preferred Richardson and Soltvedt to Willie Boland or

Martin Johansen. The squad, if anything, seemed weaker than that at the end of 1996–7. It made one wonder if Bryan Richardson's belief that quality players were being added was sustainable in the face of the evidence emerging to the contrary.

6

A Trip to Old Trafford

I had a blue card pass, and it was magic. 'Allow This Person Access To All Parts Of The Ground', it said, and damn me if it didn't work. In fact, so accommodating were the Coventry stewards that I was able to bring Bertie along as well: a breezy 'He's with me' did it every time. As soon as Graham Hover presented me with the pass, we went everywhere: to the locker rooms and dugouts, to the players' bar, into the various hospitality suites. If there was a door that looked closed to the general public, we opened it. It was the objective proof of what Bryan Richardson had promised: 'Go everywhere,' he'd said, 'you can have access to it all.'

At the games, Bertie and I stood next to the pitch while the players were warming up about fifteen minutes before kick-off. The first time we did this Bertie was thrilled at our proximity to the players, who often obliged with a friendly nod, but after a time he got bored. 'Why are we out here, Dad?' he asked. 'What good is it doing us?'

I was shocked. 'Look around you,' I said, 'see all the people in the stands? Any of them down here? We're here because we're allowed to be here.' It didn't cut any ice with him, and he went back into the stands to read his programme. He lacks soul.

The experience at Torquay had taught me that it was sensible to keep a low profile. I'd been lucky in my conversations with Oggy and Salako, two of the most approachable of the players, but Torquay had been a meaningless fixture and the team relaxed and relatively at ease. As the season got underway the atmosphere tightened, the players seemed more abstracted and remote, and I could feel a perceptible closing of the ranks. I would get a smile, and the occasional query – 'How's the book going?' – which seemed designed to ward off questions rather than to prompt them. In any case, I was determined that conversations with the players ought not to be in an interview format. So I avoided making specific appointments with them, carried neither notebook nor tape-recorder and just hoped that chance would throw up the occasional opportunity for an unguarded chat. They were wary about this, and it didn't happen very often: just because I wasn't taking notes it didn't mean I could be trusted.

At Ryton one afternoon, in the week between the Arsenal and Bolton games, I was waiting to see Gordon Strachan when I found Paul Telfer sitting on his own after most of the other players had eaten and gone home. Joining him, I asked how he thought the first two games had gone – a safe enough opening question. Just then Darren Huckerby sloped up and sat down nearby. Immediately turning his attention away from me, Telfer began an innocuous conversation with Huck about the music playing over the speakers in the dining room. I listened for a while, then got up and left. It wasn't, I think, calculated rudeness on Telfer's part: I'm certain he would have intended nothing of the sort. It was a question of priority and of tone. Huck was a team-mate, an insider, a fellow professional. It was inappropriate to talk seriously with me while a team-mate was there. It struck the wrong kind of note. With team-mates around you have a laugh, keep things light.

I hung around waiting for Gordon for over an hour, but he remained closeted in his office. Just after two, I told his secretary, Jenny, that I had another appointment (I didn't), and, leaving a note for Gordon asking him to ring me (he wouldn't), went home to find Bertie for a late-afternoon game of golf. As we were hitting our drives on the third hole at the Warwickshire Golf Course, we noticed Gordon striding up the fairway of the fourth, which was adjacent to ours. He gave a friendly wave and came over.

'Sorry I was running a little late,' he said. 'I wanted you to come in afterwards to sit in on my meeting with my scouts, the lads who cover the country for me. Hear their reports.'

I assured him it didn't matter, and asked if we could meet some time soon. He thought for a while, and suggested that I came to his house on Monday (which was a bank holiday), at one-thirty. No, make that one-forty-five, he amended as he returned to his game. Bertie, who had listened to the conversation, reminded me tartly that I shouldn't get so cross when appointments were delayed. I was sure he was right. Repeating the mantra, 'Keep your ego out of the way,' I duffed my approach shot to the third. Bertie was smart enough not to snigger. As I approached my ball, I asked him to confirm what time Gordon had asked me to visit. 'One forty-five on Monday,' he said. 'Try keeping your eye on the ball this time.'

Monday, as it happened, was also my birthday. Leaving an agreeable lunch party at Max Smith's with the airy announcement: 'Back soon, I have a meeting with Gordon,' I set off into the countryside. As soon as I drove up the Strachans' driveway, though, I knew what was going to happen. There were no cars in front of the house, and it emanated that odd kind of silence that suggests there is nobody at home. I knocked on the door, without hope, several times. Smoking a cigar, I wandered round the garden, just in case he was running a little late.

Half an hour later, I was back at Max's. 'How did your meeting with Gordon go?' he asked.

'Short and sweet.'

Two days later, before the match against West Ham, I hosted a dinner for prospective publishers of the book, and my agent Giles Gordon, at Highfield Road. Anna, Bertie and Jonathan Strange joined us to swell the numbers. One of the publishers had specified in advance that he needed a vegetarian meal. 'That's him out then,' observed Anna acerbically. 'What can a vegetarian know about football?'

At one point during drinks Gordon popped over to say hello, and had a chat with the various publishers.

'I'm sorry I missed you on Monday, Gordon,' I said. 'I was at your house at one-forty-five as we arranged.'

'I waited for you,' he answered, 'at the training ground at four o'clock. There was an Under-Twenty-One game. I was there all afternoon.'

'No, you said to come to the house.'

'I never see people at the house. I said at the training ground.'

'Never mind,' I said as cheerfully as I could, 'it just shows you should never make appointments while you're on the golf course. More important things to think of. But the main thing is, can I come up with the team to the game at Old Trafford on Saturday?'

He paused for a moment. 'I'll have to think about that one. Give me a call at Ryton tomorrow.'

'What time?'

'Nine-thirty.' He said goodbye, individually, to the little group of publishers, friends and children, and departed. Unable to restrain myself, I immediately told the story of the missed appointment to the people down at my end of the table to see what they made of it. Bertie, sitting at the other end, was called upon for confirmation of my memory of events. 'That's right,' he agreed. 'Definitely at Gordon's house at one-forty-five.' I was inclined to believe that, with so many things to remember, Strachan had just forgotten, or got muddled. But I could not understand why he should have seemed so certain of his erroneous memory of events.

'Look,' said Jonathan Strange, 'he didn't win fifty caps for Scotland by admitting he was wrong.' That seemed facile to me, and like a lot of facile remarks, it was probably true. Self-doubt is not a quality you see much of in sportsmen. Though they must have it, the idea is not to let it show. Gordon, no doubt, believed he was telling the truth. He was on auto-edit, some self-installed process in which events come out the way he wants them to. It made me wonder what the players made of him.

I called his office the next morning at 9.30. Jenny told me he was busy, and to try again in ten minutes. I tried again every ten minutes until 10.20, then again, on her instructions, at eleven, when I got through. I was welcome to join the team at the Manchester hotel on Friday night, Gordon told me, but I had to make my own way, as the coach was going to be full – he was bringing a large contingent of players. Jenny rang me later with the directions.

I arrived at the De Vere Mottram Park Hotel on Friday afternoon at about five, just as the Coventry coach was pulling up. There were twenty-four people on board – only two or three more players than usual – and plenty of empty seats. I had expected as much. Gordon greeted me cheerfully as he got off – 'Had a good trip up?' – as we noticed a bit of a log-jam at the entrance to the hotel, presided over by an elegant, balding gentleman in a stylish grey suit, presumably the hotel's manager. On closer inspection, he turned out to be Birmingham City manager Trevor Francis, exchanging pleasantries with some of the Coventry players as his team prepared to depart for their evening match against Stockport County.

Peter Ndlovu, recently sold to Birmingham City by Coventry, and hence now playing in a lower division, greeted Strachan warmly. Strachan was pleased that Ndlovu was scoring a few goals for Birmingham, and a number of the other players, including Telfer and Salako, said hello to their former team-mate. 'Sometimes,' Strachan was to say later, 'players stop improving and they need to move on. Peter was like that; if anything, he'd gone backwards at Coventry. He needed a new challenge. I never stayed at a club for more than five or six years myself. Change is good for you, good for the family.'

The hotel was typical of the kind frequented by Premiership teams. A substantial country house of Georgian origins with undistinguished modern wings and additions, located in Prestbury, outside Manchester, it is of comfortable four-star status, with a health club, swimming pool, golf course and pleasant and extensive grounds. The Germans stayed there for Euro '96, and it is the England cricket team's home for Test matches at Old Trafford. The rooms are generous and utterly without character, the bars and lounges indistinguishable from a thousand such round the world. There is not a single picture anywhere in the hotel that is worth looking at, but none that actively offends the eye. The major aesthetic principle is bland and safe.

In the lobby, waiting to go into the dining room before dinner, Dion, Gary Mac, Shawsy, Willo and Telf were sitting round a table, passing the time in a desultory way. As I entered, there was a distinct, if hardly perceptible, reaction from the group – they all hunched their shoulders inwards and there was a slight lowering of heads as they sought to avoid eye contact. It wasn't even conscious, but the instinct of self-protection was clearly at work. It suggested the behaviour of a herd of timid animals sensing the advance of a predator. I walked past them breezily, as if unaware of their presence, and headed off in search of a drink, or two.

The food served at Mottram Park is unambitious, though it is marketed in the modern mode. The à la carte menu posted outside the dining room features an awful lot of things enhanced with a coulis. Not that Coventry City players, on the night before a match, were likely to consume much coulis. We were given a buffet of chicken, pasta, steak, various vegetables and fruit salad. Most of the players were drinking mineral water. No alcohol was drunk, either with the meal or afterwards.

As Darren Huckerby came in to dinner, casually dressed in a tracksuit like most of the players, and his ubiquitous baseball cap, he was sharply reprimanded by Gordon: 'Huck! The hat!' Huckerby looked at Strachan blankly, uncertain what he had done wrong. Gordon, cool but not unfriendly, eyed him like a strict headmaster. 'Show a little respect, son.' Huckerby, bemused, wandered back towards the lounge, away from the dining room, to return a few minutes later with the cap turned round in the Spike Lee kids-in-the-hood style. It would be nice to think this was some kind of statement on his part, as if to suggest that some cap styles are more respectful than others, but he had just flipped it round and tried again. Huck isn't exactly an ironist. Maybe he thought it would be less noticeable with the visor at the back. He didn't get away with it; nor did Dion Dublin, following him in. It doesn't matter if you're worth £4 million, if the boss says take it off, off it comes. 'Righto, gaffer,' said Dion, without any perceptible trace of resentment.

I love this 'gaffer' and 'boss' stuff. It is reserved for Gordon. Pendrey and Miller are called by their first names. It is a throwback to the world of factory workers and their managers, an anachronistic bit of Victorian class relations, made foolish by the fact that many of the players calling Strachan 'gaffer' make as much, or more, money than he does. And while he can buy and sell them, the likelihood is that many of them will be at the club longer than he will. And this, of course, is part of the point. 'Gaffer' is a generic term; it means 'whoever happens to be manager at the moment', in the same way that 'king' signifies a position and not a person. So to call someone 'gaffer' is to signal one's respect for a position of authority, tacitly to acknowledge the right of the person bearing the title to direct your life, for better or worse. Like 'your Majesty,' the word 'gaffer'– or its surrogate, 'boss' – lends a little formality and distance to what is a complex, and some-times strained, relationship. 'After all,' said Oggy, 'the gaffer is always going to be the most unpopular person in the room. How many players here? Twenty-four? Only eleven of them get to play.'

From the other side of the divide, Strachan was equally conscious of the problem. 'This is a great set of lads,' he said. 'Mind you, most of the lads on Premiership teams are all right – the bad ones have been pretty much weeded out by the time they get to this level – but these guys are a particularly nice lot. You have to keep them on their toes, though. It can be hard to get the balance right, because some of them – like Williams, or McAllister or Telfer – have the inner voice, and others, like Huck and Salako, you have to keep on at them.'

It was, in this context, an unexpected metaphor, this 'inner voice'. Rather than having the banal connotations that it might carry at a Hampstead dinner party or evangelical meeting hall, here it seemed to suggest quite a complex process of maturity and inner-directedness, which Strachan associates, in general, with the older and more seasoned professionals. If you watch Gordon at training or on the touchline, you see that the ones who need an eye kept on them get a lot of pushing, demanding, encouraging, criticising, sometimes even bullying. But it was revealing to note, a little contrary to my expectations, that he was sensitive to the notion that what will motivate one sort of man may alienate another.

'People think of me as screaming a lot from the sidelines, but ninety per cent of it is sheer encouragement. Of the rest, half is tactics, half criticism.' There was some feeling, round the club, that Big Ron had a better rapport with the players, an easier touch, a capacity to say the hard thing and then lighten it with a quip or a bit of tomfoolery. 'Gordon's different from Ron,' said Oggy. 'Just as much his own man, but with Gordon things are black and white.' A driven character himself, what Strachan most dislikes, and least understands, is lack of commitment. But he can be generous about full-hearted players who make mistakes. His response, for instance, to Richard Shaw's terrible back pass which gave away the second goal at

Highbury, was characteristic: 'I never fault a lad for an honest mistake. I thought he had a superb game otherwise, and I told him so.'

In contrast, he remembered his early days under Alex Ferguson at Aberdeen. 'He was from the hard school, and he'd try to break you down. It was always fuckin' this and fuckin' that, and "call yourself a fuckin' footballer, do you?" He'd go on and on at you. And then he'd send them out on the field, and one or two of them would think, my God, he's right, I'm not good enough, and others would get out there and try to prove him wrong. And the first sort were out of there, fast.' You could sense, as he said this, that his feelings for Ferguson were more respectful than warm. Ferguson, after all, sold him twice: once from Aberdeen and again from Manchester United.

'I think Alex saw me as a bit of a joker,' said Gordon, 'always laughing and joking. I think he appreciated that I could play. But I don't think he regarded me as a sensible lad.' There was a much-reported incident involving some tea-throwing between them at Pittodrie, but Gordon believes Ferguson has largely moved beyond that sort of behaviour. 'But he can go back to it. All that psychological warfare business. I think his enthusiasm kept him going at first, but that enthusiasm to keep on winning has made him not only a better manager but probably the best in the world.'

The De Vere Mottram Park does not have a stock of Havana cigars. I have noticed that very few hotels in the north do, though I do not know why this should be, unless the north really is less prosperous than the south. Not that the folk watching the Birmingham City–Stockport County match in the hotel Leisure Centre looked short of brass. A couple of florid gentlemen, obvious refugees from a wedding, to judge from the carnations in their buttonholes (the Daily Events Board by the registration desk announced two weddings: Yvonne and John and Yvonne and Howard), were happily sipping champagne, toasting the voracious Yvonne and watching the game on the 48-inch screen. Having had the foresight to bring my own Montecristo, I settled down next to David Burrows and lit up.

The happy wedding guests were immediately delighted by the presence of Strachan, who was intently watching the game beside Garry and Alex. 'You going to win then, Gordon?' asked the elder of the two.

'You bet,' said Gordon, without taking his eye from the screen. As the game progressed, the two men – avid Stockport supporters – gave a running commentary on the play, looking to Gordon with each comment for confirmation of their acuity. He ignored them entirely. They didn't seem to notice. They were satisfied just to be near him.

Paul Williams and Richard Shaw, wandering in from the adjacent snooker room, where Oggy, an excellent player, was plying his trade, sat down next to Burrows and me, but within a couple of minutes had moved away to a table of their own. Gordon turned his head and said, 'Cigar bothering you, Willo?' Williams nodded sheepishly. Gordon turned to me: 'Rick.' I was guilty of not having shown respect. Resisting an urge to say, 'Righto, gaffer,' I put it out. It made me feel like a surrogate member of the team. (When Gary Breen arrived back in England late from an international match in Dublin, Gordon was quick to accuse him, too, of a failure of respect: 'We were due to be practising set pieces at Ryton, and Breeny didn't turn up. He claimed that he couldn't get a flight from Dublin on time. But he could have. Three of them. I checked.')

Willo and Shaw were quickly bored with the game, and, like most of the rest of the players, wandered back to their rooms, to watch television or listen to music. This left me alone next to David Burrows, which is what I had been hoping for. You need to catch a player on his own in order to get any sense out of him. Having been at clubs like Liverpool and Everton, Burrows was one of the most experienced players in the side in big-match atmospheres.

I asked him if the noise, the sheer volume of sound, was intimidating when you played at Old Trafford.

'If you let it, it can be,' he observed, 'but you can use it as a source of energy. If you let it get to you, then you lose confidence, and when that happens it affects you physically: you have less energy, and then you lose pace and can't keep up with the game. In any game you play the first half hour on adrenaline – if you look, you'll see that's when most bookings occur – and so a big-match atmosphere can help you. And the last half hour, you play that on heart, and you can use the noise – even if the crowd is shouting for the other side – to keep you going.' Gordon, who played at Old Trafford for nearly five years, answered the question more simply: 'It only intimidates you if you are weak.'

Burrows, a typical diligent full-back, tough and reliable, is twenty-eight, and one of the side's more mature figures. He doesn't fit the visual stereotypes. He wears sports coats and trousers rather than the ubiquitous designer suits, has a purely functional haircut and drives a Ford Mondeo, about which he is mercilessly teased. But he knows where he is going. 'Some of them,' he observed, 'particularly the younger ones, the money goes right to their heads, with the clothes, and the women, the cars, gambling. They like it flash. Even when they buy a house, they buy something that looks the best, but they usually choose the best house in the wrong neighbourhood.'

Burrows was currently doing a course on property management at a local further education college. So far he had purchased at auction two flats in the Black Country, done them up and rented them out. He envisages having a portfolio of properties by the time he finishes, and is keen to be taught the relevant skills. 'The chairman says that at every club there ought to be five or six players who will be set up for life if they don't piss the money away. And I don't intend to. But you can't advise the younger ones. They don't take any notice. They're having fun.'

He was interested to hear that I had a background in

higher education, and asked me about the nature of the book. My attitude to it, I said, was similar to his attitude to property development: I am interested in the subject, and I want to be taught about it. I might be ignorant to a degree, but I'm not stupid, and I want to learn how football looks and feels to those inside the game. He seemed sceptical, and wondered if this could be done in a year. I didn't think it could, either, and it wasn't really my topic anyway. But you are more likely to get people to talk to you if you admit, however disingenuously, your ignorance than if you assume that you know what you are talking about. Thus, after the televised game was over, when I joined Gordon in his upstairs suite, the first question I put to him was: 'Tell me what I should be asking you.' He was, perfectly rightly, puzzled by this. 'It depends,' he responded. 'What do you want to know?'

The answer to this was more complex than I could, or ought, to have expressed to him, and had changed even during the short course of my relations with the team. I had begun by wishing to know, in some naïve fly-on-the-wall way, what goes on behind the scenes in a football club. But my experience at Torquay had taught me, early on and good and proper, that you can get behind the scenes without getting behind the scenes. You become a factor in what you are observing. Alex Miller was clearly not going to be talking to the others intimately, or even normally, or even at all, in my presence. It is probably all right to be a fly on the wall: a fly isn't noticed, nobody is likely to say 'Hey, let's be careful here, there's a fly on the wall.' Whereas an outsider on a team coach changes the atmosphere entirely. Anyway, I'm pretty large for a fly.

I had, at first, experienced this hostility to outsiders as a form of rudeness, excusable, perhaps, because so many football players (at least the English ones) are in general inarticulate and self-regarding, and haven't had the life experience to acquire anything resembling even a patina of charm. But if one tried to think about it from the player's point of view, the issue was rather more complex.

Players are incessantly pestered by fans, and frequently interviewed, and they learn how to handle and control the nature of the contacts: how to say as little as possible that is revealing, controversial or egocentric. Their responses are bland and safe, like the hotels they stay in. Gordon says that being interviewed is like a tennis match: questions get shot at you and you volley them back safely, knowing that your interviewer is just waiting for you to make an error so that he can pounce on it. David Burrows told me: 'It's just like reading from a script. You might as well give it to them in advance.'

Players are also used to appearing in televised games, which creates a different and more complex set of problems because the camera can see everything. They are aware that the slightest gesture – the muttered 'Fuck off', a bit of momentary retaliation, the quick, aggressive response to the crowd – can, and will, be caught, and magnified, and frozen, and discussed, and analysed – and punished. So they are trained in self-restraint to a remarkable degree. They are jeered at, kicked, abused, subjected to the vagaries of poor decisions, bad luck and bad form, prone to error, dropped or substituted, and they cannot afford to show much of what they are feeling. It may be all right (within the limits defined by the Football Association) to celebrate a goal, but at times of stress the usual and expected reaction is to show nothing.

Oggy, for instance, is ferociously competitive. At Ryton, if he lets in a goal – not even in a five-a-side, but just while practising with Jim Blyth, the former City keeper and now the goalkeeping coach – he will scream with irritation, 'Fuck! Fuck! Fuck it!' as he picks the ball out of the net. But in a League match, if he makes an error and it leads to a goal, all you will see is him picking the ball out of the back of the net and kicking it upfield. But he is seething inside, fit to kill. He knows he is constantly under observation, and that it is not the aim of the observers, be they television commentators or journalists, to find ways of showing what a nice person he is.

So when we talk of the hostility and distrust that football players manifest to outsiders, we have to understand that it is the product of long and hard training, that it is something they practise and (however unconsciously) value. There is nothing gratuitous about it, and they don't abandon it easily. In talking to Gordon, I needed to find some way round this. Or, failing that – he was never likely to become a confidant – at least to get him to talk about it. 'What I want to know,' I said, 'is something that is hard to ask. I am interested in football as a form of life. I want to be able to get some sense of what it feels like on the inside of the game, and yet as an outsider I'm not sure this is even possible.'

As I said this, I recognised that it put Gordon in a difficult position. Though he had been courteous, I had been wished on him by the chairman, and there was no use he could make of me. Worse than that, I suspected that – rightly – he regarded me as dangerous. In his dealings with the press – of whom he says, 'Of course you don't always tell them the truth' – he remained in control as long as they quoted him accurately. If he was asked a question he didn't like, he didn't have to answer it. Whereas there I was hanging about and peering into things, very present, and making judgements over which he had little control. And a book is potentially more damaging than a newspaper. An adverse or critical article in a paper is forgotten within a day or two; books are always with us. On appearing they have a first life of some months during which they are bought, read, reviewed, discussed. And they don't go away. They are sometimes reprinted; they come out in paperback. What many of us remember of Bill Nicholson and the members of his Spurs side is now largely determined by Hunter Davies's chronicle of a year with that team, *The Glory Game*.

How much of this was squarely in Gordon's mind, I wouldn't wish to guess. Football people are not, in general, readers. Even Oggy, who likes reading, and is one of the more rounded personalities in the side, admits he hasn't read *The Glory Game*, though he has heard of it. In any case, he pointed out, a lot of football players are not interested in football. They don't spend their time talking about it or watching it compulsively, and they certainly don't read books about it. On reflection, this was unsurprising. I don't suppose lawyers spend much time talking about the law. Football players, when they have done their work for the day, like most of us, go home and forget all about it. If this surprises the fans, it is because they *are* obsessed by the game, and love to talk about it. That's different.

So Gordon was probably not consciously worrying about what sort of book this might turn out to be, and exactly how he might be portrayed. He had better things to worry about, and his ego isn't that fragile. But he was, I think, aware that some uncontrollable element had entered the frame. At Ryton one day, John Salako asked me, in a conspiratorial tone, 'What does the gaffer think of the book?' I said that he was polite, but that I didn't suppose he was very keen on it. 'He wouldn't like it,' said Salako crisply. Strachan was coolly aware of being the boss, and in control. But he was not (entirely) the boss of me, and I was now a small part of a world organised so that anything within his ambit was supposed to be under his jurisdiction. Yes, of course, Bryan Richardson might fire him tomorrow, there was nothing he could do about that. But with regard to the playing side of things, his word was law.

So he didn't want me on the coach to Manchester, he didn't want me in the dressing room, he didn't want me in the dugout. He didn't want me at all. Why should he? Though I dreamed of the easy familiarity that Hunter Davies established with his Spurs side in 1971–2, I wondered if such a thing were possible in the modern game. Would any top-flight manager now allow such access to his playing staff, to the secrets of the dressing room, the tantrums, the sheer nitty-gritty? Would modern players lower their guard and talk frankly about their lives? Sure, players were big stars back in 1971, but a lot of them still lived in their old neighbourhoods, took public transport to training, boozed in the local pubs. They remained part of the community that produced them, still had roots in the working class. Whereas today's players, though still working-class in their origins, now lead the displaced lives of lottery-winners, made even more complex by their celebrity. They are comfortable, largely, only with their own.

Curiously, I understood this about the players but missed it with Gordon and his staff. They, too, were much more comfortable if you could get them alone. At dinner, in the company of Alex and Garry, Gordon had been, if not exactly monosyllabic, curtained off in his own world. No doubt my presence had had a lot to do with it. Now, in his hotel room, quietly eating grapes from his basket of fruit, feet propped easily on the table, he was relaxed, almost expansive. 'The thing you have to realise about footballers, and how they are among themselves, is that the major way they relate is through piss-taking. They can be fun, but nothing is sacred. A lad's wife could leave him for another man today, and tomorrow they'd be taking the piss out of him. It's ruthless, but not malicious.'

This sounded utterly ghastly to me, and I could not imagine a person of any sensitivity doing it. I leaned forward earnestly to reassure Gordon that I did not suppose he would indulge in any such sadistic behaviour. 'You don't strike me as the sort of person who would do that,' I said.

'Why not?' he asked in a worried tone. 'I like joining in with the boys, having a laugh.'

'No, I don't mean that. I just can't see you saying that sort of thing.' He looked at me intently, unsure whether I was accusing him of standoffishness or of sensitivity.

'Unlike a lot of managers, I want to be liked, and to have good relations with the players. It hurts me sometimes to think I might have to sell one or other of them. Paul Williams, really nice lad – I don't like to think of that.'

'Does this mean there's a lot of transfer interest in Williams at the moment?'

'No, I didn't mean that, that was just an example. The most interest just now is in Telfer and Whelan. And I don't want to have to sell them, either, though at the right price you always have to be ready to wheel and deal. Telf got a hard time from the crowd last year, but he never lost the players' respect. He's playing really well now. If he even leaves the training ground without feeling knackered, he thinks he hasn't given a hundred per cent.'

'What about Whelan? Aren't you tempted just to get rid of him?'

'I need him. And he's a nice lad, really, with a good heart. But he has to grow up: if drinking makes you aggressive, you can't do it. I've known him since he was fifteen, when we were at Leeds. And he modelled himself then on David Batty – you'd be surprised, quite an intelligent lad, and the club's joker. But Whelan really can't play that sort of role. He hasn't got the judgement for it. He just looks silly most of the time.'

He was not happy with the yield of 5 points from four games, believing that two points had been thrown away against Bolton. Though he had opposed the notion that bringing on Beardsley had turned that game, he still wondered what went wrong. 'I ask myself, if I'd done this, or that, perhaps we might have got a result. Who knows? I was very sorry for the lads. If Dion had put away his chance in the first half, the game would have been over.' But he didn't seem concerned with the details of individual games: they were over now. The problem, he thought, was that the squad was one-paced, and in need of two major signings: one in midfield, and a further striker.

Thinking of my conversation with Bryan Richardson in June, in which the chairman had said that all signings were designed to bring in genuine first-team-quality players, and particularly more athletic midfield players, I asked what Gordon thought of the additions to the

squad? To my surprise, I got something of a different story. Haworth, Johansen and Lightbourne, he said,
were purchased entirely as squad players, on the strict
understanding that the money spent on them would not
prohibit the two major signings he had been promised.
Johansen, indeed, had been purchased solely on scouting
reports, and Gordon had never even seen him play. Even
Soltvedt, heralded by the club as an important signing
after his success in the European Cup games the previous
season, was still regarded by Gordon as marginal to the
first team: 'If Whelan was fit, he'd be playing instead
of Trond.' Hedman, whom Richardson had regarded as
likely to start the season in goal, and who had looked
very solid in pre-season and reserve matches, was still
being groomed as Oggy's successor.

So, with the exception of Roland Nilsson, due to start
his first game of the season on the morrow after recovering
from a muscle strain, and a player of high quality, it
looked as if none of the additions to the squad were,
in Gordon's view, essential first-team players. He was
particularly keen to sign a high-class midfield player
– 'Not necessarily a ball-winner, you don't necessarily
need one. Chelsea don't have one. We just need a good
player next to McAllister.' He had been trying, with
Richardson, to sign the twenty-two-year-old Croatian
international Silvio Maric, of Croatia Zagreb, who had
impressed against Newcastle in the Champions' League.
Coventry have a widespread scouting network throughout Europe, with former Tottenham player Ray Clarke
acting as a full-time European scout (the only such in the
Premiership) from his base in Amsterdam, as well as an
array of agents filling them in on available players. If a
striker was to be signed, he would probably come from
Europe, though Gordon shared the chairman's distrust of
what they both call 'Latins'. ('Latins', I've noticed, seem
to settle down fine in English football when they live in
London. They do less well in Middlesbrough. But then,
so would I.)

Though the squad did not seem stronger to me, Gordon was pleased with the changes: 'Ndlovu was going backwards, and Jess, who's a nice lad and had the best training-ground skills of the lot, didn't have the heart – and if you don't have it by his age, you're not going to get it.' So the addition of strong and reliable squad players, as soon as they were bolstered by the promised major signings, represented an advance. He was beginning, he thought, to see signs of greater toughness and reliability. 'We're creating more chances, and though Dion has missed a few in the last couple of games, he's much happier this year. Last year he was a bit down, and the crowd got on him.'

According to Alex Miller, what Gordon had brought to the club was 'a higher standard of professionalism'. Though he intended no criticism of Atkinson, who left before Miller arrived, the implicit suggestion was that the team was now better prepared and more cohesive. 'The training-ground routines are laid out better, we are more clear about our set pieces, the fitness regime is better, our scouting network has improved – these are the sorts of things you've got to get right. We need to change the psychology of the club, and be positive. Not going out there and hoping to win, but believing we will win. But you can't just say this, it will only happen slowly.'

What this should mean is that you can get more out of the players, bring out what is best in the individuals, create more cohesion as a team playing together. Good management, famously, can do this. Think of Brian Clough and you understand the transforming effect a first-class manager can have on previously ordinary performers. But most managers can't perform that sort of miracle, and, in any case, Gordon's management experience is limited. Why is it that people in football suppose that a great player has the credentials to become a satisfactory manager? So what you had to hope for Strachan was that he was bright enough to learn fast, and on the job. 'I think I am getting more and more of it,' he said. 'It was a help serving under Big Ron for a time, watching and learning, but you have to do it for yourself.'

It was a constant theme in his conversation that tactics and strategies were all very well, but what really mattered were simple qualities like ability, fitness and conviction. This is not to say that he hadn't messed about with tactics like the best of them. Though he acknowledged that the side were happiest playing 4–4–2, during the course of the previous season he had occasionally adopted the current tactical fetish for wing backs, with Brian Borrows or Paul Telfer on the right, and John Salako on the left, responsible for the dual roles. It was clear to everyone that this did not work, but it had been forced on him, to a degree, by the loss of David Burrows through injury. Salako, in particular, looked like a winger trying to act as a defender, and was frequently caught out of position. It hardly seemed the way to get the best out of someone whom Strachan regarded as potentially a player of very high class. It seemed particularly unwise, too, to give Salako, sensitive to his own bad performances, and whose head is likely to go down at criticism, a role in which he seemed destined to fail.

The difficulty, of course, was that for a long period in 1996–7, the side had a problem with full-backs. Régis Genaux, signed from Standard Liège, and a Belgian international, arrived as a plausible full-back or wing back, but was already carrying an injury, and never made a contribution. His wife hated it in England, and Genaux made his own unhappiness clear, vehemently and repeatedly. ('He was the worst person I've ever known,' said both Strachan and Richardson, independently.) David Burrows was intermittently injured for several months (a problem compounded by a misdiagnosis which cost him nine weeks' further recovery time), while the elegant Brian Borrows could no longer be counted on, at nearly thirty-six and never quick in the first place, to keep up with the game. England Under-21 international Marcus Hall was not at his best at left back, never seeming, quite, to know either where he was, or where he ought to be. So the idea of wing backs, given the available personnel, had its appeal.

The clue to the tactics for the coming season was the purchase of Roland Nilsson, a right back of the highest class, with approaching 100 caps for Sweden. He had been signed at the instigation of Ron Atkinson, previously his manager at Sheffield Wednesday, who rated him then as the best right back in the top division. Nilsson's arrival did not necessarily herald the end of the wing-back experiment – Oggy pointed out that Roland was so good he could play wing back if asked – but suggested a return to a 4–4–2, with an overlapping full-back on the right.

Nilsson, though, had not been ready to play his first full game until Old Trafford. In the previous games, Gary Breen (normally a centre half) had been asked to play at right back, and looked extremely uncomfortable. It seemed hard on Breen, who was struggling to establish himself in the side, to judge him on out-of-position performances. Later the next day, at Old Trafford, he was not even on the substitutes' bench, and viewed the game from the stands, looking morose and evidently wondering how he was going to get his place back.

Steve Ogrizovic, senior professional and perhaps, as goalkeeper, the member of the side with the best view – both physically and metaphorically – of how the defence was deployed, said: 'I think that English players are happier playing four-four-two. If you're doing badly, you might have to change tactics, but I think four-four-two feels most comfortable.' Asked about how he had felt in his role as a wing back, John Salako was clearly being careful: 'I'm happier up the wing, but I'll play anywhere the gaffer says, just as long as I'm in the team.' His face and tone gave the real answer: he hated it.

The reason, though, that Gordon had reverted to a standard flat back four, at least for most matches, was that he regarded his two central defenders, Shaw and Williams, as greatly improved in the time he had worked with them. 'Willo is much better in the centre of the defence. In midfield he doesn't have enough time – he likes to have the game in front of him. But he's a footballer now. And Shaw is really much better than he was. He doesn't commit himself so quickly, keeps on his feet better, makes you beat him. If he could improve his long passing, I'd be really happy with him. And when we are more solid at the back, we can get forward better: Dion is playing the best football of his life because of it.'

After an hour and a half, as I took my leave, Gordon rose, shook my hand, and said, 'You see, I do like to talk about football.' The reference, of course, was to our first meeting at his house; was there also, perhaps, some tacit acknowledgement that he had been a little unfriendly, some implicit apology?

The following morning there was a practice on the hotel football pitch scheduled for 11.00 a.m. Before that, players are free to breakfast at their leisure, and wander in between eight and ten, sitting alone or in small groups, more than usually silent, reading their newspapers. Nilsson and Hedman were seated together, quietly perusing copies of *The Times* and the *Telegraph*, like young businessmen at a trade convention. Which is, in some substantial area of their lives, what they are. Football, even at the highest club level, is not a full-time profession in Scandinavia, and Nilsson had worked in the insurance business, while Hedman ran his own clothing business with an annual turnover exceeding £3 million. They come, Hedman explained, from different backgrounds from the English players. They leave school later – at seventeen at the earliest – are (at least) bilingual, and are trained in something other than football.

It is easy to see this in their demeanour, which is more relaxed and approachable with strangers. As I walked across to the training pitch, I had to cross the tenth tee of the Mottram Hall golf course, which was slightly backed up, with two foursomes waiting to drive, owing to the Saturday-morning congestion. Next to the tee I found

Martin Johansen and Trond Soltvedt chatting amiably to the waiting golfers, who urged them to knock a couple of balls down the fairway. Johansen (who plays off 14) hit the ball a surprising distance, about 240 yards down the left. While he teed up another ball, I had a quick word with Trond, who was something of a beginner at golf, and less willing to expose his swing to public scrutiny.

'Tell me what your impressions of English football are so far,' I said. It was a pretty easy question to evade, or to answer quickly and without reflection, but he was happy to give a proper response. In the same situation, none of the English squad members would have responded with anything other than a platitude. But Soltvedt has none of their reflexive distrust of outsiders, perhaps because he, like the rest of the Scandinavians, is used to relating to outsiders; perhaps, too, because he is still something of an outsider himself, trying to make sense of a new set of experiences.

'The major difference from Rosenborg,' he observed (Rosenborg, frequent Norwegian champions, were a successful side in the 1996–7 European Cup), 'is that there your team-mates supported you on the pitch. Here you run about and your own players are yelling at you all the time fuckin' this and fuckin' that, and get the fuck over there. It's shit. At Rosenborg we used to encourage each other all the time, not have all this criticism.'

Johansen, who had finished hitting golf balls, wandered over. Trond, rather than going silent, as one of the English players would have done when a team-mate arrived, included him in the conversation. Johansen agreed, and had a question for me: 'Have you ever been in the dressing room right after the game?' he asked, raising his eyebrows. Sadly, I hadn't, as Gordon had made it clear that I was not welcome until at least ten minutes had passed and the air had cleared.

'Why, lots of yelling?'

He raised his eyebrows even higher, and gave a little whistle.

'Like after the Bolton game?'

'You bet.'

And yet I suspect that what they were responding to was nothing unique to the Coventry side, or to Gordon's managerial style. I felt as if I ought to explain this to them – that the carping on the field had nothing personal in it, that you would observe it in other football teams, from the Premiership to Sunday League. Indeed, when I managed Bertie's Under-10 side in a Warwickshire league, I instituted a rule that, on the pitch, if you couldn't say anything encouraging to your team-mates, it was best to say nothing at all. It didn't work, even with nine-year-olds: they loved yelling at each other. How could it, when many of their fathers were on the sidelines, already screaming criticism at any boy making a mistake?

Soltvedt saw the point, and its implication. He is Norwegian, and middle-class, and he has a different set of expectations. 'The funny thing is,' he said, 'that they're a really nice set of lads in the locker room, and off the pitch. I get on with them fine.' Why shouldn't he? They criticise each other on the pitch with the same ferocity that they direct at him. They don't dislike Scandinavians, they don't dislike each other. They just scream a lot.

To have noted that there is a national, and perhaps a class difference here, however, is to miss the point. Soltvedt and Johansen genuinely believed that you get more out of someone through encouragement than through criticism. To say that your average English footballer believes that a good bollocking is the best way to get someone to pull his socks up is to beg the question of whether he is right. I put this, somewhat later, to Magnus Hedman, like most goalkeepers, a thoughtful student of the game. 'I think that perhaps what you need is a mixture,' he said, 'a little Coventry City and a little Rosenborg.' But then again, goalkeepers rarely get bollocked by their defenders, so perhaps Hedman isn't particularly sensitive on the subject.

The purpose of the pre-match meeting on the hotel pitch

was to have a walk-through of the set pieces: corners, throw-ins, defensive walls, free kicks. As they were choreographed by Gordon and Alex, the first team trudged from one spot to another, while the reserves, who ought to have been listening in case they came on, were chatting among themselves, oblivious. I was standing behind the goal, watching Oggy arrange walls for free kicks, when I was joined by a young boy who had been watching the practice.

'Think you have a chance?' he asked in a friendly voice. He was about thirteen, dressed in the standard trainers and T-shirt, fresh-faced and engaged.

I was irritated. Couldn't he see that I was concentrating on our training routine? Why did he think he had a right to come and talk to me? Did he think I'd talk to anybody? 'Sure,' I said, without meeting his eye, concentrating on watching Noel Whelan say something that made Gary Breen laugh as they horsed about in the bunch of reserves.

'Who are you, then?' the boy inquired, either impervious to my tone, or perhaps expecting nothing other than rudeness from football people. 'The chairman?'

I coughed modestly. 'Not at all.' Before he could ask, in that case, who the hell I was, I moved across to the other side of the goalposts, ostensibly to listen to a conversation Gordon was having with Dion about an alternative to our near-post corner, which involved a ball hit by McAllister along the ground to David Burrows, on the edge of the area, who could then have a shot at goal. The boy, seeing that I was engaged in serious business, politely stayed where he was, and watched the rest of the practice by himself. As it ended, he began to amble back to the hotel, just behind a group of players. Filled with remorse, I walked over to join him.

'You a Manchester United supporter, then?' I asked. Of course he was, though like a lot of them he can't get to many games because of the scarcity of tickets. But he played football himself, and basketball, and was clearly handy at golf, though modest about it. I told him something of the book I was writing, neglecting to mention that some of it was about how unfriendly football people can be to outsiders. Before he left, I briefly introduced him to one or two of the players, and he left looking happy.

Within a few weeks of joining the team, however marginal my role, I already found myself unconsciously mimicking their attitudes. If one friendly little boy could already elicit this tetchiness from me – and tetchiness puts a favourable gloss on how I'd acted – what right had I to expect interest or responsiveness from members of the team? They have to put up with this sort of thing incessantly – and do so, one might add, with a kind of resigned good grace, signing autographs and fielding banal questions while remaining on automatic pilot, their minds entirely elsewhere. If a fan, thrusting a programme to be autographed under Dion Dublin's nose – and Dion is one of the most generous in autograph-signing – were to say at the same time, 'You're a plonker,' Dion wouldn't even hear it. He would smile and say, 'Thanks, mate,' and sign the next programme.

At lunch Gordon, Garry and Alex discussed the forthcoming game, but in a desultory way, the planning already having been done. They were united in their admiration for the set-up at Old Trafford: 'I think they are the biggest club in the world, bar none,' said Gordon. 'There's a tremendous atmosphere. Let's not leave for the ground too early. You just sit around too long and get nervous and talk shite.'

The tactical plan for the game had been explained to me twice: once on the previous evening in my conversation with Gordon, and once by Alex Miller after breakfast. The key to the match, they agreed, lay in trying to counter United's pace: 'They're very two-paced, as a team, and the through-balls to Cole or Giggs can kill you,' said Gordon. 'So what we have to do is lie back in our third of the field, let the defence play deep with the midfield quite close to them, keep Sheringham or one of the others from playing the ball behind us. Then, if we can compete for the ball in midfield, we should be able to contain them.' To this end he had dropped Soltvedt, who was neither quick nor a ball-winner, and brought in Marcus Hall – 'fresh young legs' – deciding to play Salako and Huckerby on the left and right of midfield, and Dublin in front of them.

I wondered if playing five in midfield signalled a lack of attacking ambition, remembering the poor display in the Arsenal game. But Gordon felt that the problem against Arsenal wasn't tactical – 'We just couldn't pass the ball to each other, kept giving it away' – and that Dion would have plenty of support when the ball got forward. 'When it comes in from the left, Huck will push up as a second striker; when it comes in from the right, Salako will.' So playing one striker was the same as playing two strikers. Unless you asked Alex, who told me that we were being adventurous, and playing three: 'Salako and Huck will both press up, so I hope we can make some chances.'

Gordon was happy enough for me to join the team on the coach to Old Trafford, leaving the hotel at 1.30. Our police escort took us into the city of Manchester, where an astonishing number of supporters were already on their way to the ground. They viewed our coach with the mild interest a bull might occasion on its way to the ring, and one or two fingers were raised, pointing out individual players. Numerous people waved to Gordon, a former favourite at Old Trafford, but he didn't notice. I was sitting by the front window, doing my best to look like Dion Dublin, but my suit wasn't smart enough, and nobody waved to me.

On disembarking from the coach, Gordon was enveloped in a sea of warmth. Supporters wanted his autograph, stewards wished to welcome him back, an official of the club offered a handshake. Reduced to little more than a thatch of ginger hair surrounded by a waving mass of red shirts, he took the adulation easily, and, remembering the first rule of autograph-signing – keep walking while you are doing it – made for the players' entrance, with me at his side. The steward had a brief look at me – who was I, the chairman? – and let us through into the dressing rooms. Leaving my briefcase inside, to give me a reason to pop back after the match, I went out into the corridor, just as Bobby Charlton was walking past. He gave me a cheerful smile and a nod: if I was there, I must be somebody. Teddy Sheringham was lying on a massage table getting a last-minute rub-down. Ryan Giggs came out of the United dressing room, tossing his locks like a pony in a breeze. He looked at me intently, but didn't smile.

Once you're back there you can more or less do what you want. I accompanied several Coventry players down the tunnel and out towards the pitch. As you come out of the tunnel the North Stand looms ominously before and above you, an expanse of three tiers that holds more spectators than the whole of Highfield Road. But the total effect, very few spectators having yet arrived, was far from intimidating. Old Trafford has an asymmetry which seemed to me vaguely incongruous, almost comic, as if it had begun on a grand scale and then petered out, rather than the other way round. It is, after all, pretty small beer compared to the San Siro or Nou Camp, those cathedrals of football majesty in Milan and Barcelona, its pretensions to grandeur on a cosy, English sort of scale. Not a stadium at all, really, just a collection of variously sized stands, no different from the other grounds, just larger.

As I walked along the side of the pitch, John Salako trotted by, looked around him, and said, 'This is what it's all about, playing on grounds like this.' As he stopped to sign autographs at the entrance to the tunnel, and while no one was looking, I quickly put my foot over the touchline, and my toe on to the pitch, just to say I'd been there. I immediately felt ashamed, and retracted my foot quickly, before it got singed, or I got ejected. But no one bothered me. I was with the Coventry lads. I belonged there.

An ear-splitting fanfare of trumpets greeted the teams

as they emerged from the tunnel – the kind of music that would inspire the sort of person who thinks *Ben Hur* is a great movie. The game itself, aside from one or two little things, went according to plan. The defence, playing deep, cut out potential through-balls. Nilsson was solid, always in the right place, got forward intelligently, and laid on a couple of great passes. The Coventry strikers – all one, or two, or three of them, depending how you looked at it – created space and chances. Dion hit a post, Huckerby had a couple of good runs. Afterwards, Gordon was glowing in his praise of his team, and Alex Ferguson said that perhaps Manchester United would have to rethink their strategy 'for games like these'.

In the dressing room, heads were bowed gloomily. Dion was wondering how we could have lost 3–0 after such a display, Gary McAllister sitting with his head in his hands, Gordon shaking his head wearily. In the second minute, an innocuous shot from outside the box had deflected off Richard Shaw's boot and into goal via Cole. Halfway through the second half, a United free kick, flicked across goal, hit Roy Keane on the knee and went in. He celebrated as if he had intended it. And in the final minute, a perfect ball from Giggs put Poborsky through for the final goal.

I crept into the dressing room, picked up my briefcase and headed off. On my way to Manchester Piccadilly, I stopped off at the Manchester United Superstore. It was mobbed with supporters clutching children in one hand and tenners in the other. The place was crammed with overpriced tacky rubbish: kits in four varieties, mugs, scarves, ashtrays, pens and pencils, beer mugs, golf balls, footballs, duvets and sheets, stickers, hats, coats, socks. I even found a wind-up Ryan Giggs doll, but I couldn't spot a blow-up one. It would sell, and not just to the ladies.

7

Clump 2

Coventry v. Southampton, 13 September
Sheffield Wednesday v. Coventry, 20 September
Coventry v. Crystal Palace, 24 September
Blackburn v. Coventry, 28 September
Coventry v. Leeds, 4 October
Barnsley v. Coventry, 20 October
Coventry v. Everton, 25 October

Five points after five games didn't seem much of a start to me, but Bryan Richardson was unworried. 'Well, we didn't expect to get anything at Highbury or Old Trafford, so five from three games isn't too bad. But it should have been nine. The Whelan incident really hurt. He would have kept up the pace in the middle of the field against Bolton and West Ham. We would have won those games.'

'Are you thinking of selling him?' I asked. 'He seems pretty incorrigible, and this sort of thing is always likely to happen again.'

'We need his strength in the squad, up front or in midfield. After all, he's a four-million-pound player – Ray Clarke, our scout in Amsterdam, says he could play for Ajax. Dion is a great header of the ball, but he's limited: he's not very quick, and doesn't ever take people on. I can't recall him ever going past somebody – he's just not that sort of player. And defenders have got used to Huckerby by now, and they know how to read him, to lay off and double-team him. He may improve as he goes on, but only by instinct. Basically, we need to add a top-class striker.'

Gordon and Bryan had just returned from a trip to Zagreb and Monaco. Richardson's role in the transfer activity is an active one. He travels the continent widely, both with and without Strachan, and is constantly on the look-out for possible signings, though he says he would never impose a player on Gordon. Their primary target was still Croatia Zagreb's midfielder, Silvio Maric, who had been outstanding for Croatia in the World Cup qualifying games, and Strachan was keen to sign him. 'He's a world-class player, very intelligent, nice lad.'

That sounded too good to me: Coventry can attract players only up to a certain level. Above that players set their sights higher. 'Why would a player of his class, and potential, wish to sign with Coventry City? Surely he will go elsewhere?'

Richardson wasn't so sure. 'Yes, Barcelona, Internazionale and Milan are all interested in him as well, so there is no shortage of competition.' It is at points like this that Richardson's native optimism and ambition seem fool-hardy, even delusional. He responded to my sardonic grimace with an interesting explanation. 'Look. Barcelona has sixty full-time players, the Italian clubs do, too. Maric is good, but there is no guarantee that he will get right into their first team. He's not quite ready for that. So why not come to us? But you have to be honest with the boy. We put it to him that he can come to Coventry for a few years, and then, when he is ready to go, we let him. You have to make a moral commitment to the player. A couple of years playing in the Premiership would be good for his development. And if we're not greedy, insisting on a long-term contract, we might get him.'

Maric, apparently, had thought this a reasonable line of thought, and was ready to consider a move, but Croatia Zagreb were unprepared to let the player go ('The package would have come to three or four million,' according to Richardson) while they were still in the European Cup. So, until Christmas, at least, the deal was on hold. 'There will still be twenty-five games left, so that may not be too bad, as long as we're not in trouble.' So Richardson and Strachan's next port of call was the French champions, Monaco, where, it was known that Dr Campora, the president of the club – who had sole responsibility for transfers – was considering a clear-out. Richardson and Strachan tried to put together a package, valued at up to £5 million, which linked the superb young reserve striker Trezeguet with any one of the midfield players John Collins, of Scotland, the Frenchman Benarbia or the Pole Legwinski. But Monaco were still in the European Cup, and a deal with them was unlikely to happen before Christmas, either.

Richardson, displaying the optimistic sang-froid that is behind his financial planning, kept faith with his long-term strategy. 'We'll keep our powder dry. Gordon is doing a great job. The team is much improved, and the results will come. I'd rather sign international-quality players – we don't just need one, we've got to get at least two – in the New Year than common-or-garden ones right now.'

As usual, it sounded good, and, as usual, I found myself wondering. We had only five points: if not relegation form, certainly not a good start. The chairman's protestations to the contrary, we had not really improved the squad. We were competing with Barcelona, for God's sake, to sign players. And (as it was soon to be announced) we were facing a loss of £10 million in the previous financial year. Yet Bryan Richardson spoke with perfect conviction of our prospects for a good Cup run and a solid mid-table place that season, a future with international players in a futuristic £67 million new stadium, and a flotation that would, in just a few years, value the club and its associated leisure business at something over £200 million.

Let me quote something of interest here from the Coventry City chairman: 'We are going to become the Real Madrid of Europe. At Coventry, in five or six years, we shall have without a doubt the finest and most revolutionary stadium in this country, both for spectator facilities and social amenities.' The new structure, he said, would be unique in Britain, with indoor sports and leisure facilities to be let to local clubs and schools. Lounges, restaurants and bars would be open every night, and there would be a club room with the capacity to hold 2,000 people. 'There will not,' said the chairman, 'be anything to touch it.'

And now let me admit something: that wasn't said by Bryan Richardson, but by former chairman Derrick Robins, in 1970. The visionary optimism of it reminds one of Richardson, and serves as a useful reminder both that Coventry have been ambitious in the past – the following season they played in Europe – and that ambition is sometimes unaccompanied by success. I am sure that Robins was just as optimistic then as Richardson is now, and probably with greater reason: in 1970 Coventry were on the crest of a wave; when Richardson took over in 1994, staying up was about all the club seemed capable of. If that. In three years Richardson had laid down a brilliant long-term strategy that was solidly imagined, financially ambitious, businesslike and profoundly exciting to all of us who cared about Coventry City. All it had failed to do so far was produce a good team. 'It takes time,' he told me calmly. 'It'll happen.'

The following game, against Southampton at Highfield Road, provided evidence that Richardson's optimism was not unfounded, while at the same time confirming my fears (and, to be fair, some of his own) about the side. Southampton, still lacking the injured Le Tissier, were awful: utterly ponderous in defence, lacking in sharpness or vision in midfield, toothless up front. Coventry were infinitely superior, but profligate. Dublin later reckoned that he had missed seven good chances, one of which hit the woodwork. Fortunately, in the sixty-fifth minute, Dion flicked a pass into the path of Soltvedt, who gathered the ball, sold a dummy and bashed the winner past the keeper. The final score of 1–0 didn't reflect City's superiority.

Soltvedt, ironically, was only playing because Kevin Richardson had been transferred to Southampton for £200,000 in midweek. Richardson, who was made Southampton captain, had a quiet game, and was booed every time he touched the ball. It seemed a curious and unkind reaction from the crowd, who only a couple of weeks earlier had acknowledged him as the best Coventry player on the pitch, but there was nothing personal in it. A member of the tribe had defected. 'City reject – ooh-ooh – City reject!'

But to the players, this is how life works. Richardson had been told quite clearly that he was not going to get regular first-team football, so he refused to sign a new contract. Southampton offered it, so he went. It was as simple as that. The fans resent it because they think of players as if they were supporters, and supporters do not change their allegiances. But Kevin Richardson was not a Coventry City supporter. He played for them, while he could; when he couldn't, he left. After the game I asked Oggy, the longest-serving member of the Coventry side, whether it was odd to face Richardson as an opponent, having trained with him only a couple of days before, and he looked at me quizzically. 'Not at all. Happens all the time. Players are like mercenaries, I guess, but then, so are football clubs. As a player, all you are guaranteed is the wages in your contract. If I lost my place in the side, and some other club offered me first-team football, and they'd pay the wage, I'd probably be off, too.'

Speaking about the game afterwards, Garry Pendrey was dismissive of the Southampton side: 'I didn't see anything there. They will struggle. They don't have a single player who we'd want for our first team.'

'Of course not,' I said, 'not with Le Tissier absent. But wouldn't we love to have him!'

He shook his head dismissively. 'Total waste of space. I wouldn't play him if you gave him to me.'

I was astonished, and horrified. What right had Garry Pendrey – erstwhile thumper of a full-back with Birmingham City, one of the honest journeyman players and latterly coaches – to malign a player of the majestic abilities of Matt Le Tissier? Didn't it just sum up everything you need to know about English football? It was only a year before, after all, that Le Tissier's 25-yard shot at Highfield Road had not merely beaten but totally flummoxed Oggy, who could not believe that anyone would shoot from that position, much less place the ball so accurately into the corner. Matt Le Tissier, like Glenn Hoddle before him, can transform a game, transport a crowd, and with one moment of grace provide that aesthetic delight that makes as fundamentally banal a game as football seem a form of art. How could Pendrey account, then, for Hoddle's repeated attempts to get Le Tissier into the England side, and on to a stage worthy of his ability?

'Sure, Glenn tried. But it didn't work, did it? The thing about Le Tissier is you have to build a side round him, and when you do – like Southampton – it's going to be a bad side. That's why none of the big clubs have ever been in for him.'

'Chelsea was,' I said quickly, pleased to think myself knowledgeable enough to contradict him.

'No they weren't. Harding wanted him. And Harding thought like a fan. But Bates would never agree to it. Nobody at the big clubs would.'

'Anyway,' I countered, producing another snippet of supposed information, 'Le Tissier isn't available. He says he likes it there, and doesn't want to move.' (I'd always rather admired his quiet lack of ambition, and the desire to stay geographically and psychologically close to his Channel Islands roots.)

Pendrey snorted with amusement. 'Rubbish. He can afford to say that, because I don't believe anybody wants to buy him. Footballers go where the money is. You think he wouldn't sign at twice the money if he could?'

Still uncertain whether I had been listening to hard-earned wisdom or insider claptrap, I left the ground, and met up with John Salako in the car park. He was, as always, happy to talk, and chuffed with the result: 'I think this could be the turning point,' he said. 'We'll get on well from here. We'll win at Sheffield Wednesday, and then we should beat Palace.' He sounded optimistic, but there was an underlay of apprehension. I was surprised that, after only the sixth game of the season, he should already be talking about turning points, as if the first five games hadn't been a moderate success. Or did his mind dwell on failure, or on the imminence of failure? Was he already thinking about yet another fight against relegation? ('The difference between Salako and Shaw,' Richardson told me, 'is that though they both went down with Crystal Palace, Richard got over it.')

But I wanted to talk to him about something else. Supposing that he would be sympathetic to the problem, I explained to him how insular and defensive the players seemed to me, how wary of outsiders. He agreed. 'We're all like that, especially when we're together. I come to practice in the car with Trond sometimes, and I really like him, we talk a lot. But never up at the ground. What you have to do is talk to the players one-to-one, once they've got to know you.'

But how were they to get to know me if they wouldn't talk to me? It wasn't going to be easy. For the players have a second line of resistance. If they can't avoid speaking to you entirely, they can avoid saying anything when they do. They do not wish to be caught in an unguarded moment, and the unguarded moments are what I wanted to catch. But if I didn't want the sort of answers journalists get, I shouldn't be asking the kinds of questions journal-ists ask. But what could I put in their place? What was it I wanted to know? I couldn't imagine that asking Darren Huckerby what he was *really* like was going to get me far.

In any case, you don't find out what people are like by asking them. Not football people, anyway. They are not used to articulating their feelings, or analysing their inner experience. If I was going to learn anything, it was by observing, by being there with my eyes and ears open. Which was all very well, but until Gordon let me back on the coach and into the dressing room or the dugout, I was going to be too far away to see much.

At least the initial period of sheer amazement at being behind the scenes had ended, and I felt less intimi-dated by simply being there. It was time to be a little more aggressive. The next game was at Hillsborough. I resolved to follow Salako's advice, and try to go one-on-one with the players. Like a lion, I would isolate a member of the herd and pounce.

After dinner, I stalked Gary McAllister on his way out of the dining room and asked him if he had time for a chat. He made the sort of face that Trond Soltvedt had had in mind when he complained about the whingeing on the pitch. He would, he said, prefer to talk in the morning. We made a date for eleven (he didn't show up). During the course of the minute and a half this discussion took, a lot of the other players managed to make their escape as well. I tried Dion Dublin. 'Why not talk sometime up at Ryton?' he said. 'You can make an appointment with the secretary.' And off he went. He and McAllister had both made it clear that if they were to talk to me they wanted to be *interviewed*. So we had a sort of stand-off, and just exchanged the occasional smile.

But Oggy was still there. Unlike the other – and younger – players, Oggy had no interest in running back to his room to watch soft-porn videos on the telly, or to play music, and he rather liked a chat. I pounced and dragged him off to a quiet corner of the lounge. He was the only player in sight, and it was only just past eight o'clock. Perhaps I'd been misled by tabloid stories of riotous goings-on in hotels, of drunken football players and smashed-up rooms, loud music and enraged guests, but the behaviour of this lot made your average granny look like a raver. They go straight up to their rooms after dinner, and whatever they do in them is done quietly. (I'd lurked in the corridor outside their doors, listening, and you could hardly hear a peep.)

Most of them, by their own accounts, are asleep by ten. None of them ever, on these pre-match days, drinks anything stronger than tea. There isn't even, as there was in the old days, a card school with large amounts of money changing hands. A few of them have a flutter on the ponies, but only moderately. This may all be due to increasing standards of professionalism – I'm told other teams are the same – but it is certainly enforced by the presence of Strachan. 'We've never had a hotel incident of any kind in my two years here,' he said proudly. 'In fact we've had several letters from hotels saying how much they liked having us. After all, other people stay at places like this – nice places – and they expect some peace and quiet. They bring their wives and kids here. They have a right to enjoy it.'

The others having departed, Oggy and I were alone. 'Well,' he said amiably, humping his huge frame into a leather armchair and lighting up a cigarette, 'what do you want to know?'

I decided to share my problem with him. 'Well, I'm not sure that I know. But I do know what sort of book I'm not writing: I'm not interested in sensationalism, or sex and drugs and rock 'n' roll in the dressing room. I don't care how many pints Whelan can drink, or how many illegitimate children Peter Ndlovu has fathered . . .'

He laughed: 'Same in each case.'

I was ashamed to admit to him how little I had been able to formulate what it was I wanted to know. It had seemed easy: you get behind the scenes, and then . . . You Know. It becomes clear, it hits you. You put your finger in the air, like Huckerby does when making a point, and say, 'So this is what it is all about! Who would've guessed?'

'I want,' I said hesitantly, 'to get some feel for what this life is like, what the individual players make of it all.'

'I don't think that we are *like* anything,' said Oggy, a little severely. 'I hate the stereotyping of football players. Players are different from each other, just like other people are. Just because we didn't stay in school to do exams – because you can't, especially these days – it doesn't mean we are stupid. Some of the guys have surprising tastes – opera, reading, classical music – but they won't talk about them. We're very private, like a closely knit bunch of nomads. Most of them don't much like outsiders, don't feel comfortable with them.'

Oggy is something of an exception to the rule. Aged forty, and with a career as a policeman behind him before he came into the professional game, he is comfortable and reasonably forthcoming with strangers. And I liked his assertion that people tend to stereotype sportsmen, to assume that they are stupid, inarticulate, philistine. I have always believed, I told him, that the capacity to play football (perhaps most sports) at the highest level is in itself a form of intelligence. Oggy looked at me quizzically, wondering how the term might be applied, say, to Huckerby or Whelan.

'What does "intelligence" mean, after all?' I responded in my best seminar-room manner. 'Surely it involves the ability to see problems, to locate options? It is subtle, hard to predict, full of variety. It is a kind of quickness. And that is a description of both, say, Salman Rushdie and of Gianfranco Zola.'

I was rather proud of this, but Oggy clearly thought it was bullshit. 'And Paul Gascoigne?' he asked, in traditional academic style producing the most telling counter-example. Presumably my argument breaks down at some point, and Gascoigne is it, though I still wonder if physical

alertness is as different from mental cleverness as it is
sometimes assumed. Which involves, then, the implicit
idea that Paul Gascoigne can't be as stupid as he makes
out. I suspect this may be true, you know. And if it isn't,
it ought to be.

Buoyed by his philosophical victory, Oggy continued
with some good advice. 'You've got to take it slow with
the players. Don't forget, we don't talk much football
among ourselves. It's really a pub-culture sort of thing
– talk about girls, films, have a bit of a laugh. At least
twenty per cent of them have no interest in football
at all. They just do it for a living. They won't admit
that to you, but once they get used to your face they
may relax a little. You'll know when they start to take
the mickey out of you, because that's the major way
we relate to each other. And keep an eye out for the
Company – every side has one – who are the major
piss-takers: Telfer, Shaw, Huckerby, Whelan, Willo. If
you're interested in intelligence, that's where you'll find
it – in the piss-taking in the dressing room and up at
Ryton. Some of these guys are really quick and inven-
tive.'

Oggy had been the butt of this form of wit during a
training session earlier in the week. Paul Telfer, lying
on the massage table, looked up to find Roland Nilsson
gliding by, glowing after his shower, freshly and immacu-
lately dressed, as if ready for a shoot with *Vogue*, his
sweater casually swinging over his shoulders. He looked
every inch the athlete superstar. 'Ooooh!' Telfer gasped,
'an airline pilot!' Nilsson smiled good-naturedly, and
walked out. He usually has a smile on his face, even
during a game. Why shouldn't he? He was followed in
by the grizzled figure of Oggy. 'Ooooh!' said Telfer, 'a
baggage-handler.'

'I love all that, even if they do call me "the fossil",' said
Oggy, 'and if you are ever going to get to understand all
this you need to see it where it all happens. But you'll
have to get in with the manager. If you've just been

wished on him by Bryan Richardson, he'll keep you at arm's length.'

'I think that is a problem,' I said. 'Why should he let me in? What good will it do him?'

'That's right. It might even do him a lot of harm. He doesn't know what you are going to write. Look what sometimes happens; look what happened to Graham Taylor. If I were you I'd keep quiet, just hang around. Like Don Howe. When he first joined Terry Butcher here, he said that for the first week he wasn't going to say anything at all. Just hung about, looked at things, let people get used to his face. Do that, and then maybe later ask Gordon for more access to the dressing room or the dugout.'

'What is he like compared to Big Ron?'

'Much more of a black-and-white sort of guy. Ron was like John Sillett, liked a laugh, was relaxed with the players. Good at handling people.'

'Is Gordon bad at it, then?' I asked, eager to seize the implication.

He wasn't prepared to go that far. 'No, I don't mean that. Gordon isn't as easygoing as Ron or Sillett. The side that won the Cup in '87 were a great bunch, really worked together. Maybe they weren't individually the best players, but everyone knew their role, and Sillett got the best out of them.'

I wondered if this was an oblique reference to the frequent changes of tactics and formations under Strachan, or the experiments with wing backs.

'Tactics are all right if you have the right players. Telfer and Salako are basically midfield players, but if you use Roland and Marcus you could have wing backs. But you have to do what works. If it doesn't, you have to change it.'

He was reasonably confident that we wouldn't be involved in another relegation dogfight. 'I think we're getting better, and we ought to finish mid-table. You don't go from near relegation to the top seven in a year.

It will take time, but this is a very well-run club. Under Richardson we have a much higher profile. He's got an ego – gets up a few people's noses – but that is no bad thing. He's ambitious. He's found money to spend – but these days you need to spend it just to keep up with the others.'

He stretched and stood up. A youngish couple and their two kids came over and shyly asked for an autograph. 'Where you folks from?' inquired Oggy, as he signed and exchanged a few meaningless but appreciated words with them. The children beamed up at him as if he were Father Christmas.

'I'll tell you what you ought to do,' he said to me as he took his leave. 'You ought to have a word with the team as a whole, tell them what you are doing. A lot of them are asking who you are.'

'But Oggy, I did that in Torquay. You remember, at lunch before the game.'

He shook his head. 'I must have been somewhere else.' He had totally forgotten not only my little fiasco of a self-introduction, but our talk on the pitch afterwards.

It was no wonder no one wanted to talk to me. I wasn't unimportant, I was fucking invisible.

An hour or so before kick-off, the players, still dressed in their suits, like to have a wander round the pitch. The stadium is empty, save for a few stewards, and they can graze peacefully about the grass, look up at the stands, check the weather. Pitches differ across the League, in size and texture. The grass is cut at different lengths, the stands are varied in height, cast shadows in odd ways and are situated at different distances from the pitch. The players' brief peaceful reconnoitre is done without any obvious analysis of all of these factors; it resembles, instead, a contemplative stroll in a park, a bit of looking about, smelling the air, taking in the view. Without being conscious of it, what they are actually doing is registering the sizes, shapes and conditions, what many of them call 'getting the feel of the place'. Some of the players like to do it together – the Scandinavians are often found in a little huddle, passing the time of day – but John Salako always does it alone.

He had particular reason to be thoughtful today, because Gordon had just told him that he was going to play up front with Dion. Huckerby was unfit, and Lightbourne hadn't looked particularly impressive. So Salako – 'for his pace', Gordon said – was going to get a chance. We gazed up at the stands together. 'The irony is,' he said, as if thinking aloud, 'that it is so great to play in places like this – each time could be your last – but you can't enjoy it. It passes so quickly, and you are concentrating so hard. The pleasure comes afterwards, remembering it.'

It doesn't always. After the game, he trooped off the field ashen-faced, having missed five good chances in a goalless match that Coventry should have won easily. He had missed from the left, and the right, and the middle, and been one-on-one with the keeper twice. He missed, sticking a foot out, from a yard away. If there are any further ways to fail to score a goal from open play, no one has thought of them. Other than that, curiously, he had a great game. He had made the chances himself, seen opportunities without seizing them, looked quick, direct and confident – until the moment of committing himself to the shot. And, at that point, you could not merely sense, you could actually see, the self-doubt. It was painful to watch.

After the final whistle, I waited the statutory ten minutes, then went down to the dressing room. Salako was nowhere to be seen, though it was unlikely that he could have showered and dressed so quickly. Perhaps he was hiding in the loo. It was very quiet, all the players aware of the missed opportunity. 'We dropped two points, simple as that,' said David Burrows.

'Did they give Salako a hard time?'

'What do you think? They called him "Slasher".'

That seemed, even by dressing-room standards, particularly unkind. By way of mitigation, Burrows observed that they always call him Slasher, and that his performance showed why. I don't suppose that would have made John feel a whole lot better.

At the press conference, Gordon said that Salako had let himself down: that he had all the talent to be a top player, but that it was up to him if he was going to achieve his potential. I was a little surprised that he should go public like this. He usually didn't, though there were a couple of times in the previous season when he had criticised the team harshly at post-match press conferences. But what really surprised me was that he expected the gamble to come off. Though Salako had, at Palace, occasionally played as a second striker, it was something of a risk to use him up front. He has never been a big goalscorer: he got only four League goals in his first two seasons at Coventry, and never more than eight in the League in a season at Palace.

That morning, as we got on the coach to Hillsborough, I had suggested a deal with Gordon: if we got a result, I got a ride back to Ryton with the team. If we lost, I had to go home on the train. Reckoning that I had won, just, I got on the coach, hunkered down in the front seat and resolved to keep myself to myself. As Salako entered he looked me in the eye and shook his head, less in weariness than in despair. A couple of hours later, as we arrived back at Ryton, I saw him off as he got into his Subaru.

'I think I'll go home and commit suicide,' he said grimly, closed the door gently and drove away. I stood for a moment in the darkness of the Ryton driveway. Failing to kick a ball into a net, that's what he was guilty of. It seemed a pretty small cause for such a weighty dose of desperation. Failure to kick a ball into a net. 'I'm in danger,' I thought to myself, 'of getting too close to all this.' I got into my own car and drove home, reminding myself that football, when it comes to it, isn't very important, or shouldn't be.

It is to John Salako, though. Nevertheless, he'd get over it. You have to, as a player. But I know fans who won't forget the performance, or forgive it, for years. John would hear them at Highfield Road for the next few months.

A draw with a nippy and confident-looking Crystal Palace side at Highfield Road was followed four days later by a televised goalless draw at Blackburn, which gave further evidence of the side's improvement. Blackburn, under the new management of Roy Hodgson, had started well, and we'd been murdered in the League at Ewood Park in 1996–7. Under siege for much of the first half, the defence, with the greatly improved Breen happily situated at centre half, looked solid and composed. An occasional chance was created, and missed, and the feeling among the TV commentators, and in the later match reports, was that Coventry were becoming a hard side to beat. They were also, as Gordon noted sadly, a hard side to get wins with, and the pattern of draws was becoming slightly worrying. 'But at least we are now putting ourselves in positions where we should be winning games,' he said, 'rather than being relieved we didn't lose them.'

The Blackburn game would be remembered for the sending off of Dion Dublin early in the second half, when he rose for a header and a flying elbow appeared to deck defender Colin Hendry. To Hendry's credit, he immediately rose from the ground and seemed to try to intercede with the referee on Dublin's behalf. From the stands it looked the sort of challenge that centre forwards make all the time – certainly Everton's Duncan Ferguson would never be left on if you got a red card for the odd flying elbow. The call against Dion had been made by one of the linesmen (or referee's assistants, as they are now called), rather than by the referee, and was for 'dangerous play'. Yet Dublin insisted, and replays confirmed, that no contact had been made between his elbow and Hendry's head.

Dublin, and Strachan from the sidelines, were incensed, and the club appealed against the verdict, with its incumbent three-match suspension, using video evidence that clearly demonstrated that no contact had been made. Hendry, sportingly, agreed to testify on Dublin's behalf, and a recent precedent had seen a red card against Manchester United's Gary Pallister rescinded on the basis of video evidence. But the FA refused to convene a tribunal to reconsider the verdict, which Strachan repeatedly and publicly called 'a farce'.

'It was strong language,' Gordon told me, 'because I wanted to force the FA's hand. I was trying to provoke and intimidate them. They shouldn't have let me get away with it, and I repeated it as often and as loudly as I could. I was trying to get them to have me up on a charge – bringing the game into disrepute or something – so that the matter would have to be looked into publicly. But they didn't want to do that, so they just ignored me.'

The key to the incident, according to Strachan, was not merely that it had been a bad call, but that it had been the wrong one. After the match, Strachan accosted the linesman in question and asked him what sort of foul had been committed. The answer, 'dangerous play', was what he wanted to hear. 'It meant that if Dion's elbow didn't make contact with Hendry, then it couldn't have been dangerous play.' If the call had been for 'violent conduct', that could have warranted a sending-off whether or not there had been any contact. 'The video showed no contact, so the question was what call the ref had made. It can't be one law for the rich and one for the poor. If Pallister had been let off on video evidence, why shouldn't Dublin be?'

Strachan believed there was more to it than that. The real reason that the FA didn't want to hear the appeal was not so much that the Manchester United case had gone the other way, as that it would constitute yet another precedent for the consideration of

idence. And such evidence, repeatedly used,
undermine confidence in the performance of

A full month after the incident, Strachan said that he
was still so angry that it gave him stomach pains just
to think about it. 'The referees don't want to use video
evidence, it can make too many of them look a fool. Why
should they? It will only add to the call for professional
refs, and they want to stay part-time. They can keep their
jobs, and a ref who does two games in a week can make
a thousand pounds.'

Bryan Richardson, while agreeing that an injustice
had occurred, had a different angle of vision on the
incident. 'I'm in a more complex position than Gordon
is, as both a club chairman and a member of the FA
Council.' He was most unhappy, it transpired, about
the way in which the appeal was handled and dis-
missed. The film of the incident, as is customary, was
sent to the FA Disciplinary Committee for viewing.
That committee had the power, if it so wished, to pass
the film on to the referee for his comment. But this
never happened.

'When the film was seen by Graham Kelly, the chief
executive of the FA, he said that it didn't warrant sending
on to the referee. My objection is that Graham is simply
not qualified to make that decision. He was never a
footballer, he's an administrator. If the film had been
sent to someone qualified on the FA – someone whose
judgement I respect like Jimmy Armfield or Howard
Wilkinson – then we would have accepted their judgement, even if we disagreed with it. But Graham Kelly?'
He winced. 'Gimme a break.'

Dublin, whatever his perceived limitations, is a Coventry
talisman: when he is out of the side, the team almost
never wins. 'We believe,' said Richardson, 'that it cost
us at least two, and possibly four, points.' By this
sort of reckoning, adding the points notionally lost
because of the absence of Whelan to those caused by

the suspension of Dublin, Coventry might have been in the top four . . .

But the pattern of drawn games pertained: of the next three League matches, two were home draws (with Leeds and Everton), sandwiching a 2–0 defeat away at Barnsley. It was pretty pedestrian stuff, the failure to win games at Highfield Road in danger of becoming endemic. Though Richardson talked of the need for a striker, what we actually needed was more and better service for the strikers we did have. The previous year's problem of linking the midfield with the attack seemed to remain unsolved by the additional presence of Soltvedt, who was in and out of the side, took up good forward positions but didn't score goals. McAllister was once again being asked to do too much, running about like a petulant chartered accountant, overdrawn and overwrought.

During the days between the Barnsley and Everton games, Soltvedt was quoted in a Norwegian newspaper as saying that he hated the whingeing of English football players, singling out McAllister in particular. As soon as the story was reported in the English press, Trond was quick to deny it, but it seemed obvious that he had been feeling like this since the start of the season.

'Trond came to talk to me about it,' Gordon admitted, 'and I tried to explain to him that it was just part of the English game, with nothing personal in it. After all, at Rosenborg they only had a couple of tough games a year. Here you have them every game. I told him to get used to it.'

McAllister, speaking to me a little later about the incident, just said: 'It's fuckin' ridiculous. I took worse than that when I was fifteen. It was you fuckin' cunt this and you fuckin' cunt that till I started to wonder if I could play at all. But I got over it. It doesn't do you any harm. Toughens you up.' He puts the problem down to cultural differences. 'Scandinavians don't grow up in families that are obsessed by football. They don't understand, at first, how passionate people are about it.' For many British players, the vast majority from working-class backgrounds, if you didn't fight your way up the football ladder, scrapping and cursing, there was little in the way of an alternative life. You gave up the chance of an education, if you were bright enough, to further the possibility of a career. Making it didn't mean a lot, it meant everything. As Gordon was to point out, as we sat in his hotel room on an away trip, 'Where I came from, it was either football or boxing that got you out of there. Those were the only chances for a lad . . . This suite is bigger than the whole house I grew up in.'

Could a middle-class Norwegian understand all this? One of the first things Trond did, after moving to his new home in Kenilworth, was to take his wife and five-year-old son to see Warwick Castle and Shakespeare's birthplace. He didn't meet Huckerby at either. The cultural gap is considerable. 'They don't get the piss-taking, either,' said McAllister, 'except maybe Magnus – he's starting to make a few jokes.' I had recently observed Oggy doing a little innocent teasing of Martin Johansen, who, after a moment's reflection, responded: 'Ah, this is the piss-taking, yes?'

To which Oggy had agreed, like a weary schoolteacher, 'That's right. It's how we make fun of ourselves.'

Johansen nodded sagely, docketing it in his Strange English Customs file.

Encountering Soltvedt, I asked whether he was satisfied with the explanations he had been given; whether they reconciled him to the whingeing. He shrugged his shoulders with a good-natured smile. I guess he was philosophical about it. Or perhaps he was toughening up.

He needed to, the same as everybody else. After twelve games, and 13 points, Coventry were fifteenth in the League, and had won only two games. Gordon and

Pendrey had said on the coach to Torquay that after a dozen games we'd know where we were. We did now. We were in trouble.

8

Clump 3

Wimbledon v. Coventry, 1 November
Coventry v. Newcastle, 8 November
Derby v. Coventry, 22 November
Coventry v. Leicester, 29 November
Aston Villa v. Coventry, 6 December
Coventry v. Tottenham, 13 December

'It's a lovely day for a football game.' Gordon was finishing his fruit salad at breakfast at the Croydon Park Hotel. He looked out of the window at the early-morning sun and clear blue sky, drumming his fingers on the table as he sang to himself, which he often does when he is tense and abstracted before a game. The tune of the day, appropriately enough, was 'I Believe in Miracles'.

'Yes, an excellent day,' he added, looking at me directly. He smiled, and his eyes twinkled a little. Gary McAllister, sitting across from us, nodded to himself in agreement, keeping his head down as he read his paper with a studious air.

'That's exactly what always happens,' I said, 'whenever I ask that question. Nobody will answer. I got the same sort of evasive response last night from Garry and Jim Blyth, while we were drinking in the bar.'

'Quite right,' said Gordon, a little waspishly. He is good at waspish: his accent is just right for it, and he has the kind of buzzy authority that suggests you are about to get stung.

'But why won't anybody talk about it?'

'Because it's nobody else's business.'

'Well,' I replied, not exactly waspishly, but with a hint of asperity, 'it's mine. After all, I am writing a book about the club, and how can I write it if nobody will talk about the departure of Big Ron?'

I got a long look at the Strachan eyes of blue: 'That's your problem, then.'

Righto, gaffer. McAllister kept his head down.

It was almost a year since Ron Atkinson had resigned his post as manager, announcing that it was time for Gordon to take over responsibility on the field while he stepped up to become director of football. It was all as planned and agreed, except that it happened earlier. The original idea had been for Ron to see out the 1996–7 season as manager and then hand over responsibility to a Strachan who would have had a couple of years to learn the business at the feet of the master before taking control. It had seemed, at the time Strachan joined the club, a sensible plan, not least because Gordon was still, at thirty-eight, the best player on the team. But results had been terrible, Big Ron announced his resignation, spent a restless and essentially unprofitable few months as director of football and left the club when his contract terminated at the end of the season.

And nobody wanted to talk about it. In previous discussions, Richardson, normally the most open of men, had tended to get a little opaque on the topic of Atkinson's departure. In the office, Graham Hover and Neil Bryson clammed up, both saying, 'You'd better ask Bryan about that one,' as if they had learned the sentence by heart. Hover promised to try to arrange a meeting with Atkinson, but nothing came of it. There had been much speculation in the press that the resignation had been forced, and rumours in the *Mirror* that the key figure in the 'sacking' had been Geoffrey Robinson, but all questions about the affair were politely stonewalled.

The same policy was clearly in place up at the training ground, but with a distinctly different tone. While the folk at Highfield Road didn't much want to talk about Atkinson, the players and coaching staff did. The players declared themselves ignorant of the circumstances of his departure, while Strachan and Pendrey, in particular, regarded questions about it as invasive. Most people spoke of Atkinson with the kind of respect reserved for the newly dead. They didn't want to hear a word said against him. They recalled his virtues fondly and respectfully. They regarded his demise as sad and premature. There were repeated hints that had he received better treatment he might have survived.

There was one recurring theme in responses to my questions, no matter with whom I was talking, and that was the suggestion that this was an internal matter. A problem had been dealt with 'in house', and it was not to be discussed with outsiders. And if this, in itself, indicated that there was something to hide, it was by no means clear what it might be. Managers leave football clubs all the time, and Atkinson was, in any case, only a few months from his move upstairs. He had not been fired, but announced his own resignation. So what was going on? Why did the players and coaching staff seem to feel that he had been badly treated?

They loved talking about him. 'He's a great fellow, Ron,' said Gordon, back at the breakfast table. 'He was up the ground just last week – showed up in his kit, about three o'clock, saying, "Who wants a game, then?" and we played until dark. That's Ron. He has the heart of a thirty-year-old in the body of a man of fifty-seven.' It is a typical anecdote about the Big Man, who is remembered at the training ground as a man of moderate habits and immoderate goodwill.

'What he liked,' said Pendrey, 'was his pot of tea, and to

sit round after a training session talking football. He was a great man, had a way of getting the best out of everybody. He could bollock a player one minute, and the next you'd see them off together, Big Ron's arm round the lad, having a laugh. He really knew how to get on with people.'

But getting the best out of them was, in fact, what Atkinson had failed to do. If the players had liked and respected Ron, they hadn't been performing for him. Reflecting on that 1996–7 season – his first for Coventry after the highly publicised transfer from Leeds – Gary McAllister said: 'I could tell we were in trouble from the first game.' He was not referring to the 3–0 home defeat by Forest on opening day, but the previous week's 7–2 rout by Benfica in the friendly at Highfield Road. 'And I'd played against that Benfica side before. They weren't a top team. It was fuckin' embarrassing. You could tell the writing was on the wall. I felt numb for a month.'

Some thought it was the players' fault. Managers are too frequently blamed for mistakes that occur on the field, but I had seldom seen a side that seemed so underprepared, and so tactically uneasy, and that is the fault of the manager. So it was no surprise that early results were terrible. Once Strachan had taken over, the results under him (32 points from twenty-six games) were such that the team wouldn't have been in trouble at all had they been under his guidance from the start. Indeed, it had been widely reported in the press this very week that one of the contenders for the presidency of Benfica had announced that, if he won, he would want Gordon Strachan as his manager, so impressed had he been with the way in which Strachan had kept Coventry City up.

If anyone at the club could talk about the affair, it was Richardson, just as, in politics, there are certain sensitive topics agreed to be the sole province of the prime minister. I arranged a meeting with the chairman on the day after the Wimbledon game, determined to get his version of the story.

In the meantime, there was a game to be played. We

tend to do well at Wimbledon, and Alex Miller was very confident. What we were going to do, he explained, was play Gary Mac just behind the front two – in effect, to mirror the same sort of formation that Wimbledon used. 'They're direct, a very up-and-down sort of team, and we reckon that if we push Gary Mac up, it will give him more space, and also help create space out on the wings, so we can get some crosses in.'

It worked a treat, and Coventry raced to an early 2–0 lead, with goals from Huckerby and Dublin. Crosses rained in from the flanks, and chances were created every few minutes. Though Wimbledon pulled one back against the run of play, the result was never in doubt. It was the first away win of the season. Encountering a pleased Miller in the dressing room after the game, I asked him why, if these tactics worked so well, everybody didn't use them.

'Haven't thought of it, have they?' he said with a twinkle. Gordon was looking chuffed, too. He was considering a new five-and-a-half-year contract, though he was realistic about the immediate prospects: 'People tell me I have a fair chance of success. I think I have a fair chance of failing and won't promise anybody anything. When I think of all the managers, like Gordon Milne, Bobby Gould and Ron Atkinson, who have succeeded in maintaining Coventry's status . . . I have to continue that tradition and I realise now just how tough the job is. I don't know how much ability I have as a manager. All I know is that when I am either sacked, finished or just walk away, I don't want to have any regrets. I must enjoy this job as I haven't taken to drink, my wife is still with me and there are not too many grey hairs.'

It was odd, I thought, that he should be deferring to previous managers just because they had kept Coventry up. It sounded like a thoughtful reflection, but I didn't quite believe it. Gordon doesn't think he is without ability as a manager, though I think he knows that, at present, his major strength is as a coach and a motivator. His words, I suspected, were really directed at the team. He continued: 'How can I ask players to commit themselves to Highfield Road if I am not prepared to do exactly the same? When I get my teeth into a job, I like to do it properly.' And if the players were to do the same, the implication was, then we wouldn't have much to worry about at the end of the season. For once.

The next day I bearded Bryan Richardson on the matter of Ron Atkinson. 'Let me put in this way,' I said, being a little economical with the truth. 'I have had a lot of different versions of why Atkinson resigned, and I need to know what really happened.' Richardson made one of his usual quick decisions: after all, if he had sanctioned the writing of a book about the club, he could hardly suppress one of its more interesting stories. 'All right,' he said at last. 'It happened like this.

'We had lost at Sunderland 1–0, and we didn't play at all. Sunderland were a poor side, and after the match I could see the depth of worry and frustration Ron felt about why the side weren't performing. He knew he had good players, better players than the teams in the bottom places in the League, and that they simply weren't producing the results we all expected from them.

'I talked to Ron about this a few weeks later, and he knew that I was concerned about the situation. Almost half the season had gone by, and we were in danger of losing touch. At the board meeting, the Friday before the Everton game, the topic had come up. Certainly, at that board meeting, some of the members were concerned, though their feelings were largely unspoken, but the least comfortable was Geoffrey Robinson.' And Robinson, the club's largest financial backer, was the key figure on the Board at that moment.

'You know, football is a hard game, and it has a lot of hard men in it, and a lot of harsh critics. But aside from the usual – "Oh, he's made himself a pile of money out of the game," that kind of grudging remark, I've never heard anyone in football say a bad thing about Ron Atkinson. He's great fun, full of goodwill. Who else could say, down at a training ground, "OK let's have a little game: blacks against whites," and get away with it? The players loved him.

'After the game at Sunderland he was really down. It was a terrible period for him anyway. His father Fred was dying of cancer – great fellow, Fred, everyone loved him, and he and Ron were close the way a father and son ought to be, and so often aren't – and Ron was really feeling it. And the team just weren't performing.

'The thing about Ron, when he's under stress, is that you can tell it from his face. It gets all swollen up, and red, and it had happened three times lately. You could see that things were getting on top of him. On the day after the Everton game, which was on a Monday night, I met with him, at lunchtime, up at Ryton. I put it to him that I didn't like what I was seeing. Ron wasn't being Ron, not bubbly and larger than life. He wasn't doing himself justice. I was afraid that he had lost faith in himself, that he really no longer believed that he could turn the team round.

'So I put it to him: why not hand over the day-to-day stuff to Gordon, as we had agreed he would do at the end of the season, only bringing it forward? But I did not fire him, and if he had said no at this point, I would have let him go on, though maybe only for a few games unless things turned round. But I wanted him to handle the turnover in his own way: that he announced his resignation, so that he would be in control of the presentation to the media, and be able to make his position clear. And, by and large, that is what happened.'

There was, however, a further, and unexpected, twist to the tale. Most of the media duly reported that Atkinson had stepped down, or up, depending on how you saw it. But the *Mirror*, crediting an undisclosed source, claimed he had been sacked. Richardson would only say that the leak did not come from within the club, and that, in any case, Ron wasn't sacked, but had resigned. It is widely rumoured, though, both within the club and outside it, that the story emanated from the office of Geoffrey Robinson, and was leaked in order to undermine Atkinson's future role at Coventry City. Robinson would not comment on this rumour. But Atkinson was clearly incensed when he made his sole remark on the affair to the media: 'Suffice it to say that I won't be voting Labour at the next election.'

Ironically, Atkinson's relative achievements at Coventry had been largely dependent on the money provided by his new antagonist. Though no longer on the board since his appointment as paymaster-general in the Blair government, Robinson has been a key figure in the club's recent development. His offer of financial help had guaranteed the chairman the luxury of a financial vista long enough to enable him to think strategically about the future of Coventry City. By the time the money eventually had to be repaid, we would be several years into the next century, with a new stadium and probable subsequent flotation, which would ensure that substantial new capital was available.

Atkinson's time as director of football was not entirely wasted, but his position had been undermined. He was responsible for the signing of the excellent Roland Nilsson, but it was clear that there was no longer an Atkinson-shaped space to be filled at the club. He was seen less and less frequently at Highfield Road, and rarely appeared at games or functions. When his contract expired no one felt it advisable to renew it.

But according to Richardson, the arrival of Atkinson was 'the biggest thing to happen to the club since we won the Cup in 1987. He turned us round in a very short time. Don't forget the team that he inherited from Phil Neal – with Sean Flynn, Julian Darby, Steve Morgan, David Rennie, Ally Pickering – would never have survived. They were a nice bunch of lads, but not top-quality players: they wouldn't have had a chance. Such a lot of money had come into the game from Sky that standards were rising quickly and dramatically. So we had to go out and spend, and spend fast. There were a few mistakes, sure, like Isaias, but Ron brought in a solid core of genuinely good players, as well as Gordon. It took them all some time to bed down, and they struggled, but they stayed up. And he left us in a much stronger position than the one he found us in when he came. It gave Gordon the basis on which to build.'

But the win at Wimbledon did not break the developing pattern. In the next match, at Highfield Road against Newcastle, Coventry once again went ahead and seemed to have the match under control only to end up with yet another home draw (making a total of eight draws in fourteen games). Newcastle started slowly, and it was no surprise when they went behind to a Dion Dublin goal after just four minutes. What was surprising was the nature of the goal: Dublin, having chased a ball at the far post, had run off the field of play while Shay Given gathered the ball. The Newcastle keeper rolled it in front of himself in a leisurely fashion, preparing to kick it downfield, at which point the alert Dublin zipped back from behind him and knocked it into the net. I don't think any of the players – or referee Paul Durkin – had ever seen anyone do this before, and everyone stood about, with various expressions of admiration, bemusement and outrage on their faces. The Newcastle players protested – a sort of 'Hey! That's not fair!' kind of protest – and the Coventry players protested back 'Yes it is!', eventually convincing Durkin to check with the linesman, in case he had a view. He didn't have any doubt about it: the goal stood. Afterwards, Kenny Dalglish claimed that Dion had re-entered the field of play without permission, which was pretty silly.

Following an equalising goal from the surprisingly sprightly Barnes, Newcastle looked to have taken the upper hand until Dublin put in a rebound from a shot by Paul Williams. It seemed all over, but with a few minutes to go, and Coventry hanging on, Robert Lee picked up the ball, some 30 yards out, looked up, noticed that nobody seemed much interested in closing him down, and with a this'll-show-'em look on his face, placed it high into Oggy's top corner.

It felt, once again, like 2 points lost rather than 1 gained, and I could imagine Bryan Richardson adding another couple of points to his Fantasy We Should've Had League table. But we did have 17 points from fourteen games, which gave no immediate cause for alarm, unless you had looked at the fixtures coming up in December. Gordon, who professed never to look a clump ahead, had his usual word for it: 'horrendous'.

At one o'clock on Saturday, following the midweek Coca-Cola Cup fixture at Arsenal (which I will treat separately, for reasons that I'll explain later), Bertie and I got into the car to go to the game at Derby. I wasn't looking forward to it. We had lost to them three times the previous season. In the fifth round of the FA Cup (with a home draw against Middlesbrough in the next round for the winner), we had gone two up within thirteen minutes, and while Max, Guy and Bertie were celebrating the second goal, I was filled with dread. I hate 2–0 leads, especially with a lot of time to go. I turned to Max and said, 'I don't like it.'

He was still beaming. 'It's OK, it's OK, we'll be all right.'

'If they get one back, we will need at least one more to get something out of the match.'

They got two before half-time, and went on to win 3–2. As we walked, speechless with disappointment, back to the car park, Max had had tears in his eyes. Later in the season, a vital home game against Derby – the penultimate game of the season – was lost in an absolutely flaccid display. 'We thought that was it, we were down then,' David Burrows had told me. 'We were awful.'

'You know what, Bertie?' I said now. 'I can't face it. I

don't want to go. Derby to win is the home banker of the day.'

He was amazed, and not a little censorious. 'You're kidding, right? You have to go.'

'Do I? Just watch.' We drove up to the Warwickshire Golf Club, where we had lunch, played nine holes and arrived back at the car to hear that Coventry were 3–0 down at half-time. During the interval, I was later to hear, an irate Strachan had confronted referee David Elleray, a schoolmaster at Harrow, and words had been exchanged about an alleged handball incident before Derby's third goal.

Huckerby got a meaningless seventieth-minute goal to take the full-time score to 3–1. After the match Strachan made a statement about the referee in the post-match press conference: 'He can go back and tell the schoolchildren that he had a good laugh at the weekend. Referees can be flippant because it is a hobby. It is a vehicle to be a celebrity. I went to talk to him at half-time and he said something to me and then he seemed to want to retract it and tried to stop me leaving the room. It was astonishing what he said. I didn't know whether to laugh or cry. I think it must be time for full-time referees to be judged like players and managers. I would like to be a part-time manager and an accountant during the week.'

In 1996–7, Gordon had got into trouble after being sent off during a reserve game and refusing to go, and was fined £2,000 by the FA. After overenthusiastically protesting about a bad error at Chelsea, when the referee failed to notice a blatant handball by Dan Petrescu (which was followed twenty-one seconds later by a Chelsea goal), Strachan was again brought before a disciplinary committee, though he escaped punishment. This season, of course, had already seen the incident at Ewood Park and Gordon's subsequent fruitless attempts to get himself up on a charge by making vociferous public comments about the refereeing.

And now this. What had Elleray said that had sent

Gordon into such a tizzy? The referee would make no comment, and Gordon had so far not repeated the remark. 'It'll only cause more trouble if I tell you,' he said. 'I think I ought to keep it to myself. But I pointed out to him that he must have known that he was wrong about their goal, because after that he gave every decision to us. It was getting embarrassing.'

I had known that we would lose at Derby, so there was nothing depressing about the result. But the forth-coming match with Leicester felt like a critical game, perhaps some sort of turning point. I was starting to feel like John Salako. For the first time in the season we had lost two matches in a row (counting the Coca-Cola Cup defeat at Arsenal), and a third would be bad for confidence – particularly at Highfield Road, where we were still unbeaten. But the worst news was of the res-ignation of Alex Miller, who had just been appointed to the manager's job at Aberdeen. His tactical shrewdness and positive nature would be missed, and his resig-nation had come at a bad time, with the team only just beginning to show signs of cohesion and, however intermittently, confidence. He was the only member of the coaching staff with whom Gordon felt completely comfortable.

A few days before, I had been surprised to hear that a transfer of David Burrows to Sheffield Wednesday was imminent. Combative, mature and reliable, he had been solid as a rock in defence, and hadn't missed a game after his troubled period with injuries the previous season. It was predictable enough that Ron Atkinson (recently reinstalled at Wednesday in place of David Pleat) would want to sign Burrows, who had played for him at both West Brom and at Coventry. Even more than most man-agers, Ron likes signing players he knows. The reason that Richardson considered the deal was that Wednesday were prepared to offer Mark Pembridge for Burrows plus some cash.

A Welsh international, and Wednesday's Player of the

Season in 1996–7, Pembridge was the sort of grittily competent midfield player that we had needed ever since the failure to sign Craig Burley over the summer. A crisis in midfield was fast approaching. Whelan was still out, moping disconsolately round the training ground, kicking balls with his left foot; John Salako had been in and out of the side since Hillsborough, due to a niggling hamstring injury, and the rumour circulating at the club was that he was just seeing out his contract and had no particular desire to play. Physio George Dalton, commenting on the injury, would only say wryly, 'He doesn't feel he can do himself justice. It's the sort of injury we used to play right through in the old days.'

The continuing failure of Soltvedt to make a place for himself had left a midfield in which Willie Boland was now more likely to be a starting player, alongside McAllister, with the improving Marcus Hall on the left and the excellent Telfer on the right. Though Strachan, earlier in the season, had been dismissive of Boland – 'He's not going to make it' – Willie had been improving steadily. 'When I took over,' Gordon said, 'he was overweight, walking round with stubble on his face. His attitude wasn't right. But over the summer he went and got himself fit, and he's coming on.' Pembridge would have been a good signing, though he would hardly have solved the problem, because if Burrows were to go, then Hall would move to left back (where he is more mobile than Burrows, and better going forward, but a less solid tackler), still leaving a place to be filled in midfield.

The squad, it was becoming apparent, was very thin. The arrival of Soltvedt and Johansen hardly compensated for the loss of Jess, Ndlovu and Richardson in midfield; up front, Nuddy and Jess would have provided better cover than Haworth and Lightbourne. The squad wasn't stronger, it was weaker. And if we had the sort of money available to contemplate the Maric or Monaco signings, surely it was getting time to spend some of it? Presumably the Burrows transfer was just such a move?

I'm too soft for all of this: I like David Burrows, and it seemed cruel to sell him out of the blue, just like that. How could it have made him feel? I know how it made me feel – terrible – and the night after I heard the news I had a sort of compensatory dream, in which Burrows was alone with Gordon, who was telling him not to be sad, because he was his third or fourth favourite person on the team. This made David feel better, he and Gordon were reconciled, and I woke up feeling relieved. My unconscious was working overtime making sure everyone was happy.

The possible transfer left some bad feeling in the club, though, because Atkinson had approached Strachan directly, to see if he would be interested in a deal for Burrows plus cash, rather than going through the chairman. Burrows would only comment, 'It's a hard game these days. That's what it's like.'

Burrows, curiously, was left out of the side for the Leicester game. I found him in the players' bar half an hour before kick-off, looking a little pale and bemused. He had discussed terms with Wednesday, but the deal was still on hold because Pembridge was apparently asking too much. 'I haven't actually agreed yet with Wednesday,' Burrows said. 'I don't really want to go, but . . .' It seemed the terms he was being offered were pretty compelling. 'I'd really miss it here – I've been happy this year. It's the best atmosphere I've ever experienced, and I've been at a lot of clubs. Most clubs, you get one or two arseholes in the dressing room, but this really is a great bunch of lads. I don't really want to go. I'll have to think it over this weekend, and talk to Gordon on Monday.' As things turned out, the deal eventually broke down when Pembridge declined the move.

It was a critical point in the season. A loss would have meant a total of 17 points from sixteen games, which suggested distinct relegation possibilities; a win, on the other hand, would have left us with 20 points. But the real cause for concern was the next seven fixtures:

away games at Aston Villa, Liverpool, West Ham and Chelsea; home matches with Spurs, Manchester United and Arsenal. We would be lucky to get 5 points from the lot. If we didn't beat Leicester, it seemed to me reasonably certain that, by the middle of January, we would be in the bottom three.

Gary McAllister thought me unduly pessimistic. 'I think we'll be OK. We can field eleven quality players now, and a lot of the young players, you know, aren't frightened about relegation: Huck, Whelan – they don't think about it at all.' He smiled to himself. 'They don't think about anything much, they play on instinct. It's hard to teach Huckerby, but he's learning, and he's got talent. In a couple of years he'll be gone. This has always been a selling club; anyway, the best young players want to win something, go to an Arsenal, Liverpool, Man United.

'But the younger players,' he added with a hint of sadness and incomprehension, 'they don't love the game. I do. It's all I know, never done anything else, I'm a bit of an anorak, really, and I'd love to go in to management some day. Maybe start at a lower level, learn a bit about it, then hope to move up.' He was the only one of the players who discussed tactics with Gordon – 'We played together, don't forget' – and often made up the fourth hand in the card school (they play Hearts, as seems to befit Scots) with Gordon, Garry and Jim. Sometimes I was allowed to keep score.

Gordon provided an interesting gloss: 'I know a lot of the younger players don't love the game now, but it's not a game you can love any more. When I was young we played in the street, had fun, identified with the great players, thought and talked nothing but football, lived for the Saturday game on the telly. Now there's too many games on TV. And you see the kids now in their teams at nine years old, and it's do this, do that with their coaches and parents out on the touchlines screaming at them . . .' Too much pressure, too early. It's no wonder players are more cynical, less rooted in the traditions and spirit of the game. John Salako admitted: 'I've fallen out of love with it. It's a good job, and I have a wife and two little kids to look after, but when I lie in bed at night dreaming of glory it's harder than it used to be. You have to sort of force the thoughts. But who knows? If those goals had gone in at Hillsborough, and I'd maybe scored a few more, I'd be thinking: World Cup.'

Salako, though, had his doubts about McAllister's assessment of the side. 'I think we can field only seven, maybe eight, real Premiership players, and that we still don't play to a plan. Gordon and Alex are too keen to switch tactics, so players don't really know what their role is. Take Breeny – I don't think he's clear whether he's supposed to dribble out of defence, or just clear it quickly.' Nevertheless, he didn't want a role himself; he wanted to be given free rein to go where he felt was right. 'Huck should, too – we're both that sort of player. You'll never teach Huck, it's a waste of time. With him it's pure instinct.' But he thought the season would go down to the wire: 'We haven't made a good start. It's going to be tough.'

In spite of all these forebodings, I put a bet on a draw against Leicester, which, as Bertie pointed out, meant that it couldn't be a draw, as I have never won a bet. (He had forgotten my coup at Spurs the previous year.) But Leicester, with Emile Heskey suspended, looked a little toothless, and the game had all the hallmarks of a low-scoring draw.

It wasn't. Early in the first half, Huckerby, chasing a through ball, compelled Kasey Keller to handle the ball just outside his area. The referee, to the crowd's astonishment, penalised the keeper only with a yellow card. From where I was sitting it looked as if Keller had made first contact with the ball just inside his area, then been carried outside it by his momentum. Given that referees have a degree of discretion in such matters, it seemed to me reasonable to let Keller off. But Strachan, commenting on the incident after the game, was incensed. 'At most games I have attended the goalkeeper would have been sent off. Absolutely no doubt about it. It's bound to make a cynic like me ask questions. Perhaps it's a case of my devious mind working overtime because David Elleray is head honcho among the refs in this country. But I feel entitled to wonder aloud whether that incident at Derby is in some way going to work against this club for the rest of the season.'

If it did, one supposes, it may well be because Gordon kept going on about it. Certainly his behaviour over the previous eighteen months hadn't been such as to endear him to referees. I am not qualified to assess what goes on in a referee's mind, but it looked as if Gordon was beginning to suffer from the occasional paranoia which is a reliable sign of stress.

By the end of the game, he had more reason to feel aggrieved. Later in the first half, a diagonal free kick bounced off Coventry's far post, and Graham Fenton knocked in the rebound. More ominously, Gary McAllister came down from jumping for a ball, immediately grabbed his knee, tried to play on for a couple of minutes, and was eventually stretchered off with ligament damage. At half-time there was nothing much to hope for, but early in the second half Soltvedt, having come on for McAllister, was put through by an adroit back-heel from Telfer, only to blast the shot over the bar. A late penalty, given when Richard Shaw brought down Muzzy Izzet, made the score 2–0. Coventry had rarely threatened, and had played without any confidence. The midfield, particularly, was so lacklustre that Paul Williams – booked for the ninth time of the season – took to kicking high balls forward from defence, where the Leicester centre backs, led by the admirably combative Matt Elliott, won everything in the air.

Afterwards, Strachan was outspoken: 'It was the worst performance in the thirteen months since I became manager, both individually and collectively. Our supporters usually get something for their money here, but this game wasn't worth the admission price.' You could hear the desperation in his voice. With Alex Miller gone, and McAllister possibly carrying a bad injury, the first crisis of the season had arrived.

Strong problems, strong remedies. At the next game, sitting in the Coventry end at Villa Park well before the kick-off, Bertie and I were astounded to see the figure of Noel Whelan, kitted out, emerge from the tunnel for the pre-match warm-up. He had not played a competitive match since the pre-season friendly during which he had initially been injured, and while he had come to training over the previous month, he'd cut a sad figure, unable even to manage sustained jogging and taking no part in the competitive practice matches. Over the preceding couple of weeks he was reported to have been at Lilleshall working on his overall fitness, but no one expected him to be back before Christmas. And there he was before us, a huge grin on his face, swapping jokes with Paul Telfer, his arm around Willo, knocking the ball about, happy as the star striker for the local under-11s.

'What's Noel doing out there?' asked Bertie. 'Is he playing?'

I certainly hadn't heard so. Though McAllister was definitely out with that knee injury (and little had been seen of Salako), Hall, Telfer, Soltvedt and Williams were all fit, and there could be no good reason to risk playing an unfit Whelan, with the chance of exacerbating his injury. Presumably, I said, he was there to get the feel of the match atmosphere again. Several of the fans around me strained to listen, knowing that I had inside information on things, and I adopted a characteristically authoritative air.

At 2.58 the Villa public-address announcer told us that, in the Coventry starting line-up, was 'Number eight: Noel Whelan!' An enormous cheer went up from the City end: 'ONE NOEL WHELAN! THERE'S ONLY ONE NOEL WHELAN!' Whelan turned to the crowd and clapped his hands back at them by way of thanks. I didn't quite know what to make of this act of spontaneous generosity on the part of the crowd. Had they forgotten that this was the very dope who had kicked in a window, come within a quarter of an inch of severing his tendon, and was now making his first appearance in the seventeenth League game of the season? That we were in serious trouble, to some considerable degree due to his self-inflicted injury? But the City fans loved Noel Whelan, and more than one of them has himself got pissed and kicked in the odd window. He's a bit of a lad, Noel, and they rather admire that.

Football is a game of tradition, facts, statistics, folk memories. But no one can remember Coventry winning a match at Villa Park, in twenty-five attempts, because we never have. This time we never looked like doing so. The atmosphere was, even for a local derby, particularly unpleasant, with 'Shit on the Villa!' chants escalating from the Coventry end until the crowd seemed like a single hydra-headed organism of hatred. Much of this venom was directed at Stan Collymore, such a spectacular flop after his £8.5 million transfer from Liverpool.

Out of temper, and sorts, and form, Collymore barged his way about to the accompaniment of chants of 'What a waste of money!' until he managed to diffuse the barrage with a neat bit of public relations. As the Coventry crowd chanted, 'If you've shagged Ulrika, clap your hands!' (Stan was dating the presenter of the show with those ter-rifying Gladiator ladies), Collymore turned to the crowd, and gave a mock clap of his hands. A huge cheer went up, and he was quite the hero for a few minutes – Stan the Shagger – until he scored a soft goal from outside the area (his first of the season at Villa Park) and the City fans decided that they didn't like him so much after all.

It wasn't long before they positively hated him again. Just before the end of the half, Collymore elbowed and barged his way past Paul Williams just outside the Coventry area. Willo returned the compliment and dragged him down, and was sent off. With ten men Coventry held on for a time in the second half, but a goal by the nippy little Hendrie put the game out of reach, and in the final moments Julian Joachim, standing virtually on the touchline, managed somehow to curl a ball round Oggy and in at the far post. With two minutes to go, Gary Breen, who had seemed out of sorts, and who had been arguing with Willo in the first half, joined his team-mate for an early shower when he, too, was sent off for a blatant, and wholly unnecessary, shove on Gary Charles.

The nine Coventry players who drooped off to a catcall of boos looked thoroughly dejected. It was the third League defeat in a row. McAllister was out with a long-term knee injury; Miller had departed; Huckerby had hurt his ankle. The only hopeful sign was that Gordon didn't blame it on the referee: 'I don't think he made a big difference. Paul Williams was a bit harshly booked, but when he dragged down Collymore, we were always worried. As for Breen, if you raise your arms, you're going to be in trouble.'

And we were: seventeen games, 17 points, just 1 point outside the bottom three.

After the Villa game, on Monday morning at Ryton, Gordon asked Oggy to come up for a chat in his office. He was, he explained to the astonished keeper, going to play Magnus in the next game, against Spurs at Highfield Road. 'It was horrendous,' Gordon said. 'He didn't see it coming at all. He was extremely upset, extremely.' He went quiet, replaying the conversation in his mind. 'It's the worst part of the job. I hate it, but you have to do it. I'd seen it coming for a few weeks. I tried to explain it to him, that he'd made a few errors, and anyway we'd spent a lot of money on Magnus, who'd been doing a good job, and it was time to give him a go.' After practice, Oggy went home and, he admitted, locked himself in a room 'for a long time'.

Jim Blyth agreed with the decision. 'Perhaps we waited

a few weeks too long, but that was only fair. But when the third goal went in at the Villa, I looked over at Gordon and we both sort of nodded. I think Oggy isn't quite as quick as he was: that goal by Robert Lee in the Newcastle game wasn't hit all that well, and the first Villa goal took a little deflection, but it took it immediately, and I think Oggy should have been able to get down to it. And I've noticed in the night games Oggy's eyesight hasn't seemed as sharp as during day games – why should it be? He's forty. The time is right for a change, and I think Magnus is ready. He's learning all the time – Oggy has helped him a lot – and he's amazingly brave, almost too brave.'

But Strachan was clear this was not the end for Oggy. 'We'll offer him a one-year contract next year, and then I hope he'll stay on at the club, in one capacity or another. He's a qualified coach, and he knows his football.' In fact, Oggy would quite like to become a manager one day, though he noted that very few goalkeepers ever get a chance to do so.

It was poignant seeing Oggy in the dugout at the next match, against Spurs at Highfield Road, and the crowd had responded to him generously – 'Oggy! Oggy!' – when he had come out for the pre-match warm-up. Though privately despondent, and still smarting with a sense of injustice, in interviews he was as fair and professional as ever: he wished Magnus good luck, and said he would work his socks off to be ready if there was a need for him. He had, after all, made 587 senior appearances for Coventry. During the match, standing and shouting encouragement with Gordon, Garry and Jim, he looked more a member of the managerial team than one of the substitutes.

I love it when we play Spurs: they give me such happy memories. Not only do they usually play attractive football, they roll over at White Hart Lane whenever we need them to. In two of the previous three years Coventry wins at Spurs had saved us from relegation. And it was particularly pleasing to see them this year, because they had been terrible all season. Equipped with an obscure new manager called Christian Gross, who seemed to think that all the side needed was to train twice a day, and with their fancy squad of internationals heavily hit by injury, they had lost their last match, at home to Chelsea, by 6–1. If we couldn't beat them we were in real trouble.

So much of football, though, is a matter of confidence and momentum. It was the sort of game that would be won by the team that scored the first goal. And for much of the first half the more likely team, without question, was Spurs. Shots flew by the post, one hit it, and Hedman, quick and assured, made a couple of good saves.

To compound Coventry's problems, Gary McAllister injured his knee again, and had to be substituted. This time he would probably need an operation. But the game turned with that crucial first goal, which Huckerby crashed in after latching on to an adroit flick from Dublin. After that, Spurs, looking demoralised and tired (it must take it out of you training twice a day) gave up further goals to Breen, another long-range beauty from Huck, and a cracker from Marcus Hall: 4–0.

After the game Dion was lavish in his praise of Huckerby: 'As long as he keeps listening and learning I'm convinced he can play for England. I've seen some good strikers in my time and I know Darren can go all the way.' Huck responded, modestly and in kind, with a tip of the old hat to Dion. 'That was more like it. Dion has been working a lot with me, and it's paying off. I should have had a hat-trick really, but two will do for now.'

The win lifted City to fourteenth in the Premiership, but I have yet to find a player who cared, or even knew, about where the team stood in the table. That sort of statistic is for the fans. Twenty points from eighteen games – that most of them knew. And they knew what it meant: there was hardly a moment to take a deep breath before the frightening set of fixtures to come.

9

The Coca-Cola Cup

When I was an undergraduate at the University of Pennsylvania, I shared a flat with a wacky boy called Dick Zneimer, who came from New York City. He hated going to college in Philadelphia. To get from Philadelphia to New York, you have to take the New Jersey Turnpike, then go through the Lincoln Tunnel, and in hardly any time at all, there you are. But Dick Zneimer refused to do it. Instead he would go cross-country, traversing the most godforsaken, smelly, polluted parts of New Jersey on back roads, rather than use the equally smelly, but direct, Turnpike.

The reason, he explained to me, was simple. If he took the Turnpike, he would have to pay a toll, the proceeds of which went to the state of New Jersey; on the back roads, he didn't have to pay. When I objected that he seemed perfectly happy to pay the toll on the Pennsylvania Turnpike, his eyes lit up with delight: I had fallen into the trap.

'That's because I don't mind paying money to the state of Pennsylvania,' he said. 'But never to New Jersey. It shouldn't exist, and I'm not going to support it: it should be a part of either New York State or of Pennsylvania.'

Dick Zneimer didn't believe in New Jersey, and I feel

the same way about the Coca-Cola Cup. I don't like going to the games, and I don't like having to write about it. It is a tax on the pockets and credulity of supporters, and on the energies of players, and its continued existence is yet another testimony to the avarice and shortsightedness of the game's administrators. English Premiership football-ers play too many games: with twenty teams the Prem-iership is one of the largest of European top divisions, and the nature of the football played in it is acknowledged to be exceptionally physically taxing. Furthermore, almost no other European country I can think of has two such cup competitions. The Coca-Cola Cup is wearisome, and I hope it will one day be abandoned.

Coventry's progress to the fourth round of the compe-tition was an adequate illustration of the reasons why I dislike the Cup. In the second round (when the Premier-ship teams enter the competition), matches are played on a home-and-away basis, because Premiership teams are kept apart, and it was presumably felt to be unfair on the teams in the lower divisions if they didn't get a chance of a home fixture. As a result of this worthy but muddled thinking, Coventry had to play Blackpool twice. Having lost a first leg 1–0 away, City then won the return match at Highfield Road 3–1 to go through to the next round, where we slaughtered an abject Everton side 4-1, with Lightbourne and Haworth up front and looking a surprisingly good partnership. After the match, Howard Kendall was so furious with his side's performance that he actually smacked one of his players round the earhole, in full view of the departing crowd, and to its delight.

But I went to Highbury on 18 November: there's no sense letting your principles get the better of you, especially when your team is in the last sixteen of a Cup. Arsenal had looked good in the second game of the season, but we had been playing some attractive football, and were more resilient now. I was feeling chirpy and hopeful as we sat round the dinner table at the Swallow Hotel at Waltham Abbey the evening before the match.

Huck had his hat on again, backwards. He was trying to eat his dinner, but he was swarmed over by Shawsy, Willo and Telf. Next to them, Dion Dublin chortled with amusement. A man of few words, Huckerby is the constant target of a catalogue of cruel jibes on the theme of how thick he is. On his own, he is amiable, if slow-witted, but he has learned to be careful, and expresses himself simply and directly. (Questioned about the effect of the prolonged absence of Noel Whelan, he would say only: 'We need him. He works hard. He's a good player.' His sentences rarely get longer, or more complex, than that.) But he liked the attention, and his head turned, with a grin, from player to player as they teased him.

'Huck,' asked Gordon, from the next table, 'did you bring the bag with the videos in it?' Huckerby considered this, as a hoot of obscene suggestion echoed round him. Gordon waited patiently, then turned to Garry Pendrey. 'I think the hat is for keeping his brain warm.' It didn't seem to be working. Huckerby continued to ponder, his mouth half-open, like Pete Sampras. Dion leaned towards Gordon. 'Leave him to it, gaffer,' he said, 'he's punch drunk.'

As Huckerby thought, Pendrey observed that Huck had been away at the weekend, watching his brother, who is a non-League player, in the first round of the FA Cup. 'Brother idolises Huck,' said Pendrey.

'Oh,' Gordon replied, 'bet he's a striker who runs about like an arsehole.' Presumably it runs in the family.

Eventually Huckerby shook his head to indicate that he didn't have the video bag, and Gordon motioned to the nearest waitress. A tall blonde girl of majestic proportions and good cheekbones, she had been courted by half the team over dinner, but had taken the flirtatiousness in good spirit. 'Do me a favour,' said Strachan. 'Would you tell Huckerby over there that it is against hotel rules to wear a hat in the dining room?'

She smiled. 'Shall I get the manager to do it, sir?'

Gordon cheerfully agreed.

Huckerby's hat had so far defeated Gordon, and he wanted to have a little fun. His face, a good mirror of his inner world, registered a mixture of irritation and amusement as he watched the black-tied hotel manager suggest to Huckerby that the offending object be removed. Huckerby looked puzzled, but took it off politely, and put it down next to his soup. Why shouldn't he wear a hat?

The day before, at the training ground at Ryton, I had confessed to him that I had dreamed about him the previous night. 'That's not a dream, that's a fucking nightmare,' said David Burrows, lurking nearby.

'Oh, yeah?' said Huck, ignoring him.

'Yeah. I dreamed that you were writing a novel.'

Huck's mouth dropped a little further open, then snapped shut decisively, like a turtle's. 'I could write a novel,' he said. He lifted a finger into the air: '"Huckerby on the Meaning of Life."' This was greeted with hoots of derision. Noel Whelan, kitted out though still unable to train, looked at Huck fondly. 'Wouldn't have anything in it, would it?' Whelan, himself both shy and inarticulate, had nicknamed Huckerby 'Forrest Gump'. Huck didn't mind, though he did object to his previous nickname – 'Trigger', after the character in *Only Fools and Horses*. Perhaps he thought it made him sound too horsey.

I think I had my dream because the constant teasing of Huckerby made me uncomfortable, and I'd been labouring inwardly to maintain the belief that he was not – couldn't be – as stupid as he made himself appear. Any teacher is familiar with the kind of child who, seeking attention, will court the approval of his peers by allowing himself to become the butt of their jibes, even if this necessitates suppressing qualities in himself that would disprove the taunts. Huckerby, surely, had learned to act the fool. This does not necessarily mean that he is one. And so, my unconscious tells me, the Huckerbys of this world all have their own story to tell, or novel to write.

Encountering him the next day in the lobby of the hotel, I asked him how the work on the novel was going. He looked at me blankly.

I had surprised – indeed, I think, horrified – the managerial staff at dinner by mentioning (after telling them the Huckerby story) that I read four or five novels a week. That was more, Garry Pendrey told me, not without a hint of pride, than he had read in his entire life. But Alex Miller was intrigued. 'What sort of novels? How do you find the time to read them?'

'I go to bed at about ten, and read for three hours. That'll usually finish an average novel, or a thriller.' I did not admit to him what was in any case implied by his question: that I read them because I am indolent, and that, yes, I did have better things to do. I just like to put off doing them.

Miller, an interesting and intelligent man, thoughtful and curious across a wide range of subjects, was slow to warm up, but had a cheerful openness that no one could have divined on the basis of his behaviour on that coach to Torquay. Like Strachan, he reads regularly in the areas of history, biography and autobiography, generally eschewing works of fiction as somehow not very useful. But both he and Gordon had read Nick Hornby's *Fever Pitch*, and admired it.

'It's an excellent book,' said Strachan, 'but it's about people who are obsessed by football, for anoraks. I'm not obsessed by football, but it was good, well written. I tried to get my kids to read it, but they aren't readers.' He looked sad at the thought. 'Always say they're too busy to read.' He didn't like the film of *Fever Pitch*, though. 'It misses out most of the good lines. Only five or six get in.' Gordon is, if not exactly a student of the cinema, widely knowledgeable about popular contemporary films. His favourites are Woody Allen's.

'I love his stand-up comedy routines. We have a common,' he said. 'We have the same problem.

both neurotic about being short.' I was slightly surprised. I had supposed that the 'wee man,' as Atkinson, among others, used to call him, was comfortable with his stature, just as a cheetah would presumably not worry because it was smaller than an elephant. The taste for Woody Allen, though, makes some sense. Woody Allen's trademark – the ironisation of his own failures and anxieties – must ring some sort of bell with people who spend so much time teasing and piss-taking, deflating both each other and themselves.

But Huckerby, the subject of so many of the team's jokes, surely could not like it, any more than he was likely to be an admirer of Woody Allen. (His favourite actors are Al Pacino and Robert de Niro.) 'Doesn't he find the teasing painful?' I asked Gordon.

'Not at all. He loves it. Just as long as he's the centre of attention he doesn't mind what they say, and they know when enough is enough – they've stopped kidding Whelan since he's been injured. But Huck still hasn't figured out that they really are laughing at him, not with him.' I found this hard to believe, but perhaps that was my problem. If you tease me because I am a worthless football player, I will beam and encourage you to say more. I would be a little sad if you were to say that I was stupid, or ignorant, or crass. Presumably, for Huck, the reverse is true. He is a terrific footballer, certainly the most valuable commodity on the team. He must be worth £5 million. He was teased, at times mercilessly, about his tactical naïveté, or about missing chances, but no one doubted his ability, his capacity to take players on, his pace. If they did, he would defend himself stoutly, and regard it as unjust. But to say that he is stupid – so what? He isn't paid to be smart.

Willo, Telf, Shawsy and Huck soon moved into the hotel lobby and ordered tea. As I walked past, they invited me to join them, which hadn't happened before. Pleased, I sat down and filled a cup. They were anxious, Willo said, to make sure that I put in the book 'who the thickest player in the team is'. I looked him in the eye, and said that I would, so long as he didn't mind. The others chuckled happily, but Willo wasn't much amused. It wasn't true, so you shouldn't take the piss about it. Though it is hard to catch him in an unguarded moment, he is a thoughtful fellow. He had recently approached chief football reporter Adam Dent with the suggestion that he write, himself, a column in the *Coventry Evening Telegraph* that focused on what football players are really like. Adam liked the idea, but his editor (I think wrongly), regarding the market for such pieces to be limited, declined.

'No,' said Telf. 'It's Huck. He has to be in the book. Me, you don't want me. Nothing interesting about me. But you gotta have Huck.'

'Well,' I said, 'let me tell you a story about Huck.' Huck looked up, vaguely alarmed, as many players will be if you start a sentence, 'Let me tell you a story about . . .' How did I know stories about him? What stories? I felt, to a small degree, that I was betraying a confidence, but I was sure Richardson would forgive me. 'I was talking to the chairman last week' – now I had their attention, even Huck's – 'and he was telling me the story about when Huck was signed from Newcastle.'

Huckerby joined Coventry from Newcastle for £1 million late in 1996, having spent a brief period on loan to Millwall, for whom he had scored three goals in six games but who couldn't afford to sign him. Coventry had previously tried to buy him from Lincoln City, where Pendrey had gone to watch him play ('He scored a break-away goal in the first few minutes. I didn't have to see any more'), but were pipped by Newcastle, who had sent both Kevin Keegan and Terry McDermott to have a look at him. But Newcastle, who unaccountably had no reserve-team football under Keegan, couldn't offer Huckerby much in the way of prospects, what with Shearer, Ferdinand, Asprilla and Beardsley competing for places as strikers, and he was anxious to get away. So isolated was he from their first-team set-up that when

Newcastle agreed to sell him to Coventry, it was several days before they could find him to tell him.

I had put my theory that Huck played the fool, but wasn't one, to the chairman, who went along with it with good grace. 'When we negotiated his contract,' Richardson said, 'which took over four hours, he argued his case very well. He just listened, stood his ground and kept arguing; he kept saying, "Chairman, I'm worth more than that."' While this sentence is unlikely to qualify Huckerby for a spot in Bartlett's *Quotations*, it seemed evidence of a kind of level-headed self-confidence. The players looked at Huckerby with mild surprise, though nothing approaching respect. Huck nodded, his face radiating self-belief. His index finger went into the air. 'I held my own,' he said.

Telfer was concerned, though, that I got the Whelan story straight. Taking me aside for a moment, he asked earnestly if there had been any reports from the Leamington nightspots.

'Not really, it seems quiet on that front.' (Bertie and Anna have expert ears to the ground in that milieu.)

'I really think he's changed,' said Telf, an assertion with which Gordon, whom I had previously consulted on the subject, seemed to agree. 'I feel hopeful,' Gordon said, 'but when you are in that pattern it's hard to get out of it.' He had gazed round the room as the players finished their dinner, his eyes alighting on a few of them. 'We've got some good role models here: Oggy, Roland, Gary Mac, Dion – good pros, you can learn from them. But you've got to want to learn.'

Whelan was the focus of countless jokes about his drinking and laddishness before his major screw-up, after which the boys cut it out, and urged him to change his ways. Telfer's description of the glass-kicking incident – 'just madness' – and his acknowledgement of its seriousness helped change the way the players dealt with Whelan. He was treated with a new gentleness – not all the time, of course, that would be soft – but his drunkenness was no longer implicitly condoned. Gordon noticed the change: 'I think the boys really tried to help him,' he said. 'They knew how stupid he'd been, and how much he'd let us all down. And they knew it was his last chance.'

There are, then, some rules with this piss-taking stuff. It is one thing to call Roland an airline pilot and Oggy a baggage-handler, another to say that Huckerby isn't very bright, and something else altogether to tease a disconsolate Salako after the Hillsborough game, and call him 'Slasher'. In each case the charge is proven (Roland is pretty and Oggy is not; Huck is not Brain of Britain; Salako is not a good striker), but in the first case one feels a genuine affection is also in play, with Huckerby there is a kind of underlying tenderness in the teasing, while with Salako the barbs have an undeniable harshness. Even here, though, there are some limits: you can call John 'Slasher', but not (except in the heat of battle) a 'useless cunt'. There's no wit in that, and wit imposes distance.

Because taking the piss, implicitly, balances affection and hostility, it is both a form of intimacy and a denial of it. Players are team-mates, with common ends, but they compete with each other for places. They are dependent on each other, but fiercely pursue their own interests. 'Selfish' is a term of approbation in this world, and denotes a singleminded commitment to one's job. I have met a number of players who would privately admit that they would rather have a great game and draw than a terrible one and win. 'At least when you've played well,' said Oggy (in another context), 'you can be sure of your place.' It's a risky business: you can lose form, be injured, or dropped, or sold, without warning, at a moment's notice. You have to get what you can out of it, while you can. You are in it, fundamentally, for yourself. And if you can't take it in the dressing room, you're sure not going to be able to take it on the pitch.

So most of the mickey-taking is a kind of free-for-all,

designed to show that between team-mates there are no boundaries, anything goes. 'They like to tell me what great tits my wife has, and how much they'd like to shag her,' Gary McAllister told me. 'And I just go all quiet, and stare at them and say, "OK, cunt, that's enough!" And they go all quiet . . . But I don't mind, really, I'm just teasing them back, it's all a bit of a laugh. After all, I've played in a lot of peculiar places round the world, in front of really hostile crowds, and if you can take that, you can take almost anything.' Teasing and being teased shows you are one of the lads, that you can take it, and dish it out. It can, as Gordon observed, get rough, but what you really worry about, as a player, is not when they are teasing you, but when they're not.

The contrast between Strachan and Huckerby in contract-negotiation was instructive. Huck, belying his dopy image, toughed it out; Gordon, who is a tiger, was as easy as a pussycat. Though the story linking Gordon with the managership of Benfica had run in the national papers a couple of weeks before, there had never been an offer on the table, and Gordon was already, in any case, considering the new contract with Coventry. 'He's very straightforward to deal with,' said Richardson. 'He told me to draw up a contract, put in it what I thought he was worth, and he would sign it. So that is what I've done. And he will. That's the sort of person he is.'

Richardson had been working on getting the players on to long-term contracts. England Under-21 international Marcus Hall had just signed a new four-year contract, and the only players whose contracts would expire at the end of the season were John Salako and Oggy. And each time one of the team signed, it was still reported in the press as 'Player X Pledges his Future to the Club.' But this is nonsense, an old use of journalistic rhetoric that has lost meaning in the new financial and contractual climate. There is now no sense in owning a player unless you own him for a decent period of time, otherwise he will just play out his contract, become a free agent and go for nothing. So players must be on long-term contracts in order to protect their value. It is just as accurate to say that the club has them on a long contract in order to sell them as in order to keep them. In some ways, post-Bosman, it comes down to the same thing.

On the coach to Highbury before the Cup fixture, I laid on the table in front of me a copy of the catalogue for the current exhibition in my gallery. The show was dedicated to the works of an illustrator called Mike Wilks, whose book *The Ultimate Alphabet* was something of a cult success in the mid-1980s. Putting the catalogue out was intended as a kind of bait, and slightly to my surprise, I got a bite almost immediately. Alex Miller reached across the aisle and picked it up, while I studiously kept my face in my newspaper. He read the introduction by Sir Tim Rice, then looked through the illustrations slowly, his face flickering with a mixture of concentration and bemusement. He didn't look as if he liked the pictures very much, but then again, neither did I, though some people seem to love them to bits.

Handing the catalogue back to me, he asked, 'Is this what you do, then?' It was an innocent enough question, but it was the first time that any of the managerial staff had asked me a single thing about myself: who I was, what I did. From their treatment of me thus far you might have supposed that I was some sort of manifestation, a spectre which mysteriously appeared on occasional match days, or at Ryton, and then equally mysteriously disappeared. The notion that I might have some kind of life beyond these recurrent appearances had been of no interest to them at all.

'It's part of what I do,' I said. 'I have a shop in Bloomsbury, and we deal in rare books and manuscripts, and sometimes we have picture exhibitions. But I like to do lots of things, so I'm also writing this book, and sometimes I give bits of talks and lectures.'

'You wouldn't do very well in football, then,' he said. 'There's no time to do other things. You have to work a hundred hours a week just to do the job.' He pointed to the catalogue. 'Tell me how this works, then. How do you put prices on the pictures? Do people come in and bid for them, or what?'

'No, we price them, and then it's first come first served.'

'What if someone offers more for a picture than the person who first wants it?' he asked, envisaging, I presume, a situation not so much like a Sotheby's auction as a bidding war between clubs for the services of a player.

'Too bad, first one gets it.' He looked perplexed: surely that was a stupid way to do business? Gordon, in the meantime, had picked up the catalogue, and was looking through it with the same concentrated attention that Miller had shown. I asked if he liked the pictures.

'No use asking me,' he replied. 'I don't know anything about art. Don't understand it.' I admired his refusal to join the 'I know what I like' school of aesthetic appreciation. He was looking into another professional world: like his, it required training and knowledge, without which he did not feel qualified to offer an opinion. Miller nodded his assent. 'I don't know what to make of it,' he said. Garry Pendrey had by now had a leaf through the pictures as well. He didn't, either.

They're pros. They are entirely and unashamedly willing to own up to great chasms of ignorance about what they don't know: about literature, or foreign languages, art or classical music, haute cuisine or fine wine. They are entirely without pretentiousness, and they do not fake responses. They live in a world in which any form of pretence is savagely pilloried, and they have great respect for genuine professional competence. This is what makes them so short-tempered – contemptuous even – with the sort of football fan (almost all of them, in fact) who thinks he understands the game and knows better than they do.

Having observed this from the start, it was thus an

essential part of my strategy to claim ignorance, and to ask to be instructed. Because while the pros are polite to supporters, they think them fools. Not because they always have the wrong opinions, but because they hold them without having earned the right to them. Because they don't know what it is like, haven't served their time.

I was reminded of a conversation I'd had with John Salako. 'Fans,' he said, 'most of them, are sad. They think the game is more important than it is, it says something about the miserable kinds of lives they must lead. They get things out of proportion.' The way in which fans overvalue the game is not, in general, congenial to the players, one of whom (who did not wish to be named) would only say, 'Fans? Come on. Players hate fans.' For the great majority of the players football is not an obsession, but a profession. It takes training, and skill, and a lot of ability, playing or managing.

Gordon can be particularly scathing about fans who try to tell him what to do. I had recently observed him at a club function, rendered absolutely mute by four supporters, each of whom was giving Gordon his opinion on what he ought to be doing. 'They were saying the most amazing, the most stupid things,' said Gordon. 'Then they'd slag off a player, and want me to agree with them. And that player is my player, maybe my friend. I just kept quiet. What can you say?'

Gordon's silence was perceived by a couple of those fans (I asked them afterwards) as dour Scots stuff. It brought to mind a question I had been wanting to ask Strachan: why is it that Scots seem to be so successful as managers of English teams? 'I think,' he said, 'if you look at the current lot – Kenny Dalglish, Alex Ferguson, George Graham – they all have the same quality. I have it too. We're extremely stubborn. We work very hard, we're desperate for success, and we will stick to our guns. But there's more to it than that. I think we are like that, when we come down here, because we want to prove ourselves. Maybe it's a political thing, but I don't think we ever forget the history with England, how Scots have been treated.'

'Does this have a downside?'

He laughed, and Miller, across the aisle, nodded his head in shared amusement. 'Sure it does. We can be arrogant, not take criticism. Sometimes I'm so stubborn that even when I know I'm probably wrong I still carry on. And old Alex Ferguson, he'll never admit it even when he knows he's wrong.'

'Does that get him into trouble with players?'

'Sure, it can. But then the player doesn't stick around for long. He's out.'

'Is that what happened to Andrei Kanchelskis?' Press reports had suggested that the superb Russian international winger had fallen out with Ferguson after a series of disputes about the player's fitness, and his apparent capacity to play at international level while being simultaneously unable to appear in club matches. Relations eventually broke down, and Kanchelskis was sold to Everton.

Gordon, Alex and Garry all gave a guffaw.

'What's so funny?'

'Nothing at all,' said Miller. 'Rumour has it that Kanchelskis was represented – owned – by the Russian Mafia. When they told him to leave, he left, and they took part of the action. Maybe that's why he left Everton for Fiorentina as well; it made them some more money. He goes when they say he goes.' Gordon and Garry nodded their assent.

The Russian Mafia? I suppose the look of incredulity on my face must have indicated a degree of disbelief, because Miller assured me, 'It's well known in the game. They control a number of other Russian players, particularly in Italy and Spain.' I looked across to Gordon for confirmation.

'For sure,' he said, rummaging about in his bag. He didn't seem to be kidding. He eventually found what he was looking for, and handed it to me as we arrived at Highbury. 'Use my ticket tonight,' he said. I took a look at it. Affixed to it was a yellow stub that proclaimed 'Manager's Ticket'. The seat number was Directors' Box, Row A, Seat 1. I resolved to keep it, to give to Jonathan Strange to add to his collection of Coventry memorabilia.

I love Highbury. It's such a shame that Arsenal play there. As you ascend the marble staircase, flanked by oil portraits of former Arsenal luminaries, there is none of that tackiness that even some of the more famous English grounds exude. Only at Ibrox, Alex Miller told me, do you get a similar sense of gravitas, only (of course) more so: 'There's no equivalent at any English ground,' he said proudly.

Taking my usual pre-match stroll round the pitch, this sense of well-ordered symmetry and, yes, tastefulness (the first time I've been tempted to use the term about a football ground) was reinforced. But Kyle Lightbourne, strolling about with me, was oblivious of it: what he liked was how small the pitch is, and he looked up and down it yearningly, wishing he could get a game.

'But surely,' I said, 'that's bad for a striker. Don't you need room to run about and find space?'

He shook his head. 'This is one of the smallest pitches in the whole League. That's partly why Ian Wright scores so many goals. If you get behind your man at all, and somebody gets the ball to you, you're gone. There's no time or space for a defender to catch up with you.' Fortunately Wright was being 'rested' on the night, as was David Seaman – evidence of the low priority manager Arsène Wenger was according the Coca-Cola Cup – but Bergkamp, coming back from suspension, would be playing.

And the match, eventually, came down exactly to what Lightbourne had described. Arsenal, kept in the game by Seaman's excellent young Austrian understudy, Alex Manninger, scored in extra time when Bergkamp got a step ahead of Richard Shaw, who didn't have time to catch him, and coolly chipped Oggy. It looked simple, and wasn't, like so many things that Bergkamp does. A few minutes later Huckerby got behind the Arsenal defence, went one on one with Manninger, and missed. And that, you may say, is the difference between high class and high promise.

I watched the game from my seat upstairs, flanked by Bryan Richardson on my left and, across the aisle, Arsenal vice-chairman David Dein. The contrast was interesting. Dein sat perfectly still and silent throughout the match, blazingly intent, like a Roman emperor watching Christians being eaten by lions, though with less sense of fun. Richardson, on the other hand, twisted and shifted about, accompanying the play with a running commentary. I liked to think his talkativeness was because I was there, while Dein was sitting alone, but that's rubbish. He was talking to himself.

Dion got some stick. 'Come on Dion, run! God, it's one of those nights when he's not in the mood to play . . .' Paul Williams was struggling a little in midfield: 'Come on, Willo, for Christ's sake, you've got a foot like a hammer!' Simon Haworth, struggling just as badly up front, was spared criticism, though. His better touches were applauded with 'Good boy, nice touch, now move, find some space!' I suspect that Richardson knew Dion and Willo could take some criticism, while Simon, the new boy, needed encouragement, and so he unconsciously behaved, like most fans, as if they could hear him.

I liked his engagement. At one point, when Bergkamp turned a Coventry defender with yet another artistic little touch, and brought the ball down smoothly with one movement, flicking it off at a gorgeous angle, I turned to Richardson and, making a contrast with Williams, said, 'Doesn't he have wonderful soft feet?' This seemed to me simple, but eloquent. He didn't answer. He didn't want to talk, except to himself, and he didn't give a damn about Bergkamp's feet. They belonged to an Arsenal player.

Some time at the start of the second half the scoreboard announced the attendance: 30,000 plus. Richardson looked about the largely full ground. 'Fuckin' place holds thirty-nine thousand,' he muttered to himself. 'You see nine thousand empty seats? And we get thirty-five per cent of the gate . . .' At the final whistle, disconsolate, he wandered off, wishing me goodnight, and I headed off in search of my dinner partners, Bertie and Jonathan Strange. We were joined for dinner at an Italian restaurant close to the ground by the writer Tony Holden, his agreeable American wife and son, and a couple of his pals.

Nick Hornby was there, too, and Holden introduced us, thinking that my fan's-eye view book might be interesting to him. He is pleasant and unassuming, seemed to like the idea, and talked a little about the reception *Fever Pitch* had had from the Arsenal players. 'As far as I know, they all read it. Ian Wright said the most interesting thing. He said that he has never understood supporters, why they get so worked up, and that the book had made him understand.'

After about an hour, Arsène Wenger came in, and everyone in the restaurant rose to applaud him. Except me and Bertie and Jonathan. Why applaud some Arsenal bastard when they'd just put us out of the Cup? No one noticed our lack of respect, but it made us feel better. Anyway, it was only the Coca-Cola Cup. Who cared?

10

A Trip to Anfield
and a Half-Time Report

The Haydock Thistle Hotel is located in the middle of a field just off the M6, about £20 worth of taxi ride from Liverpool Lime Street Station. To get there from Leamington Spa, you can either take the team coach from Ryton, arriving two hours later, fresh and cheerful, or catch a train from Leamington Spa, arrive late in Birmingham, miss a connection, wait for an hour, get the next Liverpool train, catch the taxi to the hotel, and turn up too late for dinner. I had taken the latter option. The team coach, Gordon had told me, was full.

After four hours of travelling on loathesomely over-heated, crowded, Virgin trains – which manage wonder-fully to duplicate the misery of flying Economy Class – I reached the hotel at 7.30, just as dinner was finishing. Telf, Whelan, Huck (without hat) and Shawsy were already out in the hotel lobby, watching the Christmas revellers. It was party night, and the place was teeming. A lot of local firms were having their Christmas parties – four-course De Luxe Meal followed by Disco – and there was that slightly frantic feeling you get in the air when a lot of people are deter-mined to have a good time in too small a space.

In the hotel lobby, greeting arriving partygoers, were five scraggly musicians with an odd variety of facial hair (two handlebar moustaches, some mutton chops and what looked suspiciously like a bearded lady), looking like vegetarians on parole. They were playing Christmas carols by ringing bells in some sort of pattern. If you listened carefully, you could catch the occasional hint of a tune – 'Good King Wenceslas', or something equally awful.

The Coventry players were checking out the women, splendidly decked out in their once-a-year finest. Or should I say once-a-generation? I hadn't seen outfits like these since the sixties. A large blonde lady shimmied by encased in a red sequinned dress that looked like a cast-off from a Julian Clary show. The players stared with the kind of awe they usually reserve for Ryan Giggs. And there was plenty more to look at: the room was aglow with the sparkle of jewels and flashing bits of glass. You could literally see the dresses reflecting against the walls. There was something lovely about it, this pre-Armani showmanship, recalling those happy days before the omnipresence of black designerwear and sleek elegance, when dressing up had something childish and extravagant about it. When you looked in the mirror and what you saw was so pleasing exactly because it wasn't you, but something heightened, transformed. When, just for the odd occasion, you got to be the peacock.

I ought to have liked it a lot, but I didn't because I was so pissed off. I'd just come from the dining room, where Gordon, Garry and Jim, finishing their meal, had fobbed me off in no uncertain terms. They looked curiously forlorn and incomplete: it was the first away fixture since Alex Miller's departure.

'Can I have a chat after dinner, Gordon?' I asked, instead of the question I really wanted to put to him, which was, 'Why did you make me spend £60 and four hours on a fucking train when you know damn well I could have come on the coach, you little shit?' And the subsidiary: 'And isn't it about time that you got over your paranoia about an outsider being around?' I'd been around now for four months. I was on easy, casual terms with a number of the players. I hadn't asked much. I'd been as discreet as a doctor in a whorehouse. Wasn't it time to lighten up a little? What did they have to hide?

Strachan looked up – he was particularly pale and drawn, and his eyes were puffy, as if he had a bad cold, or hadn't slept – and said he was going to play Trivial Pursuit Pop Tunes after dinner. Jim smiled and tried to look amiable; Garry could barely bring himself to say hello.

There was definitely a change of atmosphere. The team had drifted down the League, and the forthcoming fixtures were ominous. And – to my eye at least – Gordon had been continuing to exhibit some of the classic symptoms of stress. His persistent confrontations with referees, combined with an increased sardonic quality in his press statements about both individual players and the team as a whole, seemed to point to the loss of that little bit of control. Indeed, I wondered whether the team's deplorable disciplinary record to date – three sendings-off and forty-five bookings – hadn't to a degree been caused by Gordon's incapacity to mask his own anxiety.

A number of the bookings and sendings off had been due not to faulty or malicious tackles, but to indiscipline and mouthiness. If you have a manager who is over-fond of voicing his opinions, his players will follow his lead. Why can't footballers just accept the referee's decision and get on with it? On the whole, rugby players do, and cricketers. Presumably the football authorities implicitly sanction dissent: if they didn't want it, all they would have to do would be to instruct the referee to book any offending player or manager, however mild the dissent.

It was hard not to be sympathetic, though, because we did seem to be getting some bad decisions. (Mind you, it would be hard to find a team or a set of fans who don't feel this.) But Gordon's frustration was understandable

Football, he believes, is a simple game, not merely tactically, but in its very nature. It has clear rules, which should produce a kind of even-handed certainty in their application. One of the delights of sport, after all, lies in the ways in which it differs from life. Because there are clear rules, quality and hard work should be rewarded; there is nothing ambiguous about the process of winning or losing. Whereas life is a God-awful muddle. It is for me, at least. I rather suspect that, for Gordon, it isn't: the rules are just as clear as they are in sport. (Do your best; don't fake things; respect others; say your piece truthfully or say nothing; court neither wealth nor fame; love and trust your loved ones; behave so that you will have no regrets afterwards; admit it when you have failed.) For me, as for most of us, each of those simple precepts needs to be followed by a 'but' or an 'except when'. Which is where the muddle comes in. And when some of that muddle – inevitably but infuriatingly – invades the game, when referees are inconsistent, incompetent or unfair in their interpretation of the rules, then it is particularly galling to someone like Gordon Strachan. It seems to offend not only against the spirit of the game, but the very rules by which he has lived his life.

The problem of team discipline had unfortunate consequences. For the Liverpool match, four players were suspended: Breen, Burrows, Boland and Williams (again). McAllister's knee had been operated on during the week, and he would be out for some time. The squad looked absolutely threadbare, though it had been bolstered by an exciting new signing: a young midfield player named George Boateng, who would be thrown straight into the side the next day. First scouted by Ray Clarke, Boateng was signed from the Dutch club Feyenoord, and had captained the Dutch Under-21 international side. Although :d at some £4 million, Coventry had snapped £220,000 because his contract was up at the season. By making a move for the player in Richardson had been able to beat off challenges from several Spanish and Italian clubs, who were waiting until January to make their moves, since after 1 January the player would have been free to negotiate with other clubs without talk of a transfer fee. Thus the chairman had managed to acquire the player at a bargain price (Coventry had offered £150,000; Feyenoord wanted £500,000).

Gordon's comments on his new acquisition carried a hint of a barb in them – 'he can pass the ball to his teammates, which is always a good start' – which seemed as much to criticise those Coventry players who couldn't do so as to extol the virtues of Boateng, who allegedly could. The remark fitted exactly into the pattern of his recent utterances: the team wasn't very good, a number of the players were letting the side down, the referees were diabolical . . . It had all the hallmarks of a man looking for someone (else) to blame. Only five or six games back his tone had been demonstrably different: when the team had not been winning many games, but not losing them, either, and when Gordon's oft-reiterated public view was that we were a fast-improving side, gritty and determined, and likely to win a significant number of games with just an occasional shift in luck.

I suspect that the loss of Alex hurt him more than he would admit. He was comfortable with Alex. You saw it in the way they talked, in the easy banter, the shared reminiscences of the Scottish football scene, the lack of any deference on Miller's side. A shrewd tactician, and a former manager of Hibernian himself, now second-in-command of the Scotland team that would be going to the World Cup, Miller was, if anything, a more experienced and sophisticated figure than Strachan, and was valued accordingly.

The problem, according to Richardson, was that he had not signed anything more binding than a month-by-month contract. When he had left the manager's job at Hibs a year or so earlier, he had still been owed a significant amount of money, and until that was paid he saw no reason to sign a long-term contract at Coventry. He was, in fact, in the process of negotiating a deal with Richardson in which he could only leave (without compensation being paid to the club) if he were offered the managership of either Rangers or Scotland. But it was always going to be hard to keep him. He was simply too good, too experienced and too ambitious to stay as a number two, even to a man he liked and respected as much as Gordon.

And the back-room staff matter to a manager. They provide support and relief, serve as sounding-boards, offer criticism, cautious or up-front, report on things that the manager may have missed, add anecdotal evidence about other teams and players. Garry Pendrey, for the moment de facto number two, was a constantly chirpy and supportive presence, but fundamentally deferential to Strachan in a way that Miller was not. Jim Blyth, recognising that he was just the goalkeeping coach, modestly confined himself to a supportive role, though he was an intelligent reader of the game, and a shrewd analyst. But he didn't think it his place to have much tactical input.

That was Miller's job, and Miller was gone. Talking to a number of Coventry fans after the Leicester game, I found a widespread feeling that Gordon was not as tactically astute as Miller, and that we might well struggle as a result of losing him. Was that true? they asked me, secure in the belief that I was privy to all the secrets. But I didn't know. Nor was I competent to judge. Certainly Miller liked to talk about tactics more than Gordon did – one of Gordon's fundamental beliefs was that it is possible to overcomplicate things when you analyse the game – and I could think of a number of instances (such as the good performance at Old Trafford and the away win at Wimbledon) when I'd been under the impression that the excellence of the Coventry performance was attributable to Miller's tactical nous.

The only way to tell how significant Miller's input had been was to watch out for what happened now that he was gone. The first home loss of the season – a woeful display – had come two days after his resignation. He had gone to Scotland on the Wednesday before the Leicester game to talk to the people at Aberdeen, informed Richardson of his decision to leave on the Thursday, and (somewhat to Richardson's annoyance) never returned. 'He should have come back for the Leicester game,' Bryan said, 'because Aberdeen weren't playing that Saturday.'

Noticing the harried look on Strachan's face at Liverpool that evening, it was impossible not to feel sorry for him. He seemed a forlorn and isolated figure, and after a time, having checked into my room, had a wash and eaten a bowl of (execrable) chilli from room service, I began to feel sorry for him, and contemplated going back downstairs to join the Trivial Pursuit game.

Better sense prevailed. Instead I spent some time roaming the bars in search of a Cuban cigar (no such luck), and ended up watching some local nurses, loosening up now with a couple of drinks inside them, strutting their stuff on the dance floor. Their male colleagues were watching from the sidelines, a good few pints short, still, of the confidence to go out and join them. We all admired a particularly Rubenesque brunette in a gold lamé dress wriggling a bottom like an enormous apple, golden, delicious, a sight at once so mesmerising and so delectable that, after five minutes of serious study, I decided life wasn't so bad after all, and went up to bed.

It should have given me something better than Huckerby to dream about, but it didn't. I slept fitfully, the unresolved irritation with Strachan waking me several times. Then I lay there, my head in a whirl, feeling the injustice of his standoffishness, before drifting back to sleep, and then it would happen all over again. At breakfast, both Gordon and Jim admitted to insomnia, which gave new resonance to the theme of staying up, and we were a pretty miserable-looking trio until Gordon was cheered up by the sight of Roland Nilsson, at the next table, studying the *Times*. He had a pimple on his chin.

'Hey, Roland,' Gordon called across the table. Nilsson looked up quizzically. Strachan pointed to his chin.

'I know,' said Nilsson, waiting for what came next. Nothing did, so he went back to his newspaper. Presumably it was part of the role of Premiership managers to keep an eye on the cosmetic imperfections of their players.

'Mr Perfect . . .' said Blyth, with a smile.

'It shows there is a God,' said Gordon. His good humour thus innocently restored, he joshed happily with the lady at the next table, who had forgotten where she had left her handbag, signed a few autographs and had his picture taken with some kids.

But it's too hard. The job of being a Premiership manager is really six jobs, and no one man at any club can hope to do it adequately with or without the right staff. Gordon readily admitted he was feeling the pressure. 'In the last few days, aside from all the normal things, I've seen two matches at the School of Excellence – I love that, it's pure football, the boys can play for the love of playing – a reserve match, then had the Spurs game. Then, on Sunday, which is my day off, I flew to Belgium to see a player. It's too much: any Premiership manager will tell you that.'

I suspect he is a bad delegator. Just recently he had had to waste a lot of time rounding up players to make a Sunday appearance at a chain of local sports shops: 'I've got to call them myself. They wouldn't do it otherwise.' In fact, he ended up going himself. But, he said, whatever the pressure, 'I'm getting stronger. You have to. And you have to remember, you have to keep reminding yourself, all they can finally say is "You're not a very good manager." It's hard, not like normal life. You're in the national limelight all the time – there are only twenty Premier League managers. But if the worst comes to the worst, all you can say is that you did your best. After all, it's not like something happened to your family.'

This is a constant reference point for him, and at stressful times you often encounter him quietly reasserting the values on which he has based his life, getting things into perspective. 'I've been very privileged. Not for the money: that's obscene. But because you get your afternoons off every day of your career, you're done training after lunch, and that means you can get home, see the kids' sports days, go to the school concerts. You can be a father to your children, not just leave them for their mother to bring up like most blokes, away from home at eight, back at seven. It gives you a chance of a proper family life.'

The solution to the loss of Miller, he hoped, would involve something more than the appointment of a new number two. The papers had linked Coventry with Stewart Houston of QPR, but there had been, Strachan insisted, nothing in it. 'We're not looking for a number two. We need something more than that, to create a bigger job, and find somebody who will oversee the development of football at Coventry for the next ten years. Even when I'm gone, it doesn't matter who the manager is. Someone who can plan, take over the work with the youngsters, be involved in signings, get the structure right throughout the club. And be involved on the coaching side with the first team, if he wants.'

'I presume you mean a director of football?'

'I don't know what it should be called. The problem with that title is that it didn't work for Kenny at Blackburn, or Ron here at Coventry. But what I mean is some sort of supremo who can oversee the development of football over the long term.'

It wasn't clear to me what this meant, but it was clear what was intended: to find a figure who would have almost the same status as Strachan, but different obligations, thus ridding the manager – who often tends to be renamed the first-team coach in such structures – of a number of his non-essential duties. 'There are so many different jobs here, and I have to concentrate on working with the first team.' It is too easy to lose sight of the fact that the essential, the fundamental, arguably the only, duty of most Premiership managers is to stay in the Premiership. This is not, of course, true for the Fergusons and the Wengers, but ask Martin O'Neill or Jim Smith, both of whose teams have done very well of late, and they will be certain about what their priority is. Staying up. The rest – the Cup runs, the chances of playing in Europe – are just bonuses.

Talking to Strachan, this fundamentally decent man, harassed from all angles, trying to keep things in balance, I felt a sudden rush of remorse for my anger with him the night before. It was foolish of me: after all, the only time I had gone from Coventry to a match on the team coach was for the friendly at Torquay. I was not welcome there before a real game. (Pendrey had recently told me, pointedly, that in twenty-five years in football he had never seen an outsider on the team coach. 'Not even the directors. The chairman's only done it once.') I was totally unaware of the magnitude of what I had been asking for, and my irritation at not being granted access only indicated my own ignorance. It seemed as if I had begun to experience, in some unanalysed way, some of the pressure that Gordon experiences daily, and which he sometimes unwittingly sheds on those about him, like flakes of dandruff.

It marked a new stage in my relationship with the team. I'd begun unconsciously to assume that I had rights. I was starting to feel, just a little, that I belonged. And of course I didn't, really. I was still an outsider, and the fact that they all knew me a bit, and I them, didn't mean that I was in any sense a part of the team. So I had overreacted. Gordon was the gaffer, and my role entirely subject to his judgement. I was the Trond Soltvedt of writers: unsure of my place, in or out depending on the day, unable to feel certain of my plans or expectations, looking eagerly to Gordon to give me a break. Presumably the players are used to this, to the myriad ways in which a manager may, wittingly or unwittingly, transmit the pressure he is under to those around him. But it was new to me, and I wasn't very good at coping with it.

'Gordon,' I said, 'we need to sort out some ground rules, because there is obviously some problem with me coming up on the coach that we haven't talked about. But it isn't full. We both know that.'

'Of course,' he acknowledged. 'But before a game I'm just not comfortable with an outsider around. Sometimes on the coach we need to be able to talk freely, and we can't if you're there. You've been discreet, that's not the problem. It's just that everyone is keyed up before a game, and the presence of somebody from the outside changes the atmosphere.'

'That's seems reasonable. I wish you'd said this to me before. Then I wouldn't have asked.'

'I guess I should have. But the same goes for the ride down to the ground from the hotel. That's a time we really need to be alone. You can come tomorrow, but after that you should make your own way. But you're always welcome to come home with us after the game. It's over then.'

This made a serious difference, and I was chagrined to hear it. The richest part of this whole experience – the one that opened the most revealing and varied vistas – began with the coach ride down to a new ground, then the disembarking from the coach at the players' entrance, the sight of a new set of dressing rooms and internal corridors, the view of the home team roaming casually about in their own domain, the walk through the tunnel on to the pitch, the chance to wander round and see Hillsborough, or Old Trafford, or Anfield, as a player sees it: from the middle of the pitch. To sample, however briefly, the atmosphere in the dressing room before the game: the announcement of who will be substitutes, the players slowly getting into their kits, perusing the programme, oiling their legs. To sense the quiet descending, as the first-team players, concentrating on the coming game, slip back into themselves, the banter easing, the pre-match anxiety increasingly palpable, the trips to the loo more frequent. (Garry Pendrey recalled that, in the fifteen minutes before a match, 'I'd go for a piss four or five times, and even then when I went out on the pitch I'd be worried I would dribble in my shorts. But once the whistle went, it was fine.')

I loved all this behind-the-scenes stuff. I would miss it. I wondered if we could do a deal? Could I meet the team as the bus arrived at the ground, and then join them and go in via the players' entrance?

'Sure,' Gordon said amiably, unaware of any apparent inconsistency: if the team needed to be alone on the way to the ground, why didn't they need to be alone once they got there? I decided not to point this out. Anyway, maybe he was doing it because he was feeling generous.

'OK,' I said. 'At the same time, though, I'd like to begin to get closer to the action in other ways . . .'

'What sort of ways?'

'I guess a little like it was at the friendly at Torquay. More time in the dressing room, maybe some time in the dugout?'

He thought for a bit. 'That sounds possible. But not the dressing room at half-time. That's sacred. Things can get said in the heat of the moment, and afterwards they are forgotten. It's just among ourselves. It wouldn't look right in print.'

'Fair enough. When can we start to make these changes?'

He was quite clear about that. 'Not yet. Let's wait till we get through these fixtures, then sort it out in January.' The implication was obvious: if we didn't 'get through' the fixtures, if they got through us, forget it, pal. And since I was certain that, by mid-January, we would be out of the Cup and languishing in the bottom three, I didn't think that giving me greater access to the team was going to be high on Gordon's list of priorities.

'After all,' he added, 'you've been down to the training ground, been on the coach, gone into the dressing rooms and on to the pitches, eaten with the players. What else do you want to do, sleep with them?'

As we entered Anfield through the main gates a sign read, 'You'll Never Walk Alone', while on a lowish brick building to our right another sign announced: 'Care in the Community'. It was impossible not to think of these same gates, on the days following the Hillsborough disaster, decked out with scarves and flowers, a number of examples of which are still housed in a showcase in the upstairs boardroom. My only disappointment as I walked out on to the pitch at about 2.15, was the famous sign, 'This is Anfield', which is displayed at the top of the tunnel just as you enter it from the dressing rooms. Of legendary status, hailed by newspapermen as the most intimidating of messages, I had built up this notice in my mind to something of Dantesque proportions (as in 'All hope abandon, ye who enter here'), but in reality, it's a tacky piece of red and white plastic, which might as well read 'Drink Coca-Cola'.

But once you're out on the pitch, there's something at once homely and majestic about the stadium. Unlike Old Trafford, it does not tower above you, and the proportions between the four stands are more harmonious. But what is most striking – and must be intimidating to a visiting side – is how close the stands are to the pitch. Indeed, the famous Kop, now replaced, of course, by seating, extends right to the very rear of the goal, perhaps 6 feet away, and then, rising above it, dominates it completely. I tried standing in the goal, then looking backwards. Jim Blyth walked over. 'I can remember keeping goal here, and you can actually feel the heat of the crowd behind you. It must be ten degrees hotter at this end.' It was a perfect metaphor.

When the crowd, just short of a sell-out, sang 'You'll Never Walk Alone' five minutes before kick-off, it didn't quite have the expected power, because they didn't entirely have their hearts in it. They thought, foolish souls, that this was a home banker. But we'd won two of our last three games at Anfield, and Gordon was tolerably confident. 'We just have to keep them quiet for the first twenty minutes or so. Not do anything foolish. Compete for the ball, not let them get behind us. And we can't afford to give the ball away. Give them too much possession, and they'll eventually get to you. You can't play them at their own game.' He wasn't happy with the team he was putting out – 'They're all I have' – and the major attacking plan was to get the ball upfield in the air to Simon Haworth and see what developed. When I suggested this was rather a big role for Haworth to play, Strachan would only comment, 'We'll see how he does. It's the biggest game he's played.'

In the pre-match kick-about it was obvious that Boateng was a terrific athlete. He moved about like a panther, accelerating effortlessly, touching the ball deftly, flicking it on. He seemed entirely at home in his body, comfortable, luxuriant in his physical sense of himself. I could hardly wait to watch him play. He had been thrown in at the deep end, because of the continued absence of McAllister, Salako's long-term injury and the four suspensions. Dublin was playing in the centre of defence, and Soltvedt in midfield, with Haworth and Huckerby up front.

It was a makeshift team, and it began by playing like one. Though Boateng seemed to settle in straight away, he was later to tell me that he was astonished by the pace of the game, and struggled to keep up for the first twenty minutes. You could hardly tell: he looked confident, creative, athletic. But, like the others – particularly Soltvedt, who needed more time on the ball than he was being given – he gave the ball away too many times, too early. From one of these lapses, after nearly fifteen minutes, Redknapp gathered up the ball in midfield and shifted play wide to the right, where McManaman took it on to the touchline, and squared a mean pass across Hedman. Michael Owen knocked it in with his left foot from a yard out.

And that, more or less, was that. For the rest of the game Coventry huffed and puffed, made an occasional chance (the best of which Marcus Hall volleyed over from inside the box) but were reliant on Hedman for a couple of good saves to keep the score down. McManaman, working hard, dictated the course of play, and Owen shot about like a little rocket, fizzy and dangerous.

The next day the headlines concentrated on the 'Owen For England' theme, but Roland Nilsson, talking to me after the game, was by no means convinced. 'I think he is going to be a very good player, but he isn't ready yet. He's fast, but people are learning to lay off him, and let him run himself into trouble. I'm not sure he makes good runs a lot of the time.' He was, in fact, more impressed with McManaman, but added, 'They are asking too much of him. Every movement seemed to go through him, and he tired. When you have a player that good in midfield it's better if he plays flat out for ten minutes, then has a rest, then comes back into the game. Otherwise he'll burn out in the second half.' Nilsson had been impressed by Boateng, too, but had some reservations about how well he would play with Gary McAllister: 'They both like to have a lot of the ball, and I'm not sure two people next to each other can both do that. We'll have to see how it develops when McAllister comes back.'

After the game, Strachan was obviously furious. 'We had a clear plan,' he said, 'and they didn't play to it. We could not afford to give the ball away. We had to contain them in the first twenty minutes. And we didn't do it. We can't compete with them in footballing terms, we don't have the quality – I don't get a lot of phone calls from Roy Evans asking to buy my players. We have heart, so what we have to do is compete.' He made it sound as if the third form were playing the upper sixth – a version of the 'two leagues' argument – and it didn't seem to me that it was an entirely positive line of thought, or one to console and encourage his team. We had, after all, been missing several first-team players, and we weren't by any means a bad side.

Nor, indeed, did the charge that the team had failed to follow instructions bear much scrutiny. They had followed them to a T, and had tried to play conservative football without giving the ball away. The failure had not been the abandonment of the tactics that Strachan had planned, but an inability to carry them out. Nobody was giving the ball away on purpose, or through inattention. The side were simply under too much early pressure, and were closed down so quickly that they could not deliver enough accurate passes.

The team that trooped back on to the coach was subdued, but many of the players felt that a draw would have been a fair result. (Presumably the game looks different from the pitch.) We settled down while Garry distributed the sandwiches. Marcus Hall looked at his with distaste. 'Asda? Thought we could have had Marks and Spencer's by now. And just look at this coach . . .' Most of the players hated the coach, which McAllister said was the worst not only in the Premiership, but probably in the whole of the League. I quite liked it, but I wasn't very keen on the sandwiches, having tried a variety of them on the trip home from Sheffield Wednesday, so I got in early and chose my favourite, Spam and cement. I settled alone into the front seat, ate some of it and thought about the club's facilities.

Though comfortable by most standards, the coach didn't approach the luxurious sleekness of some of the visiting sides' vehicles to be seen pulling up at Highfield Road, and the players clearly felt ill-served by having to travel in it. It certainly didn't compare very favourably with their own cars. But that was just a minor irritation: what many of them really disliked was the training complex. The building at Ryton was erected in the late 1980s, when it was regarded as comfortable by contemporary standards. But time had quickly passed it by. The first time I visited the training ground early in August, I had been shocked by its Spartan simplicity. The cramped and insalubrious dressing rooms, tiny offices, primitive toilets and showers, tacky plastic tables and chairs, unattractive kitchen facilities and unappetising food. I had expected something swisher and more welcoming, with spacious and comfortable changing rooms, decent showers, lockers for each player, whirlpool baths, extensive gym equipment, decent dining accommodation – the sort of training complex, I suppose, that American athletes are used to. After all, many of the players who train at Ryton earn enormous salaries and are used to a high standard of living. It is hard to imagine many people on a quarter or half a million a year who would tolerate such a basic working environment.

It was a topic about which no player would talk on the record, as you may imagine, but they disliked the place and felt (though they wouldn't, quite, put it like this) demeaned by having to work there. Those of them who had come from elsewhere, and particularly those with experience of bigger clubs, were scathing about Ryton.

The contrast between the cars parked outside (not the Subarus, because most of the players ended up giving them to their wives or using them as second cars, but the many new BMWS and Mercedes) and the facilities indoors was so striking as to seem almost deliberate, as if it were the unconscious intention of the club to remind the players of their origins and keep their heads from swelling. 'Here I am,' the training ground seemed to say. 'This is where you came from. It's a working-class game, after all, and you – even if you do have a flash new car – are a working-class person. Don't you forget it.'

The training complex had a sort of seedy casualness that was comfortable, and people came and went as they pleased, but even that, eventually, caused a problem. Later in the season, when the players were out on the training pitch, thieves drove right up to the door, went into the dressing room and stole all the wallets and watches (including Trond's Rolex). David Burrows, who lost £8 and his underpants ('I wonder what they're going to do with them?' he mused), thought that the lack of security was scandalous, and sure enough, within weeks a guarded fence appeared at the top of the driveway. It was too late by then, but it kept the riff-raff out. Indeed, I had trouble getting through myself, even with my blue card pass. I finally talked my way in, but not before the gatekeeper had looked carefully into the back seat of my car. I presume he was searching for David's lost underwear.

The season was half over: after nineteen games we had 20 points, and the table looked like this:

		Total			Goals		Home			Goals		Away			Goals	
	P	W	D	L	F	A	P	W	D	L	F	A	P	W	D	L	F	A	Pts
1 Manchester United	18	12	4	2	44	13	9	8	1	0	28	4	9	4	3	2	16	9	40
2 Blackburn	19	11	6	2	36	19	10	7	2	1	23	10	9	4	4	1	13	9	39
3 Chelsea	19	12	2	5	45	19	8	6	1	1	16	6	11	6	1	4	29	13	38
4 Leeds	19	10	4	5	28	19	10	5	2	3	15	11	9	5	2	2	13	8	34
5 Liverpool	18	9	4	5	31	17	9	6	0	3	20	9	9	3	4	2	11	8	31
6 Arsenal	18	8	6	4	32	21	9	5	2	2	19	7	9	3	4	2	13	14	30
7 Derby	19	8	5	6	33	27	9	6	3	0	19	5	10	2	2	6	14	22	29
8 Leicester	19	7	6	6	23	18	11	3	5	3	12	10	8	4	1	3	11	8	27
9 Newcastle	17	7	5	5	20	21	10	5	3	2	12	10	7	2	2	3	8	11	26
10 West Ham	19	8	1	10	25	31	8	7	0	1	17	6	11	1	1	9	8	25	25
11 Wimbledon	18	6	5	7	19	21	10	3	2	5	11	14	8	3	3	2	8	7	23
12 Aston Villa	19	6	4	9	20	25	9	4	2	3	12	13	10	2	2	6	8	12	22
13 Crystal Palace	19	5	6	8	17	25	8	0	3	5	5	14	11	5	3	3	12	11	21
14 Sheffield Weds	19	6	3	10	31	43	10	5	1	4	18	17	9	1	2	6	13	26	21
15 Southampton	19	6	2	11	23	29	10	5	1	4	17	14	9	1	1	7	6	15	20
16 Coventry	19	4	8	7	17	25	10	3	6	1	14	10	9	1	2	6	3	15	20
17 Bolton	19	4	8	7	16	29	9	3	5	1	8	6	10	1	3	6	8	23	20
18 Tottenham Hotspur	19	5	4	10	17	32	10	4	2	4	11	14	9	1	2	6	6	18	19
19 Everton	19	4	5	10	17	27	9	3	2	4	11	13	10	1	3	6	6	14	17
20 Barnsley	19	4	2	13	17	50	9	2	2	5	10	20	10	2	0	8	7	30	14

Extrapolating forward, 20 points at the halfway mark translates to 40 at the end of the season. In 1996–7, that would have got you relegated. Though Coventry had not yet sunk to the bottom three, there had been no stage at which we had been more than a few points above the relegation zone.

As I looked at the table, several things were clear. First, I did not believe that Spurs could go down. Too many good players, too much of what Gordon would call quality. Of course, I remember saying the same thing about the Forest side in 1993, and I know that good players do not necessarily make a good side. Only one factor made me doubt this judgement, and that was goal difference. Goal difference is a remarkably solid indicator of which team is good, and which bad. Week in and week out, you may steal a result here or there, but comparing how many goals you score with how many you give away is certain to be revealing. At the top of the table, the teams seemed to be in the right order (with the exception of Arsenal, who I would expect to finish ahead of Leeds). Equally, if you studied the bottom of the table, you could see why Spurs, in spite of the strength of their squad, were placed so low.

Though Coventry were only a point above the bottom three, the City goal difference of –8 placed us above Barnsley, Everton, Spurs, Bolton, Sheffield Wednesday, and equal with Crystal Palace. And so tight was the League that, with only 3 extra points, we would have been in twelfth place rather than sixteenth. It looked very much like a dogfight at the bottom, and yet another season that would go to the wire.

Considering the forthcoming fixtures, I believed we would soon reach that bad psychological moment at which the number of points won is less than the number of games played: a sure sign of trouble. The next two games were at Upton Park (where West Ham had won all but one game this season), and Manchester United at Highfield Road). So 20 points from twenty-one games seemed a likely forecast, and an ominous one.

The other significant statistic, which did not show up in the League table but was reflected by it, was Coventry's 'top' (that is, bottom) place in the so-called

Fair Play League. To date we had demonstrably the worst disciplinary record in the Premiership. While Gordon had bemoaned the lack of quality in the side at Anfield, that lack was to some degree the result of four players being suspended, one of whom (Paul Williams) topped the Premiership list for number of bookings. And yet no one had accused Coventry of being a hard or cynical side. The on-pitch performances seemed to be constantly besmirched by occasional periods of indiscipline. Whether it was Williams running 30 yards to argue with a referee and getting an unnecessary yellow card, or Breen gratuitously pushing a Villa opponent and getting a red one, I had the constant feeling that a lot of the bookings could have been avoided.

I wondered if Gordon's demeanour on the touchline didn't add, just a little, to the occasional sense of desperation that Coventry were displaying. Of all the Premiership managers, he was the most active and vocal, standing on the sidelines for much of the match, screaming instructions, gesticulating, flailing about like an hysterical mechanical fox, having the occasional go at the referee or linesman. It hardly needs stating that yelling at a player who may be 50 yards away while 30,000 people scream their throats out is hardly an efficient method of conveying instructions. Listening to him, as I could from my seat in the Vice-Presidents, it was clear that most of what he said boiled down to the following: 'Stop doing what you just did!' In comparison, Alex Ferguson and Kenny Dalglish, fellow Scots and equally fiercely committed, tended to keep to their seats, rising only when the occasion demanded it. But Gordon was up because he couldn't stay down. He couldn't bear not having an input.

But the most worrying statistic revealed by the League table was, of course, the Coventry away record. With only one win and two draws out of nine away games, and the lowest number of goals scored away from home, it was obvious that something had to change, or else results at

Highfield Road (only one loss in ten games) had better stay good. It wasn't that the team was toothless: we had scored more goals at home than Newcastle, and only two fewer than Chelsea, but, on the road, the scoring dried up completely.

'I've never fully understood it,' Bryan Richardson told me when I caught up with him a week after the Liverpool defeat. 'It doesn't make sense. I can read the results as well as anybody, and I see what a difference being at home makes. But why? The grounds aren't all that different, and I don't see why having part of the crowd behind you should make that much difference. It doesn't in cricket, for instance, though the crowds are smaller, and it's not such an emotional game.'

But Richardson has never played professional football. Ask Gary McAllister, for instance, and he'll tell you what a difference a home fixture can make. 'The crowd – a good crowd – intimidates opponents, and it puts an extra yard on you. At Leeds it was worth a goal a game. But Coventry isn't a good crowd – none of them in the Midlands is, really, except maybe Wolves. It's not really a football area. Football is most popular in economically depressed areas, in the north, and in Scotland. It cheers up people's lives, and lets them feel like winners for once. They really identify with their teams, and get behind them.'

But Richardson was, as ever, hopeful. 'I don't think we'll be in a dogfight at the end. Of course, round Christmas, with players flagging a bit and suspensions, you might have a lean period. It's been a hard few weeks. The loss of Miller was a massive blow to Gordon. And we have some hard fixtures coming up. But I think we've been unlucky. We should have five or six more points.'

'Come on, Bryan, there's no chairman who doesn't think that. Look, if we had six more points we would be even with Newcastle.'

'And why not? This is a good side, and it is going to get better. I thought Boateng was excellent at Liverpool. He's got pace, can pass the ball, good touch, everything you could ask. And there's more players – quality players – coming.'

So it looked as if the gamble he had mentioned in September might just have come off: wait patiently until you can sign two or three international-quality players, and have confidence that the squad will hold its own until they arrive.

'I thought Boateng looked terrific. So why'd he sign with us?'

'There were two reasons,' he said. 'First, he wanted to come to England, he liked the lads, and was impressed by the training set-up. But what really clinched it was when we showed him the plans for the new stadium. I think it confirmed to him how ambitious we are. And we got him at the right price, and on the right terms. His salary will be maybe fifth or sixth in the pecking order – we didn't have to go mad. We need quality, and we got it.'

That ambition had been manifest, throughout the season, in the attempts to sign Maric (now injured) or to do some sort of substantial deal with Monaco, which now seemed less likely. But Richardson was particularly delighted because he had just pulled off his major signing coup of the season. Coventry had been tracking the striker Viorel Moldovan for a couple of months, and had finally completed a deal, signing him on a four-and-a-half-year contract for 8 million Swiss francs (about £3,250,000) from Grasshopper-Club Zürich. A prolific goalscorer ('seventy-seven in a hundred and three games,' noted Richardson, 'with a further forty-four assists'), Moldovan is the centre forward in the current, highly accomplished Romanian national team, and had scored virtually at the rate of a goal every two games.

'So where will he play?'

'We'll have to see. I don't see him as a natural with Dion. We need to be more mobile up front, and Dion doesn't like to run. Maybe with Huck, though I think he'd play very well with Whelan, but that's the sort of thing for Gordon to decide. It's not up to me.'

There had been rumours in the press, in the recent week, linking Dublin with a move to Crystal Palace, some of them suggesting a fee of £3.75 million. Were they true? Wouldn't the sale of Dion be bad for morale? He was a key figure in the dressing room, the fans loved him, and our record in games without him was woeful.

The chairman reached into his filing cabinet and took out a thick manila folder. 'I'll tell you what the problem is,' he said, opening it and taking out the top sheet. 'Dion has twenty months left on his contract. He'll be twenty-nine in April, and what he wants is a new contract for four more years at twenty grand a week. I think, left to his own devices, he'd stay – he's a good lad, and he's basically happy here. But twenty grand a week should not be on. So if he is going to have to go, it has to be soon, because if we delay another six months, he'll just play out his contract and go as a free agent.'

I was slightly surprised, if gratified, that he had been so explicit. But the implication of the disclosure of the details of Dublin's contract was pretty clear: he would be going. The money was on the table from Palace (and interest had also been expressed by Middlesbrough), but Richardson was interested in a slightly different deal, in which John Salako also went to Palace (whence he had come) for a further £250,000, 'which would mean a saving to us of over half a million, because we wouldn't have to pay his salary for the last six months of his contract. But I don't think for one minute that Dion will go to Palace. It's a poor-quality club in turmoil.'

Salako had become the missing man of the Coventry season. Having injured his hamstring (or something in that area: there had been no definite diagnosis, which was part of the problem) at Sheffield Wednesday, he hadn't appeared at all since the Everton game. He would go to Ryton for treatment, try to take part in practice matches, and invariably report that he wasn't right. The club had given up on him. 'None of the tests or scans show much,' said Richardson tartly, 'and Gordon doesn't want him any more. They've lost patience with him. It's too bad, he's a talented fellow, bright in a streetwise sort of way, and we made him a bloody good offer a couple of months ago.'

I raised my eyebrows, and he obligingly fished out another file. 'He turned down a new contract for three and a half years, at very good money.'

'Were you far apart?'

'He wanted fifteen grand a week, and he won't get it. Not from us, not from anybody. He'll be lucky to get five grand a week in future.'

'Doesn't that leave us with a problem wide on the left, or do you have confidence in Marcus Hall in that position? And if you do, what with Boateng, McAllister, Telfer, Whelan, who gets left out?'

'That's the sort of problem we want. That's having a good squad, not being dependent on bringing in players who aren't quite good enough, the Bolands and O'Neills. But when we were trying to do the deal with Wednesday for Pembridge, we really wanted to sell Hall instead of Burrows, but Ron wouldn't have him. And even though Gordon wants Burrows at left back we felt we had to try the deal because of our midfield problems. Marcus has come on well, but I think there is a feeling that he isn't quite the one thing or the other, but he is young, and learning daily from Gordon.'

'What would you say he's worth?'

He didn't hesitate. He knew. 'Million and a half, maybe two million.'

'It doesn't seem much for a regular in the England Under-Twenty-One side.'

'Maybe not, but that's all we'd get. And we need someone with proper international quality. I'm negotiating with another current Romanian international, Tibor Selymes, who is twenty-six and plays for Anderlecht, and has forty caps. I'm hoping to hear about that one this month. If we can sign him, then I feel very confident, not only about this year, but about the future. Aside from Roland and Gary Mac, all the players are young, and on long-term contracts.'

It all sounded great, and I could feel a wave of optimism hit me as we spoke. If this guy were selling snake-oil remedy, not only would I buy some, but I guarantee I'd feel better once I'd drunk it. I felt very much as I did after our long conversation in September, at the end of the first five games: thoroughly convinced that we were on the right course, but that we were not yet producing results. We were still gathering points at the rate of one a game, and that was relegation form, near as damn it. So why was Richardson so confident? Whatever that potion is that he's selling, he must take it himself. It sure keeps your pecker up.

The only time I had seen him looking flustered was at half-time at Anfield, where, over a drink in the board-room bar, he confessed that 'this business' was getting to him. I didn't know what he meant, and assumed he was referring to the bad run of results and the hard forthcoming fixtures. But that wasn't what was on his mind at all: it was the problem of Geoffrey Robinson.

Or perhaps I should say Geoffrey Robinson and his problems. Though I had asked Graham Hover if he could get me an appointment with Robinson, I had not yet had any luck. This was hardly surprising: since his appointment as paymaster-general, he had resigned his seat on the board and been replaced by his friend and accountant, Brenda Price – the first woman board member of any Premiership team, which seems appropriate for a club that has the highest proportion of female spectators in the Premiership. I had sat next to her during the Wimbledon match and been impressed by how attentively she watched and how engaged she was. An attractive woman of a certain age, of the sort that high court judges are wont to call fragrant, she exuded a kind of quickness and warmth that were immediately appealing. I introduced myself, gave her my card and asked if she would help me to meet Mr Robinson. She said she would try, and I hadn't heard from her since.

That was no surprise, either. Mr Robinson, it turned out, was being pursued by a pack of eager investigative journalists who thought there was something fishy, something somehow inappropriate, about an exceedingly wealthy Labour minister (who had ever heard of such an oxymoron, anyway?) whose financial affairs included extensive, if legal, use of tax-free offshore family trusts and the like. A number of the papers, particularly *The Sunday Times*, were running stories which implied that he was an inappropriate choice to carry out the agenda of a Labour Party committed to fair taxation and social justice.

'What makes me so angry,' said Richardson, 'is that they can't point to anything he has done wrong. He's done nothing wrong. The money that is at issue was never in this country in the first place. And it is taking a lot of time and energy to react to the allegations.' Richardson's previous descriptions of Robinson's role in the growth of the club had conjured up a Santa Claus-like figure with an enormous sky blue satchel full of £50 notes and gift-wrapped Players of the Highest Quality slung over his shoulder. It was understandable that Richardson should feel protective of such a patron, but odd that he should devote so much time to an affair that seemed, from all reports, to have little to do with him. If the business was consuming much of Robinson's time, why should it also be so troubling to the chairman?

The answer, according to *The Sunday Times* Insight team, was twofold. The first element concerned the dealings of the Robinson family trust, the Orion Trust, based in Guernsey, which had apparently purchased 10,619 (19 per cent) Coventry City shares in 1996. As one of the beneficiaries of the trust, Robinson was specifically precluded from having any influence in its dealings, which are handled solely by the registered trustees. The second element, however, would appear to have involved Richardson's guidance. In October 1996, the former chairman of Coventry City, Derrick Robins, now living in South Africa, agreed to sell Robinson his family shares in the club for £350,000. The deal was subject to Robinson's undertaking that 'it is to be decided whether I personally buy these shares or my family trust may wish to do so. In either event, the ownership will be with one or the other'. According to Robins, who bought 38 per cent of the shares for £5,000 in the 1960s, he was given repeated assurances that the shares would not be passed on to Bryan Richardson, which he was anxious to avoid, for reasons that he did not divulge. But six months later a company called Craigavon, a Guernsey-based Robinson family trust, transferred some 2,500 shares to Sphere, another Guernsey-based trust (and sold a further 5,568 shares to another Coventry City director, Derek Higgs, for £187,864). The net result of the dealings left Craigavon and Sphere with some 60 per cent of the shares.

The Sunday Times, with Robinson in their sights, seemed to think this sufficiently newsworthy to run front-page stories on it for a few weeks. There was speculation that Robinson, a close friend of prime minister Tony Blair (who backed him throughout), might eventually be forced to resign. Whatever was implied, from a football point of view the coverage served in the main simply to call into question the myth of the rich football patron whose financial input is seen as a service to his ego rather than to his bank balance. Was Robinson, in fact, a Father Christmas, or a shrewd investor lucky enough to combine his passion for Coventry City, which no one doubted, with the chance of making a serious profit? Yet, according to Richardson, the possible profit was a later side-effect, not a goal: Craigavon's purchase of shares came well after Robinson's initial offer of money. 'He really was a Father Christmas, and his motive was, and still is, entirely philanthropic as far as the club is concerned. That is a fact!'

Richardson had been at the helm now for over three years, and had been widely, and accurately, perceived as ambitious, intelligent and energetic. He has a genius for raising money, and for thinking in the long term. No one could deny that he was doing a terrific job. Gordon was admired and respected by both the players and the management at Highfield Road. It was time, surely, for things to improve. Both of them were confident that it would happen, and soon.

I wasn't. I'm a Coventry City supporter, and I'd been there before.

11

Clump 4

West Ham v. Coventry, 26 December
Coventry v. Manchester United, 28 December
Liverpool v. Coventry, FA Cup, 3 January
Chelsea v. Coventry, 10 January
Coventry v. Arsenal, 17 January

Christmas makes me ill. I enjoy robust health for the rest of the year, but the mere anticipation of a sustained rest, good food and drink, happiness round the tree, the smiling faces of my children, will infallibly bring on an attack of bronchitis. This year the timing was perfect, and it arrived on Christmas Day itself. Chesty, and red-nosed as a reindeer, I consoled myself that at least I didn't have to travel to Upton Park for the Boxing Day fixture.

Located in the midst of a warren of obscure streets deep in the East End, Upton Park seems to me as inaccessible as an Amazonian tribal village, though Jonathan Strange says this is my fault, not Upton Park's. But if you are trying to drive there in time for a football match, forget it: either you have to go on the tube, surrounded by numerous and hostile West Ham supporters, or navigate narrow streets which were never intended to bear any weight of traffic and tend to get gridlocked. The Coventry City coach once got so snarled up on the way from the hotel to the ground that the team arrived only fifteen minutes before kick-off, having had to send the reserve-team manager ahead on foot to hand in the team sheet by the deadline. It took the coach an hour and a half to cover two miles.

Once you get there it's not worth it. It is dingy, uncomfortable and has some of the worst fans in the Premiership – these are the folks, you may remember, who used to throw banana skins at black players – and there is an ominous and threatening feel in the air. Seated, two years ago, in one of the executive boxes with some other Coventry City supporters, I at one point jumped up to applaud a City goal, and a gaggle of simian West Ham supporters in front of me turned round and confronted me with one of the most alarming examples of malevolence I have ever witnessed, outside of the House of Commons. They hooted and gibbered, threw me the finger, shook their fists in a rage, scratched under their armpits, groomed each other, brandished bananas. If they could have found a way up the stairs to eviscerate me I genuinely believe they would have tried.

I would rather have bronchitis than go to Upton Park. I felt privileged, lying feverishly in bed listening to the match on the radio, not to be there in the cold, watching John Hartson raging about like a West Ham supporter, causing mayhem. With several players still suspended, and Dublin once again in defence, I was happy in my misery. (Bryan Richardson, of course, was optimistic: 'They're bound to lose to somebody there. I think it'll be our day.')

Coventry duly lost, by 1–0, Boateng having been sent off. The Hammers' goal, scored by Kitson after Huckerby lost the ball in his own half and didn't bother to track back and try to recover it, so enraged Paul Telfer that he ran over to Huck to remonstrate with him and some pushing and shoving ensued. After the match, Strachan, who might have been expected to come down heavily on such on-field antics, was entirely sympathetic to Telfer's response.

So it was a beleaguered side that prepared for the Manchester United fixture at Highfield Road just two days later. Though players were due back from suspension, spirits had not been raised by repeated rumours of the imminent sale of Dublin. Dion's muted response – 'I didn't ask for a move and I am happy at the club' – was designed to steady the ship, and presumably also to protect his own position in case a transfer took place. If he had asked for a move himself, he would not be able to claim loyalty bonuses or signing-on fees. But it was hardly the kind of news that was likely to reinforce flagging morale.

Including the Cola-Cup defeat by Arsenal, the team had lost six of the last seven games, and it was time, Paul Telfer reckoned, to manifest some of the fighting spirit he had displayed on the pitch two days before. 'It tests your character to see what team you are. If you play these teams and go to pieces it shows you are not cut out for it. We have to show we are cut out for it.' Though they had lost 3–0 at Old Trafford, Gordon and most of the players thought that the score had failed to reflect an excellent performance, and that they were unlikely to be overawed at Highfield Road. There was no reason to be: while United had been in excellent form, were top of the League and had already qualified for the quarter-finals of the European Cup, they had failed to win five of their ten away fixtures, and there was no reason to suppose Coventry couldn't get something out of the match. United have a funny habit of losing concentration against lesser teams, a kind of unconscious arrogance, I suppose, and I rather hoped we might catch them on one of those sorts of days.

They took the field with Solskjaer, Cole, Sheringham, Giggs, Scholes and Beckham bustling forward, a line-up designed to attack and to intimidate, but without the solidity of Nicky Butt (who didn't come on until the seventieth minute) they looked a little vulnerable in midfield. With only twelve minutes gone, Coventry, who had managed not to give the ball away too much, converted some nice touch play round the United area into a goal for Noel Whelan. It was just the sort of incentive United needed, and they replied with goals from Solskjaer and then Sheringham. City had created chances, but it looked as if United had only to put their foot on the throttle to find something extra.

With four minutes to go Huckerby swooped in from a position on the left wing, barrelled past John Curtis towards the penalty area, and was brought down inside the area by Henning Berg. The combination of vision, speed, strength and determination from Huck was particularly impressive because he had run hard, and it was the eighty-sixth minute: a testimony to increased fitness as well as to his commitment. Could it be he was starting to learn?

McAllister was the normal penalty-taker, so who would get the ball? The usual dead-ball kickers were Burrows, Telfer and occasionally Williams, but the best free-kick specialists are not necessarily the best penalty-takers. I think I'd choose Whelan first, then maybe Telfer. But as we watched, Dion Dublin sauntered over, picked up the ball from the referee and put it down on the spot. There was a hush round the ground. Bertie put his head in his hands, unable to watch.

I'd spent some time at Ryton the previous week, listening to the sound made when the players kick the ball. It's a habit I picked up from watching professional golfers. If you go to a golf tournament and hear Nick Faldo hit a drive, it produces a sound that, in a thousand years at your local club, you will never hear. A crack like a rifle shot, pure and perfect, produced with less apparent effort than that of your partners in the Sunday foursome. And the ball flies off in a perfect arc, climbing and climbing, until it seems inconceivable that it can stay in the air so long, and then climbs some more. It is the effect of perfect timing, transfer of weight, club-head speed. The same aural phenomenon can be observed with professional tennis players, compared to amateurs. They know how to strike a ball.

So there I was at Ryton, listening to the players kicking long passes back and forth to each other, with my eyes closed, enjoying the sounds, in the sort of happy meditative state one might experience listening to great music. The next thing I knew, Gary Breen was standing next to me, looking at me quizzically, wondering if he had disturbed me during some obscure Tantric practice.

'I'm listening,' I explained.

He looked at me steadily. I'd never talked to him much. On the pitch, especially in training, he has a chirpy presence, and seems to enjoy himself, but away from the field of play he often has the demeanour of a disaffected rock star – slim, aloof, all cheekbones and attitude – and I'd been wary of approaching him.

'To what?' he asked. The music of the spheres?

'The sound of the ball when it's struck perfectly. There's this crack like a rifle shot.'

Oh, that noise. 'We call it "pinging" it,' he said. 'You can hear it right away. Even most Premiership players can't do it.' (Gary McAllister, I later discovered, refers to players who can't 'ping' it as having 'diarrhoea boots'.)

'Which of the guys can?'

'The gaffer. Listen when he hits it. And Whelan. Telfer. Couple of the others.'

Dion Dublin can't. He's never been known as a pure striker of the ball, and many of his goals are scored with his head. Those he does get with his feet, if you recall them, are placed, side-footed, tapped. It is hard to recall him 'pinging' a ball, from any distance, arrow-smooth past a keeper and into the net. In the time it has taken to remember – and to convey – this, Dion had taken four steps back from the ball and readied himself to take the penalty. I decided that, if he was brave enough to take it, I would be brave enough to watch. When he missed, we would both have our own grief to deal with.

Dublin trotted forward confidently and clipped the ball crisply into the keeper's left-hand corner. Coventry were level at 2–2. Bertie and I hugged each other and tried unsuccessfully to throw ourselves into the air. In a moment of madness I exchanged a high-five with a vice-president, immediately felt guilty, and hoped we wouldn't be asked to resign our memberships. Behind me, though, I noticed that quite a few of the other vice-presidents were pleased, and one (arms held aloft in a most unseemly manner) seemed positively delighted.

Stung out of their complacency, Manchester United now had four minutes, plus injury time, to win the match, and I had no optimism that we could hold on for that long. Soon, though, a whole minute had passed without too much to be alarmed about. Then Huckerby received the ball in one of his usual channels wide out on the right, about 40 yards from goal. Instead of going down the line, though, he cut in past his man, sped up, pushed on through two challenges at the edge of the box, feinted left, veered right and then, with the poise of a pelican, slotted the ball along the ground and past keeper Pilkington into the far corner. 'He picked up the ball with three minutes to go,' said Gordon after the match, 'and scored with a minute left.'

This time Bertie and I did manage to throw ourselves in the air, a practice more to be recommended if you are fit and seventeen than fat and fifty-three. It was a remarkable game-winning goal, the kind that ten-year-olds dream of: a Huckerby special. If Ryan Giggs had scored it, the journalists would have gone mad about what a great player he was, but tomorrow's papers would attribute it to slack defending. Life with Coventry, as Gordon is fond of pointing out, is like that. A few moments later David Beckham had a chance to make it a draw when he took a free kick from just outside the City area. Max reported that Beckham was put off by the crowd in the

East Stand, who chanted 'Stand up if you've fucked Posh Spice!' as he approached the ball. The entire population of the stand – happy folks – duly stood up chanting, and Beckham missed.

The Coventry players hugged and jumped about a bit, and Huckerby trotted off modestly, waving to the crowd. It was almost enough to make my bronchitis go away. Bursting with delight, Bertie and I pushed through the crush of vice-presidents, almost none of whom were discussing the game, and headed off for the dressing room.

It was too early to go in. The game had only finished some six or seven minutes earlier, and by convention the only person really welcome in the dressing room that soon was the chairman. Outside in the corridor lurked a number of the City youth- and reserve-team players (some of them, endearingly, clutching autograph books in the hope of getting Ferguson, Beckham or Giggs to sign them when they came out of the visitors' dressing room across the corridor). David Busst was waiting to see the players, together with ex-England player Steve Hodge, a pal of Gordon's, who sometimes trained with the first team, and a great clutch of journalists. I sauntered past them all, saying, 'Wait here,' to Bertie, and went on in.

At which point something interesting, unexpected, and distinctly surprising happened. Gordon was standing off to the left, leaning against the wall, chatting quietly to Pendrey. I bounded over to shake his hand and offer my congratulations. 'Don't say it to me, say it to them,' said Gordon, nodding his head towards the players. Noel Whelan was spraying his chest and underarms with deodorant; Huckerby was buttoning his shirt; a naked Paul Telfer was sitting on the bench next to Whelan, drying his hair. Williams and Dublin were just emerging from the shower, towels slung round their shoulders. No one had noticed me, so my presence had not affected the atmosphere. There was no atmosphere. The feeling in the dressing room was virtually indistinguishable from the feeling in the dressing room after a loss.

I don't know why this should have shocked me so much. I expected the players to be sharing the same intensity of delight that Bertie and I and the rest of the City fans were feeling. The result was to be the lead football story of the day, yet in the dressing room there was no whooping and hollering, no American-style high-fiving, just a bunch of football players savouring the quiet satisfaction of a terrific win, and feeling the exhaustion of having run and run and run. They're professionals, and things are kept in perspective: it was, after all, said Oggy, 'just three points, part of the jigsaw'. Gordon was clear about it too. 'The feeling after a win is never as intense as after a bad loss. The winning feeling goes away. A defeat hurts more and lasts longer. You remember it. Like the news. News is bad news – it's human nature.' So the players get showered and dressed, maybe go out for a couple of drinks, get home, hope the wife isn't too exhausted after a day with the kids, maybe get a meal in, catch *Match of the Day* on the telly, hope to get an unbroken night's sleep for once. Tomorrow there will still be a nice glow, but their thoughts will already be turning to the FA Cup match at Anfield.

David Burrows, musing on the way in which the sharp delight of a victory like this wanes, offered an explanation. 'You play for an intense hour and a half a week. After a game you are knackered. You can't live at that intensity – you'd go mad. You have to walk away and get on with your own life. You can't invest as much in it as the fans do. They are over-the-top.' So he'd go back home (he had his young son with him as we talked – 'He's just like his dad when he plays: kicks everybody') – maybe go out for a couple of drinks in the evening, and slowly release the tension. After a game, like the rest of the players, he is still lost in a fug of concentration and doesn't like to talk. 'Even to my dad.

At first, he didn't understand. But now we just wait till Sunday morning, then we have a long chat about the game.'

Next to him, a showered and dressed Noel Whelan stood up, ready to go home to do some hoovering and drink some fruit juice. By all reports he was a reformed character. My scouts still reported no significant Snowy activity in the Leamington bars, and he was playing with great verve and commitment. (Mind you, he did that when he was drinking a lot anyway). And he had just signed a new contract. 'A whole lot of managers would have given up on me,' he said, 'but not Gordon Strachan. I've been a fool, but he gave me the chance to grow up and I have.'

Huckerby emerged from the dressing room and quietly went through the usual routines with the press: yes, he was very chuffed, especially for the lads; yes, it was one of his most satisfying goals; no, he always thought that we were in with a chance; yes, you sure do have to keep running and trying; no, you never can tell what'll happen. As he talked, Bryan Richardson walked by and patted him on the back. Heading in the other direction, Gordon announced that he wanted to see his wife Lesley before he went to the press conference. Alex Ferguson, looking composed, emerged from the United dressing room, signed some autographs for the Coventry kids, and admitted that United had perhaps been a little complacent. He'd said much the same thing at Old Trafford, but they'd won that match pretty comfortably. Perhaps he subconsciously believed you could get away with a little complacency against Coventry. Or maybe we were slowly turning into a useful side?

Seeing Ferguson, and having just encountered Dion as he came out of the showers, reminded me of a story of Bryan Richardson's. He had never met Ferguson, he told me, until some time after Coventry had bought Dion Dublin, when they met at a football function. 'So there's me,' says Richardson, 'meeting the greatest football manager of the last ten years, and he comes over to me to ask if Dion has settled down all right.'

'I said, "Very well, nice chap, fits in well, scoring some goals . . ."

'"Never mind about that," Ferguson said to me. "Have you seen his dick?"'

Richardson, somewhat surprised at the question, conceded that, yes, he'd come across Dion in the dressing room, and that, sure enough, it was a big one.

'Big?' said Ferguson. 'It isn't big. It's magnificent!'

Richardson agreed: yes, it was a very big one.

'Magnificent!' said Ferguson. He had, he told Bryan, seen some whoppers in his time, but Dion's was something else.

I had not failed, I must admit, to notice this happy appendage a few moments earlier, and had been suitably impressed and not a little jealous. I reported the sighting to Bertie, who was reassuring. 'Everybody gets something,' he observed. 'Dion got athletic ability and a big cock. You—'

'—got brains and charm,' I said hopefully.

'—got a big stomach,' Bertie said.

My wife Barbara (to whom I did not relate this story) wouldn't let me go to Liverpool. It was stupid enough, she said, sitting out in the cold against United, which had only made me feel worse, but travelling to Anfield to watch us lose a Cup match would be madness. She's very strict. We did a deal: I wouldn't go on the Saturday, but I got to go to Ryton for an hour at lunchtime on Friday, just to keep in touch. The coach was due to leave at three o'clock, and there was some light training scheduled before departure.

I hadn't realised it, but there is apparently a kind of tradition that supporters gather at the training ground before the team leaves for a fixture – especially for an FA Cup match. So there were a bunch of people, maybe a hundred, clustered about, many of them congregated round the entrance to the training complex, clutching autograph books and cameras. I went on in, pausing for a moment to listen to John Salako giving an interview, very carefully, to the new *Coventry Evening Telegraph* chief football reporter, Andy Turner. He was getting stronger, he said; he would soon be fit and he hoped to sign a new contract ('We're not far apart'). I ran into Gary McAllister, who was looking bright-eyed and hopeful. He was going up to Anfield with the lads, and should be ready to return to the side by the end of January. And when he said he thought that we would get a result at Liverpool he looked like he meant it. 'Players are back from suspension. We'll have Dion up front, and he'll win balls in the air. They don't look very solid in defence. And I think this time Huck will get a freer role. In the last game we had Simon up front with Noel and Huck pinching in, and it didn't work. I feel pretty optimistic.'

I went back outside and found myself in the midst of a little group of fans, a couple of whom I knew by sight, just hanging out watching as players arrived. The major topic was whether Dion was going to be sold. There was a strong feeling among them that the club was being stupid in letting him go. Various passionate but uninformed opinions were bandied about. When I said: 'He's asking too much money. He wants four more years at twenty grand a year. The club won't pay him, it would ruin the wage structure,' conversation ceased, and I was looked at with respect. No one else knew this, and I should probably have kept quiet about it, but I couldn't. 'If he doesn't get what he is asking he'll play out the eighteen months left on his contract and bugger off as a free agent. So if we don't sell him now he won't be worth anything soon.' As I talked David Burrows and Marcus Hall walked by. 'Hiya, Rick,' they said as they went through the door. The looks of respect were replaced with something that, if I say it myself, approached awe.

As we hung about talking – or, to be honest, as they hung about listening – I was consumed by a great feeling of happiness. How did David Burrows feel about being sold? (Pissed off.) Did Big Ron really offer £7 million for Hall, Dublin and Burrows? (No.) What is this guy Moldovan like? (Looks like a Mafioso; plays a bit like Gary Lineker.) Life behind the scenes had been difficult, sometimes grim, a slow war of attrition to get myself accepted. Some barely perceptible progress had been made over the months – Roland walked over to say hello, then sauntered off gorgeously – but nobody could have called it fun. It was hard work. But I had learned a lot. I'd been there. I was the fan who knew players, who chatted to Gordon and the chairman, who wasn't dependent on rumour or speculation or the odd snippet on ClubCall. It felt terrific. It was the best part.

At the same time as I was feeling this amazing high, burbling away, a fountain of information, I also felt a little ashamed that it should bring me so much of a thrill. How pathetic. Feed him a few little snippets of secrets and bits of information, and he thinks he's important, a part of the club. It was a perfect example of referred status – the sort of thing you experience with arrogant medical receptionists. The only consolation I could offer myself for this shameful bit of psychic inflation was that what had happened to me was representatively interesting and right. It would happen to any fan allowed so extensively behind the scenes. The best part is not actually being there, but talking about it to people who wish they were.

On Saturday, as I sat listening incredulously to the match commentary on local radio, we murdered Liverpool, who had won their last four games in the Premiership. After giving up an early goal to a Redknapp free kick, which sneaked past Magnus at his left-hand post, Coventry dominated the game. Huckerby equalised before half-time with another superb solo goal, and in the second half created chances from which Dublin and Telfer scored. Boateng, who had a superb match, missed an easy chance, and Whelan might have had a couple of goals. No one could have claimed that it wasn't the better side that won, which an unhappy Roy Evans was keen to stress in his post-match interview.

Gordon was, of course, delighted. 'We came with a plan to make it difficult for Liverpool, and it worked perfectly. Everyone was brilliant.' And he had his usual ambiguous enthusiasm for Huckerby's efforts: 'Darren was terrific. He knows he's got natural talent but if he's going to improve he's got to listen. Today he listened.' Huckerby, to give him extra credit, tends to accept this mixture of praise and criticism. 'I like a laugh and a joke and maybe need to grow up. I take a bit of stick but I know if I can get my head sorted I can be a decent player. It's all down to me.' He had terrorised the Liverpool defence, making Robbie Fowler look utterly ordinary, and an impartial observer, on the day, could have had no doubt which of the two was a future England player.

Coventry drew a home tie with Derby County, who had beaten us four times in a row, in the fourth round of the FA Cup, to be played on Saturday 24 January. So sure had the club been that we were going to lose at Anfield ('We reckoned we would have a free Saturday on the twenty-fourth,' said Graham Hover) that, amazingly, they had scheduled a friendly match with Bayern Munich on 27 January at Highfield Road. Gordon, following the win at Liverpool, was discreet: 'It'll be a useful fixture. They are a class side, and I have a couple of players coming back from injury and suspension that can have a run out, and we can give Moldovan a game.' But he didn't look entirely happy about it. What, I asked, if someone got injured in such a meaningless fixture?

'That can happen any time in training. You don't worry about it.' But he was delighted by the changes he saw in what he regarded as a quickly maturing team. 'I think we'll keep Dion, and I have great hopes for Moldovan. If we can add a left-sided midfield player, we'll be a top ten side, maybe better. We'll be able to field a side of eleven quality players.' And in the papers, Coventry were being treated with some respect. Coming after the Manchester

United result, the win at Anfield was not reported as a fluke. Could the momentum be maintained at Chelsea?

I would have to be the new team doctor, it was the only solution. As we sat in the locker room at Stamford Bridge, an hour before kick-off, Gordon was unable to locate a complementary ticket for me, and the match was a sell-out. So he said I could sit in the dugout – which I'd been wanting to do all season, up close and personal – as long as I maintained a nice look of medical readiness on my face. Please God, I prayed, nobody gets seriously injured.

About an hour before kick-off I had my usual stroll round the pitch. Behind me loomed the huge new Chelsea Village development, complete with a bar called Willie's which several Coventry City supporters had pretended to mistake for the Gents'. The pitch itself was very soft underfoot after all the rain, and distinctly patchy. David Burrows gave it a little kick, and observed that if it were his back garden he'd have it relaid. But it hadn't stopped Manchester United scoring five goals on it the previous week.

Viorel Moldovan had joined the side, and had seemed pleasant and relaxed at the hotel the night before. ('He's good,' said Gary McAllister. 'I've watched the videos of him, but he'll have to play at his international form to do well here, because of the gap between this and Swiss football.'). Moldovan had tolerable basic English. (Gordon had suggested that he improved it by watching television with subtitles, and the club had organised lessons with a tutor for him.) He was accompanied by a pleasant Romanian from Fulham called Nick, his agent and minder, who looked just like him. (All Romanians look the same to me: is this some form of racism?) Though Moldovan was not yet fit following the winter break in Switzerland, he would be in the dugout as well, together with the other substitutes: Haworth, Oggy, Gavin Strachan (Gordon's

nineteen-year-old son), Soltvedt and two more players, Lightbourne and Johansen, who were not kitted
out. There were twelve seats, and thirteen candidates,
counting Pendrey, Gordon, Blyth, George Dalton, Nick
the Minder and me, the doctor. But that didn't matter.
Pendrey and Strachan don't sit down. Though their
range of movement outside the dugout was severely
restricted by a marked-out area outside which they
were not allowed to venture, they paced within those
confines like caged animals. Though the crowd could
hear occasional comments from them, I was rather
looking forward to being able to hear all of them.

You might as well listen, because you can't see a damn
thing. Not only was I in the third row, with Pendrey
and Strachan bobbing around in front of me like Punch
and Judy, but we were directly at ground level and
looking straight into the sun. 'Funny, you know,' said
Lightbourne, 'but it doesn't glare nearly as much as this
in the Caribbean, even on a summer's day.' Haworth and
I reckoned it was the effect of the particles of pollution in
the air.

The Coventry side had an odd look about it: this
time it was Hall and Boateng who were suspended, and
Nilsson had the flu. According to news reports, at least
five Chelsea players did as well. 'Bullshit,' said Gordon.
'They've used that as an excuse for the last couple of
results. They've got a couple of players with knocks,
that's all.' In fact Chelsea fielded virtually their best side,
while Coventry needed to use Shaw at right back, and
Boland and Salako – to everyone's surprise – in midfield.
Salako still hadn't signed a new contract, and though he
had been quoted as saying that he and the chairman were
'not far apart', they were, and he would be leaving. And
he knew it. So this chance to prove some form and fitness
was particularly pleasing to him.

In the early exchanges the shape was wrong. Pendrey
was shouting maniacally across the field at Salako and
Burrows, trying to get them to spread out, while on the

other side he was trying to get Telfer to push up. 'Stop playing like a fuckin' full-back, Telf!' In between admonitions, he turned to Gordon, repeatedly saying 'This is a fuckin' nightmare!' Up front, Dublin was being urged to play more centrally – 'Keep in the fuckin' centre, Dion!' – in order to pinch the three Chelsea centre backs infield and create some space wide. At one point Pendrey was yelling instructions to Willie Boland, who looked up to listen while the man he was marking flew past him with the ball. Boland, looking shocked, charged back, having entirely lost position. And whenever Huckerby, the man on form, got the ball, he was mauled: double-marked, shirt-pulled, pushed, hacked down. After one particularly brutal challenge by Frank Leboeuf, Strachan and Pendrey went berserk, Gordon screaming at the referee, 'Ref! Ref! They're fuckin' assaulting him!' and Pendrey running down the touchline to the linesman, yelling 'Fuckin' tosspot!' for his failure to inform the referee of the brutality of the challenge, which had taken place right in front of him and hadn't led to a booking.

All of this had its funny side, because Huckerby, it seems, rather responds to a bit of rough treatment. Gordon, earlier in the week, had attributed Huckerby's astonishing form in the United and Liverpool games to the altercation that Huck and Telf had had on the pitch at West Ham. 'I know Paul Telfer gave him a bit of a slap and that looks to have done the trick. It has knocked him into gear. Suddenly Darren realised he must have let his colleagues down and was determined to do something about it.' So the only problem Huck had being mauled about at Stamford Bridge was that the wrong person was hitting him. I half expected Pendrey to shout 'Telf! Go and slap fuckin' Huck!'

On the Chelsea sideline, Ruud Gullit, lounging about in his little area like a boulevardier, looked over at the Coventry duo as if trying to reassure himself that they weren't about to charge over the white line and bite him. Behind the screaming Pendrey, one of the

Coventry players smiled to himself and put his finger to his head, twirling it round in the universal gesture that means 'What a loony.' The antics of Strachan and Pendrey seemed particularly ironic to me, because the previous season one of the Coventry City stewards had given Bertie a telling off for shouting what he called 'an audible obscenity', which is not allowed at Highfield Road (By Order of the Chairman). As the team doctor, I would diagnose an overdose of that male hormone that my wife is pleased to call detesterone, which consists of equal parts of machismo and rage.

It's enormously passionate, all this yelling and jumping about, and Gordon's admirers would consider it an example of his intensity and ability to drive a side onwards. But its effect on the players seemed, from my vantage point, an unhappy one. A manager who won't let you get on with it can hardly give the impression of one who has faith in his side's capacity to work things out for themselves. The players were constantly glancing over at the bench, and didn't talk much to each other, so keen were they not to miss any instructions. Gordon had said that he did all this shouting from the sidelines because they were a young side and he wanted to be able to help. But I don't believe that for a second. He would do it if they were a geriatric side. Anyway, they were not as young as he made out: the average age of the players used during the season was nearly twenty-six.

A lot of the shouting, in any case, was at the referee and linesmen. The day's ref, Mike Reed, cast several long and not very friendly glances over at the screaming pair in the Coventry dugout, and within forty minutes, three Coventry players had been booked: Salako, for an unmalicious but inept tackle; Huckerby, for a foul on Leboeuf; and Dublin, for a late tackle. Bookings of indiscipline, really, and it would take a lot to convince me that it wasn't partly caused by the contempt for the referee that emanated from the sidelines.

Maybe I was wrong. I don't understand this business,

and the levels of sheer aggression that it elicits and requires are foreign, and not a little distasteful, to me. Perhaps what I perceived as loutishness is experienced by the boys on the pitch as passion and encouragement, though from the look on the faces of some of them I rather doubted it, and they wouldn't have told me if they did object. I may be casting myself in the role of the soldier and aesthete whose only comment, on returning home from the trenches in the First World War, profoundly shocked, was 'The *noise*, my dear! And the *people*!' If a close-up view of football entails encountering a lot of the sort of people one doesn't meet at dinner parties, hurling imprecations and limbs at each other, then to complain that it is aggressive and vulgar rather misses the point.

More to the point, if you don't like it, don't go. My friend the publisher Tom Rosenthal, who steadfastly refuses to promise to read this book because it is about football players, asked the pertinent question: 'My God, can you imagine having dinner with Paul Gascoigne?' He shuddered. And I, unembarrassed, admitted that I sure could, I'd love to: the problem was he wouldn't want to have dinner with me. Or with Tom. I'd like to do it, but it is hard to imagine that I'd enjoy it, save as a source of future anecdotes.

Once you are inside the game, even to the marginal extent that I have been, it is fascinating, and you pretty much have to accept things on the terms on which they are offered. The fun of doing all this – and it was, at last, starting to feel like fun – was that I was in a position to ask direct questions, rather than having to ponder and speculate like all the rest of the fans. So, earlier that morning, I'd asked Gordon why it was that the team had such a terrible disciplinary record.

'It's horrendous,' he said. 'I think it's partly my fault.'

Aha, I thought to myself, Gordon doesn't usually analyse himself in this way; maybe he is reconsidering some things. He is capable of self-criticism – this tactic or that selection, he may later admit, might have been wrong – but he is less likely, like all of us, to reconsider and amend the deep-seated habits and reflexes of his own personality. He knows what problems his 'stubbornness' can cause, though he confesses he remains as stubborn as ever. Could it be that he believed he was setting a bad example to the players?

'You see,' he went on, 'when I was a player, and I could be a niggly little bastard, lose my temper, all of that, if I got a booking I'd not only feel I'd let myself down, I'd feel I let the side down. It didn't matter if you fined me or not – the fine, the money, didn't mean anything to me. But I felt bad for my team-mates, and so I had to learn how to control myself so as not to let them down. And I thought it would be the same with this lot – they're a good bunch of lads, and I haven't had a system of fines. That didn't work, so we've got a new policy: sending-off – two weeks' wages; bookings – depends on why and what for, but maybe a fine for that. I've told the players, and they accept it, and I think we are slowly improving. We can't afford all the suspensions.'

At this point I didn't say that, in my view, what he would no doubt see as his passion, encouragement and leadership the players may well experience as pressure, anxiety and lack of confidence in them. I did not say this because he would not give a damn: he is surrounded by people trying to tell him what to do, and of them I am by no means the most knowledgeable. 'Everybody has an opinion,' he said, commenting on the trials of being a manager, 'and you just have to stick to your guns and have confidence in yourself. And they're out there saying, "Strachan should be fired," and why doesn't he do this or that? There's this blonde girl on the telly, never kicked a football in her life, telling me what to do. You just have to get on with it.' He looked wistful as he sai a little lonely. It was such a shame that gone. 'After all,' Gary McAllister observed, was here it was really like having two man we were never going to be able to keep him. It's a massive loss for Gordon, very hard on him, but he'll get over it.'

Coventry were doing all right without Alex so far. In the first half Telfer scored, and Huckerby had a goal disallowed for a push on the keeper by Dublin, and then missed another chance. Magnus made one super save, but was otherwise underemployed. At half-time Chelsea trooped off looking dispirited, with Coventry well in control of the game.

I stayed in my seat in the dugout, doing some deep breathing exercises and trying to relax. I'd never felt so anxious at a football game in my life. Not even at the 1987 Cup final. Being in the dugout – to return to my war metaphor – is like being in the trenches rather than reading about them or observing them. You are right in the thick of it. Not playing, to be sure, though that seems easier, in a way. At least you get to run about and do something with all that energy and aggression. Whereas on the bench, in the middle of the substitutes, with Gordon and Garry carrying on in front of me, and players whizzing by like human bullets, it felt dangerous and terrifying, and, if I didn't get my breathing regularised soon, life-threatening.

And it wasn't like that just for me because I was an outsider and not used to it. Simon Haworth, one of the substitutes sitting next to me, was not, naturally, wearing a watch. Every few minutes he turned to me anxiously and said, 'How much time gone by?' Each time I checked, neither he nor I could believe the answer. Chelsea were attacking and attacking, though Coventry were defending competently, but time was standing still. At one point Simon was moved to claim that the time had gone backwards by three minutes since he last asked. It was astonishingly tense, defending a lead in the face of a lot of Chelsea pressure, dreading the almost inevitable counter-thrust.

It came, sure enough. In the fifty-ninth minute, Gullit

came on for Zola (who didn't look anything like the player he was on the opening day of the season), having already substituted Granville, with an obscure twenty-year-old called Mark Nicholls, whose major claim to fame was that he believed he was the best player in the world, a delusion which Gullit, rather than regarding as a form of psychosis, professed to admire. Within a few minutes, Nicholls, playing as if he were right, had scored with a header.

Ten minutes before, Strachan had taken off an exhausted Salako, and brought on Moldovan. (You could tell the Romanian was coming on, because a moment before Gordon had dispatched one of the other substitutes to the dressing room to fetch a pencil and pad, on which he had quickly sketched out the position Moldovan was to occupy, and shown it to him.) The change of formation, with Coventry playing three strikers, was, Gordon was later to admit, probably too aggressive: he actually believed, he said, that Coventry were so in control of the game in the first half that they couldn't lose it. Lacking Salako, the entire defence lost shape, and Graeme Le Saux had a lot of fun running up and down delivering crosses. From one of these, the excellent Nicholls scored with a deft flick; not long thereafter he supplied a pass for Roberto Di Matteo to score an easy third. After the second goal went in, Coventry heads went down, and even Gordon and Garry hushed up and seemed to accept the inevitable. At last I could relax. By the end the dugout seemed a little haven of peace and tranquillity, and dejection.

After the game, Gordon was once again critical of the referee, feeling, in particular, that Huckerby had been given inadequate protection from the attentions of his markers, Leboeuf in particular. Certainly, and not without a certain irony, Paul Telfer was in no doubt about it. 'Huckerby was being kicked all over the place and the referee gave us nothing. It was blatantly obvious but the referee was having none of it.' David Burrows called the tackles that Huck endured 'nothing short of a disgrace – not too far away from being career-threatening. The referee looked after their players and we just wanted a fair rub of the green.' What was interesting was that this time players were going on the record in support of Gordon's campaign against bad, and what was felt to be prejudicial, refereeing.

From the dugout it certainly looked as if they were right, and it is astounding that the human frame can tolerate the amount of abuse to which savage tackling subjects it. Seen from up close this is much more violent than it appears from the stands. It's like being a first-time ringside spectator at a boxing match, amazed at the blood, the welts and the gasps of pain that are imperceptible to the audience seated further back. After the game Huckerby was bruised, abraded and limping. It was a testimony to his strength and fitness: anyone less resilient would have been in hospital.

It was hard to see where it would end. Gordon, now overtly supported by his players, was on a collision course with the referees. It is too easy to suppose this to be an unmitigated bad thing, a looming disaster, but Wimbledon used to make something of a fetish of thriving on the basis of a paranoid closing of the ranks and some tough and uncompromising football. Fortunately, the referee for the forthcoming Arsenal match at Highfield Road was to be Steve Lodge, an official of liberal disposition known for his approach of trying to let the game flow. Not only had he given out the fewest yellow cards during the season, but he had yet to send a man off. Surely things would calm down.

The major talking point of the following week, though, was whether Dion was going to go. Though both he and Gordon were keeping their mouths tightly shut – 'I don't have any day-to-day problem with it,' said Gordon, 'the chairman handles that side of things, and Dion is represented by his agent, so he and I just get on with the football' – recurrent speculation was now linking

Dion with Middlesbrough. Richardson, rather against his better judgement, had raised his offer to £16,000 a week over three and a half years, and he and Dion were now 'not that far apart'. But the club had agreed a transfer fee of £4 million with Middlesbrough, subject to Dion discussing personal terms with them.

Dion, sensibly enough, kept to his policy of saying nothing: when approached by reporters from the local press, even before they opened their mouths he would say, 'No, no comment. I'm not going to talk about it.' But if he wasn't, everyone else was.

As it happened, I was a guest on the Sky Blue phone-in on local radio (BBC Coventry and Warwickshire) on the Friday before the Arsenal fixture, when feeling was running high on the Dublin issue. Callers fell into two camps. The first felt that Dion was being greedy, disloyal to the club and to his team-mates, and ought to be booed during the Arsenal game. This group not only felt very strongly about the issue, but took it personally: this was something that Dion was doing to them. He was a traitor, and if he returned to Highfield Road, he could expect a roasting of 'City reject!', catcalls and boos. One caller believed that it was only 'a small difference of money' for which Dion would be leaving. When I pointed out that, in fact, it would actually amount to £800,000 over four years, he was contemptuous: 'He's already been offered sixteen thousand a week: what's the difference?' And from the point of view of many a fan, perhaps making £300 a week, you could see why, though I wonder if such a person would turn down an extra £100 a week to move to another employer, or remain 'loyal' to his present one. Anyway, the richer you are, the more you spend: rich people like, and in their own ways think they need, money as much as ordinary people do.

None of the callers did so, but they could have cited Bryan Richardson as a member of their own camp, for he had recently been quoted in the national press as saying that Dion's demand was like a form of black-mail.

> Football at the moment has financial diarrhoea. The
> money coming in at the top from TV, increased
> crowds and commercial activities, is going straight
> through to the players. Supporters have to realise
> that all players now are merely hired hands. They
> are at clubs purely for the length of their contracts
> and the money to be made from them. Agents make
> sure there is no loyalty from players any more. It is
> in the best interests of their players to move on at
> the end of their contracts to somewhere that will
> pay them more.

It was surprising that he should feel this level of bitter-ness, much less express it publicly, for this was exactly the point that he had made to me over the summer, with a shrug of philosophical acceptance. If he was prepared to admit that a change of club might, in fact, 'be in the best interests of the player', then how could he realistically oppose the trend? The really revealing moment came in Richardson's choice of metaphor (borrowed, as I remember, from something Alan Sugar had said): the 'financial diarrhoea'. How did this work? Money is presumably like food: it goes in at the mouth as nourishment and is eventually excreted as shit. And who or what is the toilet where this once valuable stuff (how did it get so noxious during the course of digestion?) is deposited? The player. By implication, if the club gets to keep the money it isn't shit; if the player does, it is.

OK, so maybe it's a bad metaphor. Chairmen of football clubs are not poets or novelists. But it may unconsciously indicate a kind of anxiety – allied, I'm tempted to say, to a kind of contempt for the players – that control of the game is passing inexorably from the management of the clubs to the players and their agents. As it unquestionably has in American sport, which has been able to exert some control over the process only by instituting salary caps, whereby no team can spend more than a set amount on players' salaries.

What did the players think? Dion wasn't talking, so I went off to find Gary McAllister, who was still roundly booed by Leeds fans for having left to sign a lucrative contract with Coventry, and is a good judge of things. 'I don't know anything about the details,' he said, 'but we're just pieces of meat, to be bought and sold.' As he said this his face creased with contempt, as if the process, from the point of view of the piece of meat, was a distasteful one. 'But at least now,' he added grimly, 'the players will be getting the money. Free agency will guarantee that. And after all, it's us who play the games.'

Listening to McAllister, you might have supposed him a victim of a heartless system in which slaves are bought and sold, without their consent, purely at the whim, and for the profit, of their masters. McAllister himself was 'sold' to Coventry for £3 million in 1996, a deal which necessitated his agreement, which he was happy to give because he was signing a lucrative contract reported to yield some £750,000 a year. He's not just a 'piece of meat' – the meat doesn't get a salary, it gets eaten. (And, we may reflect, digested and expelled as shit: the same implication produced by the language Richardson was using.)

Richardson doesn't shirk the implication: the bulk of the money is better off in the club's pockets than in the player's. 'The club can invest in more players, youth policies, programmes, better stadia, etc. Players don't reinvest. After all, who pays for them to train as kids? Who gives them the security of payment of their contracts – no sacking for players – not even for those who don't behave, or train, or try properly?'

It seems as if industrial relations in football are tied to a form of language that makes measured assessment difficult, and causes ill feeling by its very nature. Just as player–manager relations are conducted in the old language of the factory floor – all this 'gaffer' and 'boss' nonsense – so the terminology used to describe changing jobs, 'buying' and 'selling' players, distorts the reality. Both sides – the management and the players – suffer from this: Richardson accuses some players of greed or disloyalty, while the players feel the club treats them cynically, as if they were disposable objects.

In the real world, though, people move from one job to another all the time. They aren't bought or sold, they resign, sign a new contract with another business, have a change. Sometimes, if they have signed a long-term contract, their old employers refuse to let them go, or demand to be compensated. They can also be fired at short notice, redeployed, or demoted. (Whereas, Richardson notes, in football, 'players, unlike business employees, cannot be fired – they are totally protected, which is wrong in my view'.)

In other ways, though, life in the corporate world is generally less well paid, less secure and more demanding than it is in the world of professional football. The resentment that players feel about 'being sold' is probably created more by the language used to describe the process than by the process itself.

This all has a tendency to descend into stereotypes: the gentleman chairman who considers himself a model of good business behaviour, and the hypersensitive player who thinks he is being treated as a disposable commodity. So we get these mildly farcical confrontations, with each party taking up his allotted role. The chairman regards it as a straightforward business, and makes this clear to the player: 'My dear fellow, another company wants your services, and will pay you a higher salary. We would be sorry to lose you, but they will compensate us, of course. But it is up to you: do you wish to go?' Who could object to that? But the player, whether he chooses to stay or to go, feels demeaned, as if he were a mere slave. 'Lawdy, lawdy!' we can hear him thinking. 'Whatever will come of me? What'll happen to my wife and all my little chilluns?'

Thus the language that football has inherited – that

players are 'bought' and 'sold' – obscures the greater complexity of the reality, and influences the way people think and feel about the process. Why should Richardson really feel bitter about Dion Dublin going to a better club at a higher salary? Why should Gary McAllister feel he's just a piece of meat?

A second set of callers to the radio phone-in, more sedate in tone, took the attitude that football is a business, and that if Dion had got a better offer, then good luck to him, much as the club would miss him. This lot said that they intended to clap Dion on to the pitch, to thank him for his services to the club. I was rather inclined to agree, albeit with some misgivings. Dion Dublin, after all, is not a servant of the club, but an employee. He is, by profession, a centre forward. He has played League football for Cambridge United, Manchester United, Coventry City and, more than likely, will play for other clubs in the future. To talk of disloyalty seems to me to involve what a philosopher would call a category mistake: loyalty doesn't come into it. From Dion's point of view, what he is considering is a change of employer. He was never 'one of us'. As I've remarked before, players are not supporters of their clubs.

Is this a little cold-blooded? The area in which I had some misgivings concerned Dion's obligations not to the club, but to his team-mates. It was, after all, mid-season, and Coventry were hovering just above the relegation zone. Though a replacement was ready in the wings, there was no guarantee that Moldovan, however impressive his record, would settle in. And Coventry's record in games that Dion had missed, since he came in 1994, was appalling. In his three and a half years at Coventry, in which he had scored fifty-five goals in 139 games, Dion had missed seventeen games through injury or suspension. In these matches Coventry had scored just five goals, and won only a single game. But if you talked to the players, they were ambivalent about the situation. On the one hand, they are a team, and they need Dion; on the other, they know that football is a business, and that players have their own interests to think of. If you get a chance for a profitable move, you take it.

There was, however, a nice counter-example available in Marcus Hall. Coventry had agreed a fee of £1.5 million for him to go to Sheffield Wednesday, who hadn't wanted Marcus as part of the Pembridge deal, but made a separate bid for him afterwards. Ron Atkinson had offered Marcus a generous long-term contract. But Hall, born and bred in Coventry, turned it down. He didn't want to be sold, so he wasn't. 'Why should I go?' he asked, 'I'm happy here.' This was widely regarded as a form of loyalty, but it didn't strike me as that. What Marcus was doing was looking at his quality of life: why move from a situation which pays well, and which you are enjoying, to one in which you might be better paid, but not as happy? And though his first-team position was by no means secure, he was still young, and preferred to envisage a future with Coventry City. From which we may observe, once again, that generalisations about players – like that made by Richardson – are unlikely to be reliable. Marcus was thinking about personal fulfilment, Dion, it seemed, about money.

On the other hand, while most would take the money and run, the players liked, respected and needed Dion. If he were to leave, it would make the fight to avoid relegation more difficult, no question about that, and thus influence their own futures. George Boateng, already an enormous favourite at Highfield Road, put it simply: 'We all want him to stay. He is our big man. We are begging him not to go.' But Dion wasn't talking about it to the players either, and no one was sure what he was thinking.

Though he was greeted with a smattering of boos before the game against Arsenal, the applause on his arrival on the pitch was heartfelt and prolonged, accompanied by the chant, 'Dion! Dion!' There was no mistaking the affection, or the implicit plea that he stay with the club.

In the first half, Coventry played some magical football, pacy and direct, and created a host of chances. Three times Huckerby went one-on-one with David Seaman, and three times Seaman made the required save. But

Coventry were rewarded with a goal from Noel Whelan after some astute work by Soltvedt. The game might easily have been over by half-time; indeed, it should have been in the bag in the second half as Dublin, had a penalty appeal turned down after a blatant foul. But as so often happens in games like this, within thirteen minutes of the restart Arsenal were ahead. Bergkamp pounced on a poor ball from Williams, and then Anelka turned in a rebound that Hedman probably should have held on to. Huckerby was taking the usual stick, though Coventry were handing it out as well: one high tackle by Whelan on Lee Dixon, which left stud marks on his shoulder blade, probably should have seen him sent off, but he got away with a yellow card.

The sendings-off were to come, however. First to go was Patrick Vieira, after a hotly protested handball in the Arsenal penalty area, which led to a penalty once again coolly dispatched by Dublin, and the second, more controversially, in the dying minutes of the game. Dennis Bergkamp, through on goal and just outside the area, was being pursued by Paul Williams when he stumbled and crashed spectacularly to the ground. From the stands it looked as if no contact had been made – indeed, most of us were wishing we had cards to grade it as a dive – but Williams was immediately sent off (for the second time in the season), to his obvious chagrin.

The game ended 2–2, and Gordon was incandescent. Red-faced and shaking with rage, his face twitching as it only does when he is virtually out of control, he appeared in a post-match BBC interview to deny that Williams had made any contact.

The referee was an absolute joke. The standard of football and entertainment in the game is getting higher all the time but the standard of refereeing is way down. We had everything. We had skill, we had character, we had chances and we had good players on the pitch. And what do we get? A referee that spoils it for everybody, for my players and my club. It was an absolute disgrace. We hammered them, and make no mistake about that. And it was only because of the referee and a couple of mistakes we made ourselves that we didn't win. Now, I'll tell you right now, ever since I said something against David Elleray and referees, we have had nothing from referees at this club and it has gone beyond a joke today. If the FA wants to come after me they can come. We had blatant penalty claims, one where Dion Dublin was shoved out of the way, and we got nothing.

Responding to only one question, he observed that, once again, Coventry would be patronised, and once again, they would roll their sleeves up and get back to work.

It was stirring stuff. There was an immense hush in the Ladbroke Club, where I was watching the broadcast with Max Smith, Bertie and Guy. And when Gordon stalked out of the interview room, everyone rose to their feet and applauded. 'It's just like Earl Spencer at Westminster Abbey,' said Max passionately, to the general approval of those about us. But I wasn't so sure. Perhaps this time things were threatening to get out of hand?

The players, as they were now beginning to do, went on the record in Gordon's defence: Bergkamp, according to Paul Telfer, had dived. George Boateng, who had talked with his fellow Dutchman after the game, reported, 'He told me he was waiting for the touch and that is what he does because he is so clever.' Williams had previously commented on something similarly wily about Ian Wright: 'You mustn't take any notice of anything he says because he will try and kid you along that he is your mate and then he will destroy you.' Still smarting about his booking, Williams said that he had asked the ref to look again at the incident, which Mr Lodge, a reasonable fellow, agreed to do. But if it was, once again, Gordon's purpose to get himself called up before the FA, it was very likely that this time he would succeed.

What good that would do he hadn't as yet divulged.

12

Clump 5

Coventry v. Derby, FA Cup, 24 January
Bolton v. Coventry, 31 January
Coventry v. Sheffield Wednesday, 7 February
Aston Villa v. Coventry, FA Cup, 14 February
Southampton v. Coventry, 18 February
Coventry v. Barnsley, 21 February
Crystal Palace v. Coventry, 28 February
Newcastle v. Coventry, 14 March

OK, so I was wrong. At the end of the Clump of Death we were not in the dreaded bottom three: with 24 points from twenty-three games we may only have been a point ahead of the relegation candidates, but the forthcoming fixtures looked much easier, with only three games against a team in the top half of the League in the next ten. Bryan Richardson was certain that this would be the spell when we pulled ourselves right up the table. Looking at the same set of fixtures, though, filled me with nothing but anxiety. It is one thing to have done unexpectedly well against the good sides – to have beaten Manchester United and Liverpool, and drawn with Arsenal – it is quite another to do well against the teams against which you are expected to do well. (I am aware that this implies that, whether we play good teams or bad ones, I am never hopeful.) With McAllister still injured, and unlikely to make a comeback in the near future, Williams recuperating from a hernia operation and bookings and suspensions mounting, there was still plenty left to dread.

Like the forthcoming FA Cup tie with Derby at Highfield Road, for instance. Derby had been in or near the top six all season. A team assembled as if to disprove Richardson's distrust of 'Latins' – Wanchope, Baiano, Eranio – they played as if they were having fun, even in the uncosmopolitan remoteness of Derbyshire, and we seemed incapable of beating them.

On match day, who should turn up but England team coach Glenn Hoddle. For the first ten minutes of the game, half the supporters in the Main Stand were looking backwards at him, rather than watching the game, asking themselves the same questions: 'What the hell is He doing here? Can you tell from the movements of his head which players he is scouting?' Dean Sturridge was out, and not many of the other Derby players qualified for England. Could he be here to see Dion? Or Huckerby? For England? OK, Shearer is just coming back, and Fowler and Ferdinand are out of form, but Dion? Huck? Might he have been under the misapprehension that Roland was English?

Gordon, though, wasn't about to get carried away. 'Darren Huckerby,' he said, 'is nowhere near international level yet, and I'd like to keep him here at Coventry training with us.' Dion, he acknowledged, had a chance.

Whatever the reasons for his visit, Hoddle saw a really solid Coventry performance. Two first-half goals from Dublin provided a perfect platform, and the second half passed without any serious threat of a Derby counterthrust. 'Two-nil,' David Burrows was to say later, 'is a dangerous score.' You are tempted to think the game is over, but if you concede a goal, and there is sufficient time remaining, the whole pattern of the game often shifts. Momentum transfers to the other side, and it is all too easy to start cautiously defending the lead, instead of going on playing the football that got you there in the first place. 'But we never gave them a sniff,' said Burrows. 'Though you might not have told it from the stands, it was the best performance of the season. It wasn't that Derby played badly; we didn't let them play at all. We were totally in control.'

I didn't go to the next game, at Bolton. The reasons for this are obscure, even to me, and involve my prejudice against visiting northern towns beginning with 'B'. The idea of them depresses me, though I've never been to any of them, to Bolton or Barnsley or Bradford. I don't think I have some allergy to B-towns in general: I quite like Bognor Regis, which has a cheerful sky-blueish name; if you can find me a Bognor Huckerby I'll go there, even if it's in the north. But look at the names of those northern B-towns – Blackburn, Bury, Burnley, Blackpool, for God's sake – which sound like places of interest on a tour of Hell. Perhaps, too, they are linked in my mind with that crass Lancashire businessman Mr Bounderby in Dickens' *Hard Times*, and I associate them with stupidity and commercialism, with ashpits, dreary grey skies, grinding accents and poverty.

This shameful bit of nonsense doesn't make sense, even to me, because I quite fancied a chance to look at Bolton's new Reebok Stadium, if only to be able to compare it unfavourably with Coventry's projected new ground. But I wouldn't go. Bolton had only lost one home game, and we'd only won one away: why go to a northern B-town just to watch your team lose?

Your average football fan is full of odd superstitions: if he keeps wearing that same pair of socks, the side will keep winning; if he keeps to this seat, or that, has Bovril rather than tea, repeats a favourite phrase or prayer, it will have beneficial effects on his team. It would be easy to regard this as a sad form of petty egotism, but to me it exemplifies a lovely pagan view of the world, in which we make ourselves feel meaningful, and suppose a connection between all parts of nature, however insignificant. Supporters often think, after missing a game that their team has lost, 'Gosh, if only I'd been there, it might have made a difference.' They usually don't talk about this in company, but if you ask your average fan about it, he will grin sheepishly, and say, 'Yeah, I sometimes think that.'

With me, though, it's just the opposite. I have, I suppose, something of a confession to make. I may have given the impression, so far, that I actually went to almost all of the games, but I'd missed three noteworthy ones through commitments of one sort or another. I am not, in any case, the sort of supporter who needs, or even wants, to go to every match. That seems a little obsessional to me. But there is something odd about most of the games that I don't go to. We win them. The three games I missed were all great performances: 4–1 in the Coca-Cola Cup against Everton; 4–0 at home against Spurs in the League; 3–1 at Anfield in the FA Cup.

So I didn't go to Bolton, and Coventry duly won. Bolton took the lead, and Coventry drew level through a Whelan goal. But in the second half City goals flowed in from all over the pitch, of which Huckerby got the first two, and Dion the final two. Responsible in Gary Mac's absence for corners and free kicks, Telf placed them on heads with the delicacy and precision of a Kensington hatter. The final score of 5–1 was the Sky Blues' biggest League victory away since 1958–9. I'm exceedingly sorry to have missed it, but it is hard to escape the conclusion that, as Dame Edna would say, something spooky is going on here.

I don't really understand Chaos Theory, but a lot of otherwise intelligent people seem, these days, to believe that the flapping of a butterfly's wings in China can cause a rainstorm in Leamington Spa. I take this to mean that, in general, things are a hell of a lot more connected than one would have guessed, and that even tiny and otherwise unnoticed phenomena can have unforeseeably distant consequences. I've noticed this in my own way, with only a slight variation: things that don't happen can change the world just as much as things that do. This may strike you as obvious enough – the fact that there is no tiger in my bedroom means that I won't get eaten alive, so my children can continue to be happy and solvent – but what does it have to do with football? Why should my absence from a Coventry game make the team win? Can it really be that the general atmosphere, unaffected by my pessimism and unrelenting anxiety, is somehow cleaner and fresher, and that it actually affects the result?

Barbara says that homoeopaths call this 'metamorphic resonance', and that my energy field is obviously incompatible with that of Gordon Strachan. I think that's right, but I'm not telling Gordon. Why confirm his suspicion that my presence really is bad for the team?

At the Ladbroke Club, in the old days, I was known as the Albatross. If I arrived at an important fixture, it signalled doom for the Sky Blues. On the days when I couldn't make it, we won. The supporters in my little section of the stand used to take up a collection to keep me away when a major match was imminent. 'Here's a few bob,' their spokesman would say, 'maybe you fancy a weekend in Venice or something? Why not take my daughter?'

So I was actually looking forward, in a selfless way, to missing three City games while on a forthcoming two-week trip to California with Bertie, especially the fifth-round Cup match at Aston Villa (the worst possible draw). If we were to have any chance at Villa Park it was essential that I stayed as far away as possible. Could the flapping of my golf clubs playing at Pebble Beach actually cause a squall at Villa Park?

It caused a minor squall round Ryton when I said goodbye to some of the players before leaving: Telfer and Magnus Hedman, looking pleasingly envious, wished they could play Pebble Beach, too – all they were going to play in the next few days was Sheffield Wednesday. Oggy admitted nostalgically that his favourite place in the world was Carmel, just up the road from Pebble Beach. Huckerby, on the other hand, didn't look like he'd heard of it. Where did he like to go on holiday? I asked, expecting him to say La Manga (where Gordon and Lesley often go), or perhaps Tenerife.

'New York City,' said Huck.

'New York City?' I repeated moronically, incredulity barely in check.

He nodded happily. 'I love it. I love the excitement. Everywhere you go it feels like something is happening.'

I love it, too. This confirmed my growing suspicion that there was more to this Huckerby chap than met the eye. No lolling about soporifically on sun-drenched beaches – among the most hostile of all nature's environments – for old Huck: he's off soaking up the adrenaline on Broadway.

Bryan Richardson was going on holiday too, to Sandy Lane, Barbados, one of his favourite haunts. It was his first holiday for some years, and a chance to catch the England–West Indies Test match. But he was leaving in good heart: 'We're thirteenth at the moment, and we'll finish a bit higher than that. Nobody is even thinking about relegation. Forget that. Gordon has done a tremendous job. There's not a player on the side who hasn't improved this season: Willo, Breen, Richard Shaw particularly. Telfer is playing the best football of his life. So are Dion and Huck.'

Though it was widely suspected that Glenn Hoddle had visited Highfield Road to have a look at Huckerby, he had left announcing that Dion was the best target man in England, and Richardson suspected that Dublin would be picked for one of the forthcoming games against Chile, either in the senior side or the England B squad. 'He's playing out of his skin at the moment, and providing tremendous leadership.' Talk of Dion leaving had faded from the newspapers, and though he hadn't yet signed a new contract, Richardson still believed he would. 'After all, he was never for sale, and he never asked for a transfer. All along he has said to us that he would only leave to go to a top team: Manchester United, Arsenal, Liverpool, Newcastle. And none of them have inquired about him. Where else would he want to go? This is an exciting place at the moment.'

Gordon had said earlier in the season, in one of the periods when Dublin was needed in defence, that he was a 'good Premiership striker, but an international quality centre half'. I wondered if Glenn Hoddle was thinking along the same lines. Richardson suspected that Dion might eventually end up in defence with Coventry, with Moldovan and Huckerby up front – perhaps in 1998–9, if they all stayed. Already there were reports in the media that Alex Ferguson had his eye on Huckerby, a player he had always admired. A price of £6 million was mentioned in the *Sun*. All of a sudden, everybody wanted our strikers. 'When we signed Moldovan,' said Richardson, 'we were desperately short of goals. We needed somebody. Obviously, if things had been like this we wouldn't have signed him.' He added that Manchester United had never, in any case, been in touch about Huckerby: 'There's nothing in it. Who's he going to replace: Cole? Sheringham? Beckham? But it's a fact that the better you do, the more other clubs are going to fancy your players.'

'Does that cause problems?'

'Those are the sort of problems we don't mind having,' he said with a laugh. 'We just have to provide the basis, right here, to satisfy their ambitions. We have to continually keep fuelling their ambitions by keeping the best and strengthening the weaker elements. Confidence and ambition is changed by winning.'

The California trip confirmed my conjectures about the importance of my absence: Coventry won all three fixtures while Bertie and I slaved at the Los Angeles Antiquarian Book Fair and then played golf at Pebble

Beach and Spyglass Hill. The first victory, by 1-0 over Sheffield Wednesday, marked the homecoming (as it were) of Big Ron, who was, I gather, greeted warmly both on and off the pitch. Bertie and I learned of the victory after a round of golf at Rancho Park, the best public course in LA, which is where O.J. Simpson is now reduced to playing every day. We looked assiduously, but couldn't spot him.

In the course of an enormously enjoyable and profitable two weeks, during which we sold over $120,000 worth of books and I shot an admirable 86 at Pebble (missing four short birdie putts), the undoubted highlight came in the form of a fax from Jonathan Strange. Picking it up from the concierge at the Inn at Spanish Bay (at which you can buy a good cigar, only you're not allowed to smoke it indoors), it announced, in a banner headline: 'COVENTRY TRIUMPH AT VILLA PARK!' I let out an involuntary shout, and was glared at by a handful of rich and detestably healthy Californians. 'Sorry,' I apologised, 'but Coventry have just beaten the Villa in the Cup.' Uncomprehending and unplacated, they continued to stare, and when I began to attempt an explanation, I was firmly marshalled away by Bertie. 'Shut up, and gimme the fax,' he demanded.

According to Jonathan, the win confirmed the depth and growing spirit of the squad. Telfer and Whelan were suspended, and Gavin Strachan came into the side. He had recently been chosen for the Scotland Under-21 team, but told by his father that he couldn't go until he cleaned up his bedroom. He had an excellent game, and, aided by the frenzied industriousness of Boateng, controlled the play confidently. Dublin, who had played for England against Chile during the week, and Huckerby and Hall, who had played for England B, seemed energised by the experience. Midway through the second half, Gordon brought on Moldovan, and pushed Dion back into defence to replace Richard Shaw, who had been injured in the first half. A few moments later, Bosnich (yet again) made a good save, this time from a shot by Boateng, but was only able to parry the ball, and Moldovan stuck it in. An overjoyed Viorel, sufficiently assimilated to understand the significance of the goal, celebrated delightedly, and Coventry held on comfortably through six minutes of extra time, and an appeal for a handball by Breen inside the area, to win by 1–0.

Moldovan was getting a quick education in English ways. One of the Sunday papers, in reporting the game, had made a facetious reference to Romanian gypsies, and described his mother as some sort of clairvoyant with a crystal ball. Romanian television duly made a feature out of this, which deeply upset both Viorel and Mrs Moldovan, who prophesied a hideous fate for the offending journalist.

Our pleasure was enhanced by a further fax, the next day, announcing that Coventry had drawn Sheffield United at Highfield Road in the quarter-finals. Stifling yet another display of euphoria, I faxed Jonathan back to inquire on what day the Cup final was, and began making plans for the occasion. Four days later, another fax greeted us on our arrival at the Biltmore Four Seasons Hotel in Santa Barbara, announcing a 2–1 victory at Southampton, with two superb goals from Whelan and Huckerby in the first half-hour, and confidence oozing from every player, which put Coventry 10 points above the relegation zone. Gordon was later to describe Huckerby's peformance as 'world class'.

After the match, Strachan was apparently reported to the police by some offended Southampton fans, who were, in their genteel south-coast way, outraged by his language on the touchline. Gordon, observing that it was funny to get so worked up about it when there were wars going on round the world, suggested that they report David Burrows to the police as well, for swearing at him from the pitch. Neither of them were arrested.

It was a jet-lagged and bedraggled pair of us who

arrived three days later, direct from Heathrow, at High-field Road in time to catch the second half of the Barnsley match. Exhausted by the loss of a night's sleep, backs aching from twelve hours sitting in seats designed by sadists for people who aren't masochists, Bertie and I slumped wearily into our Vice-Presidents' dark blue extra-padded luxury. 'You're late,' remarked the vice-president a couple of seats down, intelligently. 'But you haven't missed anything. Terrible game.' I was grateful for the information, though surprised to hear him say so. I hadn't thought he was interested in football. He always left before a half ended, and took his seat a full five minutes after kick-off in each half.

But he was a good reader of a game. It was pretty awful. Barnsley looked well organised and played attractive football, but hardly created chances, and the match had faded away when, with a couple of minutes left, Burrows hit an intelligent, swerving diagonal free kick into the box towards Dublin, who seemed to be pushed from behind by a defender. Penalty, said the ref, and Dion knocked it in nonchalantly. A few moments later the whistle blew, and Coventry had won their sixth game on the trot.

Television replays showed that the penalty call was dubious, and Danny Wilson, the Barnsley manager, had good reason for his post-match protests. Gordon, the scourge of bad refereeing, was silent on the subject. You only protest about it when it happens to you, not for you. But was it possible that Coventry were all of a sudden getting the benefit of the doubt in referees' decisions?

Gordon wouldn't be drawn on the question. He was facing a disciplinary hearing before the FA on a charge of Insulting Behaviour, but was relatively unrepentant. 'I wrote to Stephen Lodge after the [Arsenal] game to apologise for what I had said, and he was good enough to accept my apology. As far as I'm concerned, that should be the end of it.' Gordon had apologised for calling the ref 'a disgrace'. He had meant, he said, that his performance was disgraceful, which (according to Gordon) was different: less personal, and altogether milder. As well as true. But he was still convinced that his post-Elleray campaign against bad referees was justified. A lot of other managers (Wenger, Gullit, Kinnear, Wilson) had picked up the call, and the subject had received widespread publicity, as well as the support of television pundits like Alan Hansen, himself rather fond of calling other people's behaviour a disgrace.

Yet it had been noticeable, of late, that bookings had become less frequent, and discipline a little better established. 'Of course it's getting better,' Gordon said. 'When things are going well a team is less tense, and they don't foul as much, or get booked as frequently.' He was partly, I suppose, talking about himself as well. For a team and its manager are like a single organism, with a single central nervous system: as results improved, he became visibly less tense, and thus radiated less anxiety to the players, who could then relax and play more freely and confidently.

Could Gordon's confrontational approach, though, actually have influenced the behaviour of referees? I thought I noticed this at Chelsea, where the more Gordon and Garry complained, the fewer decisions from referee Mike Reed seemed to go in our favour. That seemed to me a good reason for the two of them to shut up. But since then, a lot of decisions had gone our way. Could it be a coincidence that Coventry, since the Chelsea game, had been awarded three penalties in their last four home fixtures? Gordon's eyes twinkled as I put the question, and he smiled broadly.

'You'll have to make your own mind up about that one.' Of course, the penalties came, too, from the new excellence of Coventry's attacking play: the more you penetrate your opponents' penalty box, the more penalties you are likely to get.

I joined the side at the hotel in South Kensington – the one with the seafood buffet and mock-lobster that all the players like – prior to the away match against Crystal Palace. Everyone was in muted hotel mode, and after supper the usual tea party of Huckerby, Whelan and Telfer was to be found in the lobby. They poured me a cup, and inquired about my holiday in California.

'Pebble Beach,' said Telfer, 'that's the one where the eighteenth has the water all along the left, isn't it?'

'Loads of it. Whole oceanful. Sometimes you can hear the barking of seals.'

He wasn't interested in scenic observation. 'How'd you do on it?'

'Missed a twelve-foot putt for a birdie.' Thank God Bertie wasn't around to point out that my third shot only landed on the green at all courtesy of a deflection off the branches of a large tree, because I was 'the luckiest golfer in the world'. (He's the unluckiest.)

'How long is the hole?' asked Telf.

'It was playing 567 yards, and the course was wet, with no roll at all.'

'I'd get there in two,' Telfer said, without any perceptible hint of fooling around.

'Right, sure you would. The last tournament there the only pro who hit it was Tiger Woods, with a driver and a three-wood.'

Telfer mused. 'I'd have to use two drivers,' he decided.

I was rather surprised at this bit of palpable self-delusion, because professional sportsmen are usually realistic in their self-assessments. They have to be, or someone else will be realistic for them. Later in the week, I told Gary McAllister, himself a fine golfer, about my conversation with Telfer, to see what he made of it.

'I'll tell you a story,' he said. 'A couple of years ago Telfer and I went to the English Open together as guests of [Ryder Cup player] Howard Clark, who's a big Leeds supporter. He got us under the ropes, and we were watching him and Wayne Grady hit some balls off the practice range. Howard had a new driver that

Telf admired, and Howard said he should have a go
with it.

'So Telfer steps up, in his shoes and jacket, tees up
and starts hitting some balls. And all of a sudden Wayne
Grady and the other pros next to him stop hitting their
shots. They're watching Telfer, who's hitting the ball
further than any of them. And Wayne Grady says to
Clark, "Who the fuck is this guy?" and Clarkie says, "Pal
of mine." So Grady shakes his head and says, "Whoever
he is, he must be Scottish."'

As Telfer and I yattered about golf, Whelan and Huck
paid us as little attention as if we were talking about
Proust, drinking their tea in companionable silence. But
I had a question for them. 'Since I've been away, we've
kept winning – six games in a row now.' They nodded
agreeably; they knew this, too. 'What I want to know is:
what happened?' They all looked at me blankly.

Let me rephrase that, I thought. 'How does it work?
First the team is struggling, then all of a sudden it can't
stop winning.' They nodded again. That was true, too.
'So,' I concluded, 'what's the psychology of it?'

Huckerby and Whelan looked at me silently and intently,
as if waiting for Nick the Romanian to arrive and translate
this into English. Telfer, on the other hand, knew what I
meant. 'It's just like golf,' he said. 'Once you get a couple
of birdies in a row, you're on a run, you're going to get
more.' Whelan and Huck agreed, but I suspected they
were thinking of a different sort of bird.

Breakfast is the most democratic of the meals because
everyone comes down at their leisure, anytime between
eight and nine-thirty, so you just sit with whoever happens to be there, be they player or manager. In the morning I was sitting with Gordon and Noel when George
joined us.

'Where's the wife?' he said to Whelan in a deadpan
voice. The reference was to Whelan's room-mate and
best friend Telfer, who hadn't yet emerged.

'Still sleeping,' said Noel. 'Lazy fucker.'

'Hope you gave her a cup of tea in bed before you came down,' said George laconically, buttering some toast. In fact, Whelan, who describes himself as hyperactive since the age of two, usually rooms alone, because his room mates get sick of him waking them at 2 a.m. for a little chat. It's no wonder Telfer needed a lie-in.

Gordon grinned, and Noel smiled happily. Everybody liked George, whose unrelenting good humour, and quick adaptation to English ways, had been remarkable. The crowd loved him too, and only a couple of months since his arrival, Highfield Road had 'Super George' banners at every game, and the favourite chant became 'There's Only One Georgie Boateng!' He has a quick-fire way of expressing himself that makes great copy for journalists. Asked what he thought of the English game, he replied, 'Good! Tough! Rough! Hard! Fast! All together! But I'm enjoying it, and that's what's important.' Thoughtful and well educated, he was, I found, rather inclined to agree with me about the nature of intelligence: 'I think,' he said, 'that school is very important and having an education can make you a more interesting player on the pitch.' I resolved to relay this to Oggy, but, reflecting that he would only say 'Paul Gascoigne!' to me, I decided not to bother.

Richard Shaw joined us, and I asked him about the change in the side. 'Confidence,' he said. Gordon nodded in agreement. 'At the moment,' said Richard, 'we believe we can beat anybody, anywhere. If we get an early goal at Palace we'll beat them by three or four.'

The goal came early enough, on a gorgeous sunny day at good old Selhurst Park, when Huckerby stroked in an innocuous cross from the left, which wasn't cleared, and Telfer knocked it in. The goal was timed at 47 seconds, and sure enough, Coventry won 3–0. It would have been 4–0 (Richard had said either three or four) but for an extraordinary miss by Moldovan in front of goal. With the ball at his feet, and an open goal ahead, he drifted slinkily and unnecessarily to his left, sold a couple of gratuitous dummies to the defender he had allowed back into play, wiggled his hips gorgeously at the crowd, dragged the ball on to his right foot, flapped his eyebrows like Groucho Marx, and missed from 3 yards out. If he'd had a little more time, he'd have lit a cigar. He looked like someone with international-quality ideas and Second Division abilities, but he had previously scored rather a good goal, so perhaps he was just swanking it. (Ray Clarke, a better judge of such things than me, thought he had overelaborated, but said that the first touch had been world class.)

And that, extraordinarily, was seven wins in a row, a club record. Coventry City were the hottest team in the Premiership. We had risen to tenth in the table, lifted our goal difference to 0, and hadn't lost for seven weeks. Having had 24 points from twenty-three games, we now had 39 points from twenty-eight. Following a banal goalless draw at Newcastle a fortnight later, the figure rose to 40 from twenty-nine. If the rest of the season was going to be exciting, it wouldn't be because of the threat of relegation.

I didn't see this coming. I had been sitting about, more or less in the thick of things, and clearly I hadn't registered the significance of what I had been observing. Was this just a run of good form, or the sign of the emergence of a genuinely good team? I suppose all I could do was ask Gordon. He ought to know. What happened? His answer was, as usual, simple, unforthcoming and unsatisfying. According to him, nothing fundamental had happened at all.

'Take a look back, even at the start of the season. In the first twelve games we win two and draw seven – and in all of those we are ahead before the game is drawn.' (In fact, that was true of only three of the games, the others having been 0–0.) 'We lose at Highbury and Old Trafford, even though we play well there. We were not at all far away from being a very good team.'

I didn't buy that for a second. 'But Gordon, for two

thirds of the season you've been bemoaning lack of quality, saying that you are a realist and that we may well struggle, and that the players have to get by on heart because they don't have the skill. Now you're telling me we were a good team all along?'

As he sometimes does, Gordon was using the opportunity to rewrite history a little, to make it more positive and a firmer foundation for optimism. 'When I said we lacked quality that was before Roland came' (it wasn't – he was saying that long after Roland arrived) 'which wasn't until the fifth game. Then it took Noel a long time to get back into the side after his injury.' (He was still saying it then.) 'Then George came.' (Ditto.) 'So, no, we're not a top side yet, but we should be higher up the League than we are now, and there is quality throughout the side. A lot of that is down to improvement in players' form, and competition for places. Viorel has put pressure on the other two, and Dion is playing great football at the moment, and Huck's started to listen, and you can see the results. Telfer is playing his best-ever football, so is Richard Shaw – Alex Miller used to say he has a brain like a sponge, remembers everything you tell him. And Breeny is the best central defender in the Premiership at the moment, except for Martin Keown. They've all worked hard and now they are reaping the rewards.'

Talking to Bryan Richardson on the same subject was a little disconcerting, because he gave the same answer, almost exactly. He made the points about the first twelve games, about having been ahead in the draws, the coming of Roland, the return of Noel, the signing of George. It had always been a good team, a team of quality players. You might get the impression, hearing it all again, that there was some sort of party line here, like a press release. But it wasn't that at all. Bryan and Gordon are so closely in contact, get on so well together, and admire each other so much, that they had simply talked the issues out and come to a common understanding. Indeed, as I sat in Richardson's office the phone rang – the hotline reserved for Gordon – and the chairman's face lit up as they chatted. Nothing to the call really, Gordon had merely rung to recommend the new Jack Nicholson film, which he and Lesley had loved. Bryan said he'd try to catch it soon.

There is one difference between them, and it may have to do with how close to the coalface you are, or it may represent a difference in temperament. Throughout the first two thirds of the season, Gordon had clearly been driven by anxiety, his major focus the goal of staying up. He was still saying that until Coventry had 46 points they would not be safe, and that remained his priority. After that goal was achieved, he might be willing to talk of other things: of a possible late movement up the table, and a push for a European place.

Richardson, in contrast, had been unwilling from the start to contemplate the prospect of relegation. Not that he was averting his eyes from an unpleasant possibility: he had never seen it as a possibility at all. Gordon had – he knew that even good teams can go down – though he had never believed it would happen. They'd both been confident, in their own way.

Unlike myself. I have persisted, so far, in describing the difference between myself and Richardson as that between a pessimist and an optimist. That is to say, I had believed that we were looking at the same thing and describing it differently, as with the proverbial half-full glass. But it was increasingly clear that the difference between Bryan and myself is not that one of us is hopeful and the other anxious, it's that one of us knows what he's talking about, and the other doesn't. (The other, you will have noted, is me.) Both Bryan and Gordon knew that they had a decent team on their hands, and potentially a good one. I guess I saw that as well. But even when results were going badly – don't forget we were on relegation form through twenty-three games – both of them genuinely believed that things were going to be all right: Bryan with great conviction, and Gordon a little more circumspectly.

But I, like many fans, had my eye on the League table rather than on the field of play. If I had known more, been more attentive, better able to navigate the turbulence of my own anxiety, I too would have seen what was in front of my eyes. Noel's return was helping, George was a terrific player, and a lot of players were clearly getting better as the season progressed. Gordon knew this, and knew that the results should be just round the corner.

Though he would hardly say so, because the major factor in all of this was him. The improvement in the form of individual players, and in the team as a whole, was not due to additions to the squad, though they had been important. No, the boys were playing better because of Gordon, because of the excellence of his coaching, his passion and encouragement, his total commitment to the side. Player after player said so, both those who personally liked him, and those who had their reservations. Richardson, too, had no doubt about Gordon's impact. 'He has made each player improve and moulded a very happy group who want to get better still.'

Every player respected him: he'd been there, done the business, worked like a dog and would fight like a tiger for the side. Anybody who can inspire that many clichés must be doing something right. Gordon, in short, was inspiring: he made you want to be a better footballer.

'There's a definite fear factor there, too,' added David Burrows. 'He can be fierce when he feels you've let the side down. Not by making an error, but if you aren't concentrating or working hard. I've played against Gordon a lot of times, and with him a lot – and I have won a few things, though not as many as he has, but I feel it too.'

'I can take a bad game from a player, but I cannot take a dishonest one,' declared Gordon. 'It's easy for me to spot.' And when he spots it, as a number of players will testify, he is not bashful about pointing it out. 'A player needs complete honesty with himself if he is going to improve. It's a bit like being an alcoholic. He has to admit and accept his own weaknesses before he is ever going to eliminate them.' Subjected to this tough regime of realistic assessment and constant pressure (and encouragement), the team, both individually and collectively, was rapidly improving.

It was clear, too, that the loss of Miller had not been disabling to the extent that many of us had feared. Though Gordon was loth to discuss his individual tactical plans with me in the way that Miller had done, recent results gave clear evidence of his emerging tactical acuity. The run of success since Miller's departure, after an initial hiccup, had been superb. It was evidence of a team not merely tigerish, but astutely directed. If the boys were improving on the field, Gordon was clearly doing so off it. He was evolving from a manager who could lead by example and was a superb coach, to one increasing in tactical awareness and confidence.

What interests me – assuming that what we had witnessed was the emergence of a good team, not a lucky set of results – is that I hadn't seen it coming. I had been gloomily fixated for most of the season on the inevitable relegation battle, yet now we had won seven games in a row. Blinkered by history and my own anxieties, I responded like your average Coventry City supporter. It hadn't mattered a damn that the club had let me behind the scenes. You can be just as blind there as in the stands.

It rather hurts to acknowledge this. To tell the truth, I'd always believed that I could manage a football club. I had, to be sure, presented myself to Gordon and the players as someone ignorant and in need of instruction, but that had mostly been a sort of strategy. Because for most of the season, as this narrative will occasionally have revealed, I had believed I could do this as well as Gordon Strachan. Not the coaching part, I admit – I'd get somebody like Gordon or Alex Miller to do all that kicking and running about at Ryton – but the actual managing part:

buying and selling players, choosing teams and tactics, motivating individuals, planning and organising, dealing with individual players, keeping team spirit high. That sort of thing: I'd be good at that.

Sure enough, this is pathetic, you will think, but in my defence all I can say is that it is a common form of stupidity, and that almost every fan has it. It's easy to catch, agreeable to suffer, and you can never be proved wrong. If your view is that that stupid Strachan should have done this, rather than that, no one will ever be able to prove to you that it wouldn't have worked. Bryan Richardson is unlikely to invite you to become the next manager, so you can go ahead and second-guess Gordon Strachan in the full and perfect assurance that you won't ever be put to the test. And as almost every man is foolishly convinced that he is (a) a good driver, and (b) a wicked lover, so too he will believe that (c) he could manage a Premiership team.

He couldn't. And so, in all humility, I have abandoned (c).

13

Life and Death in the FA Cup

Garry Pendrey had a bad feeling about this one. He wouldn't say so, exactly, but the anxiety was there in his tone, if not entirely in his words. 'It's going to be a difficult fixture. The fans think, you know, what a great draw, we'll murder them – they're not even a Premiership side – but none of them are easy at this stage. Anyway, next year they could be a Premiership side. I think it's going to be tight, very tight.' He was saying all the right things, trying not to seem overconfident, but I suspect that he was doing more than mouthing the usual platitudes, as if he had a bad premonition.

His own experience as a player in FA Cup matches had been both a successful and a painful one: he played in three semi-finals, and lost them all. 'There's nothing worse, it's terrible. I think it is probably less painful to lose in the final; then at least you got there, had your day at Wembley. It's every player's dream to play at Wembley.' He had recently played in some sort of Veterans' Cup fixture, the final of which had been at Wembley, and had scored. 'Afterwards, in the locker room, I said that scoring that goal was even better than sex, so one of the lads goes and tells my missus. And when I get home she says to me "So, better than sex, was it?" But it was, it was. Nothing like it.'

However, with Sheffield United in disarray, manager Nigel Spackman having resigned, to be joined by chairman Mike McDonald a few days later, and the recent home defeat against Ipswich having ended their unbeaten season at Bramall Lane, surely there wasn't much to fear? United had a modest away record; Coventry had won seven in a row, and lost only once at Highfield Road. Home win, right? 'The troubles with the board and the manager won't affect the players. Might even help them – they've got nothing to lose. We'll do them,' said Pendrey, 'but I have a feeling it might take a replay. I know this sort of match.'

It had been a sad week leading up to the Cup fixture: on Wednesday, Gary McAllister had had a run-out in the reserves against Notts County, his first competitive game in eleven weeks. The cruciate ligament damage in his knee had really required an operation from the first, but he had gambled that he might be able to build up the surrounding muscle structure enough to carry the injury and make it through the rest of the season. The reason for taking the risk (which had only a one in ten chance of success in the doctor's estimation) was that, if he regained fitness, he would captain Scotland in the World Cup in the summer: for any player, a great honour; for a football fanatic like McAllister, the culminating experience of his career.

The knee, predictably, had broken down, and McAllister had limped off, disconsolate: 'I just turned and reached for a ball and it buckled under me. I knew that was it.' But the club had backed him in delaying the operation. 'It was a gamble,' said Gordon, 'and it hasn't paid off, but he felt he had to give it a go.' To his credit, Gary appeared three days later on *Football Focus* and said that, much as he hated to lose out on the World Cup, he had also greatly missed being part of the recent Coventry revival. Though the winning sequence had coincided with his absence, I did not think that anything more than a coincidence: no one could fairly claim either that Soltvedt is a better player than McAllister, or that the team pattern suits Trond's play better than Gary's.

It was one of the sadnesses of the year that we were not going to be able to see the Telfer–Boateng–McAllister–Whelan midfield in action. I wondered if we ever would. It usually takes about eight months to recover from a cruciate ligament operation, which would probably take us to Christmas 1998. It is hard to regain full fitness after such an injury, especially at the age of nearly thirty-four. And anyway, would the others still be there? Although a football team has much of the closeness of family life – the intimacy and shared emotion, the jealousies and mutual dependence – it has none of its continuity: there's no guarantee that one of the other three wouldn't have moved on by then.

Oggy was still with us, though, and back in goal in the absence of the injured Hedman, who, having twisted his ankle in training, was being treated in Sweden. Ogrizovic, said Gordon, had shown great resilience after being dropped in December. 'I knew he had mental strength, but I didn't realise quite how strong it was. He could have slipped down with the disappointment of it all, but instead he has done the opposite – he trains harder than anyone. He treats reserve games as if they were Cup finals.' Gordon had now publicly changed his tune about his reasons for dropping Ogrizovic in December. The new version was that he had 'made a change for change's sake', and that it had nothing to do with Oggy's form. This may not have had the virtue of being true, but it was presumably intended to reassure Oggy. However, Oggy, who knew better, didn't need to be reassured, he needed to play, and he was thrilled to be back: 'I never gave up hope of making a return. Simple desire for the game has kept me going. And thanks to the rest of the lads, it's going to be in a big game, too.'

I felt sorry for Hedman and happy for Oggy. They both deserved to be playing – this is the point that Gordon was trying to make – but obviously only one of them could. The success of one would inevitably involve the disappointment of the other, a process that is sometimes called 'a healthy competition for places', and gives new, and literal, meaning to the idea of the survival of the fittest. It is made more complex, and more interesting, by the fact that the people competing so savagely for places are also team-mates, and obliged to appear to be supporting each other. But if you are (let us say) the reserve left back, and you see the first-team full-back writhing on the grass after a bad tackle, no small part of you will be hoping that he is injured. Not too badly, mind you, just enough for you to get a game or two, and a chance to show what you can do. And you are certainly not likely to admit this in public.

It was a great game for Oggy to return in, because he wasn't likely to have a lot to do: it had 'clean sheet' written all over it. Sheffield United had a lot of first-team players out for the match, including the injured Dean Saunders and the Cup-tied Ian Rush. Their tactics, presumably, would be to harry and hassle, defend in depth and hope to steal a draw and get back to Bramall Lane.

In fact, and to their credit, they didn't do that. They pushed men forward in adequate numbers, and ran about fiercely, they just weren't very good. Their defence seemed easy enough to break down, and Coventry made a number of excellent chances which were either missed or saved by the excellent Kelly. But after half an hour, when Dion Dublin knocked in (yet another) penalty after a good direct run in the penalty area by Gavin Strachan, the game was there for the taking.

Dion had been having another of those magisterial games in defence, winning every ball in the air, and controlling and distributing balls from the back with an authority that would make Tony Adams dizzy with envy. But he is prone to the odd mistake, his timing and vision still that of an attacker playing in defence, for better (most of the time) or worse (occasionally). Just before half-time, when Paul Telfer failed to close down the Brazilian-born striker Marcelo, Dion launched himself into an ill-timed tackle, the ball bounced free, and Marcelo lashed it past Oggy to make it 1–1.

In the second half, Boateng, Huckerby, Whelan and Moldovan (twice) had great chances to win it, but were usually foiled by Kelly, who has the anticipation of a clairvoyant and the arms of an octopus. In the final minute, though, with all of the Coventry side except Burrows and Oggy massed in the United area, a hoofed clearance into the Coventry half was chased by the substitute, Katchouro. Burrows and Oggy both started towards the ball, both hesitated, and eventually Ogrizovic made a 30-yard run from his goal, only to have his kick charged down and rebound directly behind him, while a delighted Katchouro hared after it.

From the stands it was clear that there was no avoiding disaster. The open goal was gaping, Oggy thundering along behind the retreating figure of Katchouro, while Burrows was hopelessly trying to get back to cover the goal-line. Perhaps unnerved by the opportunity, or momentarily put off by the shaking of the earth as the mammoth Ogrizovic actually began to gain ground, Katchouro, instead of pushing the ball into the empty net with his left foot, paused for that one extra moment to bring it on to his right, at which point the terrifying figure of Oggy loomed, and Katchouro's shot hit the post and bounced safely out of play. Oggy put his hands on his knees, head down, gasping for breath. 'I've never run that far or that fast,' he said later. 'It's a good thing my kids nagged me into giving up smoking just after my fortieth birthday.'

Encountering one of the Sheffield United coaching staff just after the final whistle, as the dugouts cleared and handshakes were exchanged, Jim Blyth asked if Katchouro was right-footed, and if that had been the reason for his fatal final movement. 'Not at all,' said the chap, glumly, 'that's what's so odd about it. He's left-footed.'

Afterwards Bertie and I weren't sure what attitude we ought to take to the game. We had murdered Sheffield United, but on the other hand, their last-minute miss had been a reprieve. I preferred to believe, as the next day's tabloid papers were to put it, that we had come back from the dead and lived to fight again.

'They're a poor side. We should beat them easily in the replay.' At Ryton, David Burrows hadn't a flicker of doubt, which was just as well, because it was his error, in most assessments, that had almost cost us the first tie at Highfield Road. Trevor Peake, who had just returned to Coventry to coach the Under-21s, and who had been a member of the Cup-winning side of 1987, was clear about it. 'A keeper, especially one as old as Oggy,' he laughed, 'shouldn't have to run thirty-five yards to clear a ball when there's a defender back. David should have come over. It was a close thing, but we should beat them at Bramall Lane. It might even be easier there – they'll give us more room to play.'

Gordon, though, was looking tense and abstracted. Rushing down the narrow corridor that runs from the laundry rooms to the players' lounge and dining room, he smiled quickly – the smile never reached his eyes – at John Salako. 'How's the leg, John? All right?' Salako didn't bother to answer or to return the smile. Relations had deteriorated substantially. He was on the transfer list, and had just returned from a few days on trial at Feyenoord: 'Great set-up. Big club. But I wasn't fully fit, so they said we should keep in touch.' Though Richardson said there had been interest in Salako, no club had put an offer on the table, and he was being paid his salary while he hung about hoping to find a new club. It didn't seem an entirely unrewarding form of unemployment, at £5,000 a week, but he certainly took no pleasure in it. He looked pretty miserable.

I wished him luck, but noted that it couldn't help his prospects that he wouldn't move up north, having once turned down a chance to join Newcastle for that reason.

'Oh God,' he moaned, 'not that old story.'

'Not true?' I asked, 'It was printed everywhere.'

'It was that fucking Ron Noades,' said Salako. 'I wanted to go to Newcastle – who wouldn't have? – but the deal broke down because they signed Ginola instead of me. And Ron didn't want to admit it, in case Palace didn't get another good offer, so he made up that rubbish about me not liking the north. I was furious with him, but he just said to forget it. Now everybody thinks I have some sort of phobia.' He stared at Gordon's back moving away from us. 'What's he think of your book, then?'

It was the second time he had asked me that question. I waited a moment until I was sure that Gordon was out of hearing range. 'He's been cordial, and he fits me in when he can, but I'm not very high on his list of priorities.'

Salako pursed his lips. 'He wouldn't like it.' It was the second time he'd said that as well. I wasn't sure why: was he warning me to be careful, because he didn't like Gordon? Or telling me that the project was unfeasible? Sensitive to the emotional complexity of things, he rather liked watching the drama unfold, and being kept up to date.

'I don't think he does. But he's put up with it so far, and at least the relegation pressure is off now, so I hope to get a little more time with him. But I'm still an outsider, and he's a football person through and through. He doesn't feel comfortable with me around.'

Hearing this, Gary Breen, who had become increasingly accessible, put an interesting gloss on the subject. 'We're like this all the time with outsiders. Even new players. When someone new comes into the dressing room, we keep our distance for three or four weeks, then maybe start to take the piss a little. If he responds, we know we've got him.' This partly explained, of course, why it had taken such a time for the team to gel: when Ron Atkinson came, there was a massive injection of new players, and it took a considerable period for them to get to understand and to trust each other, and longer still for them to become a team as obviously happy as this one is.

'The trust,' said David Burrows, 'has to happen both on and off the field. On the field you don't know how the new players are going to fit in, how they will play, whether you can count on them. And in the dressing room it takes a long time before you can relax together and have a laugh. Don't forget, Ron brought in almost a whole new team, and there have been a lot of new faces since then. You've got to give it time.'

'I don't think we were ever far away,' said Salako, 'and the turning point was the Manchester United game. If we'd lost that, then we might've lost at Anfield in the Cup, to Arsenal, then away at Chelsea, and we would have struggled the rest of the way. But then Huck pulled that game out, and since then, really, it's all turned around. And Huck and Dion are on fire. If you look at teams that do well, they have two people scoring a lot of goals.'

Dion had been named Carling Premiership Player of the Month and had had his game for England (which they lost 2–0 to Chile), and Gordon was inevitably going to be announced as Manager of the Month ('I hope I won't be,' he said, 'it's the kiss of death. We hardly won a game after I last won it. Anyway, two months ago they were saying I wasn't a very good manager. I wonder what's happened since?') Just now he had an important managerial decision to make, and it concerned Dublin: he had in his side the incumbent England centre forward, and he was playing him in defence.

It was an audacious thing to do, and even Giles, my literary agent, who likes cricket but detests football ('a stupid game. They run about in shorts, you know, and funny socks') seemed to be well up on the issue as he quizzed me over dinner at the Garrick Club, London's watering hole for literary types and luvvies, about our prospects at Sheffield United. 'Is your Mr Strachan' (Giles insists on pronouncing it 'Strawn') 'going to play that nice bald Mr Dublin in the front, where he belongs, or will he persist with this obscure Romanian?' Overhearing this, a couple of the members looked at Giles disapprovingly, as he was in imminent danger of breaking the first of the club's two rules, which is that no bores are allowed. (The other rule is that one is not to be rude to the staff. Both are broken regularly.)

Moldovan, in the squad for the last few fixtures, had been desperate to get a game. After a recent ten-minute vignette as a substitute, he had showered and stomped back to the team coach, flouncing his way up the steps like a Transylvanian Greta Garbo with the shriek 'Ten minutes they give me! *Ten minutes*! I VANT TO PLAY FOOOTBAALL!' He'd been bought to provide the answer to a lack of goals up front, and since his arrival they had come in droves – only it wasn't him who had been scoring them, but Dion and Huck. Gordon, trying to look on the bright side, said that this is what competition for places can do. He understood Viorel's problem, but that (after all) both Huckerby and Dublin were now worth more than him in the transfer market anyway. 'I suppose it's a good problem to have, from the club's point of view, but it's a big problem for me.' Moldovan had recently been quoted by a newspaper in Romania as wondering whether the move to Coventry was such a good idea, but Bryan Richardson insisted that this merely indicated his concern that his lack of play would endanger his World Cup selection chances, and that, in fact, he and his wife were happy with the move. 'He understands the situation. He'll be all right.'

Gordon's answer to the problem, as we have seen, had been to try (in the absence of the injured Richard Shaw) to accommodate both Dublin and Moldovan, with Viorel up front and Dion moving forward from defence for corners and some set pieces. It would take a harsh critic to say that the change hadn't worked, but in fact the good results came in spite of the change. Though Moldovan had scored twice, and made a lot of searching runs, he looked anxious in front of goal, snatching at a number of good chances. ('He thinks he ought to score three goals a game,' said Gordon. 'He's just got to relax.') Huckerby, more comfortable reading Dublin's flicks and angled passes, seemed less easy with Moldovan up front. This was by no means all Moldovan's fault: the team were used to providing for a target man, and too many balls were being hoisted at Viorel, who is no Dublin in the air. You could sense his frustration as he made a penetrating diagonal run, creating some space, and failed to get the ball played to his feet.

'If he hadn't cost £3.25 million,' sniffed Max Smith, as we travelled up the M1 to the Cup replay at Bramall Lane, 'do you really think Gordon would be playing him? It's only when he gets taken off and Dion moves up front that we ever look like scoring these days.' Guy and Bertie, stuffed like great teenage buffaloes into the back of Max's Audi A3, agreed completely. 'I'll bet he plays Dion up front tonight,' said Guy, with more hope than belief in his voice.

It would have surprised me if Moldovan wasn't going to be up front, because during the week Gordon had not released him for a friendly match for Romania. I wasn't sure about this because I hadn't joined the team at the hotel in Sheffield. I wanted to be a proper fan on the night. Coventry don't play a lot of FA Cup quarter-final matches, and the best way to enjoy one is among the supporters, not mooning about joylessly with the players, killing time before going down to the ground. Nor did I want to sit in the directors' box at Bramall Lane – that would have been awful. The lesson is clear: if you really want to enjoy your football, keep away from the football people and stick with the proper supporters.

I wanted to sing 'Gordon's Sky Blue Army' from the stands, surrounded by 5,000 people who were singing it too.

On the way to the ground the streets were teeming with supporters, the red and white United kits contrasting with the glaring Coventry blue shirts. The orange-coated stewards and police in dark blue on horseback seemed artistically arranged, as much to add to the colour range as to direct the traffic. The side streets were jammed with rows of parked coaches disgorging Coventry fans. You could see a little smile of contentment and anticipation light up the face of most of the fans as they hit the street. There is something about night fixtures – the colours filtered through the glow of the streetlamps, the chip shops and pubs alight and smoky, that sense of being out for a special occasion – that gives them a certain tawdry magic. Max looked about him with unbridled delight: 'This is what it's all about,' he said, 'I love this,' just as a very large Sheffield United supporter approached him from outside a pub, pint in hand.

Max, who had a little blue Coventry scarf round his neck identifying him as the enemy, looked up good-naturedly. 'So, mate,' said this hulking northern person, 'you gonna win, then?'

'For sure,' said Max, a friendly smile on his face.

The United supporter, now joined by a few pint-clutching pals, moved a little closer. Bertie and Guy shied backwards marginally, and I took up a distance appropriate to authorial observation, but Max was still and receptive.

'Lemme ask you a question, then.' The other Sheffield United boys nodded their heads enthusiastically: it was the question they wanted to ask as well.

'Sure,' said Max, 'what do you want to know?' Bertie and Guy had now disappeared. Having simultaneously discovered a need to tie their shoelaces, they'd gone to find a nice spot to help each other do it.

'Where's Dublin playing?' asked the first man. His

three red-shirted cronies gazed at Max intently: 'Yeah, is he gonna be up front?'

'Where would you play him?' asked Max, always keen on a good chat.

'At the back, mate, then we'll have a chance,' laughed one.

At this point it was right, and safe, for me to step in. 'You've got a chance, then,' I said. 'He'll be at the back.' They beamed with gratitude, and wished us luck. I had a feeling we'd need it. Our in-car prognostications had run true to psychological form: Max and Guy predicted easy wins to us (3–0 and 3–1), Bertie a win for us after extra time (2–1), and me a loss on penalties after a 1–1 draw. Max never distinguishes what he wishes from what he predicts, which seems to me childlike; I don't distinguish what I predict from what I dread, which is morbid. It's probably nicer being him, but he often ends up disappointed, and I often end up right. We are, after all, Coventry City supporters. Besides, I had a nasty feeling about the fixture.

'You always do,' said Bertie.

'It'll be fine, no worries,' claimed Max chirpily.

We'd only just taken our seats, five minutes before kick-off, when there was a great commotion at the top of the steps to Entrance D, directly beside us, about 10 feet away from where we were sitting: stewards came running over, hands waving frantic but indecipherable signals to colleagues near the pitch, and a clutch of spectators were leaning over the rails, trying to look into the dank stairwell. Max moved over to ask an onlooker what was happening.

'Some guy's fallen down. Looks like he might have had a heart-attack or something.'

Three men wearing St John Ambulance Brigade uniforms pushed to the front, and soon what looked like the top of a portable drip unit was sticking up incongruously above and behind the stairwell crowd. The whistle blew

and the game began. A number of the Coventry supporters, leaning into the stairwell, hardly took their eyes from
the spectacle in front of them, looking up only occasionally to check progress on the field of play. I resolved to
breathe slowly, and not to get over-excited.

For the first twenty minutes, Coventry utterly dominated the game: Boateng and Whelan covered huge
swathes of ground, with Soltvedt pushed well up behind
the strikers, and Moldovan and Huckerby peeled away
with the grace of seagulls. The goal, when it came (in the
tenth minute) was not, surprisingly, from open play,
though there had been chances, but from a 25-yard free
kick by Telfer, which travelled entirely along the ground
at distinctly subsonic speed, but bobbled over Kelly's
outstretched hand. An enormous cheer, suggesting relief
as well as jubilation, rose from the Coventry end, and,
as I looked across, it appeared that Stairwell D had just
been cleared, as one or two fans were racing up it, arms
aloft in triumph.

After which, curiously, the game started to drift away.
United won more ball in midfield, and the Coventry
defence was anxious and fragile: Burrows, looking out
of sorts and position, got booked, and was later lucky
not to be sent off; Nilsson seemed incapable of delivering
even a simple pass to a team-mate; Dion held on to the ball
too long, and tended to overelaborate. Even so, Oggy had
only one save to make, which he did confidently, seeing
the ball well under the lights. When half-time arrived,
most of us in the crowd were relieved.

As Bertie and I moved into the stairwell, I stopped
to ask an ashen-faced steward what had happened
to the man on the floor. 'It was awful,' he said. 'He
died. Massive heart-attack. We tried to resuscitate him.
Nothing we could do. They took him away in a body
bag.'

'My God. Do you have any idea who he was?'

The steward shrugged. 'Some bloke, in his fifties. His
son was with him.'

Bertie shook his head with shock, and we wandered down the steps, over the spot where the man had lain fighting for his life, on our way to meeting up, outside the Gents', with Jonathan Strange and some of the London fans. We told them the story of the dead supporter. They paused for an appropriate moment of silence, looking solemn and flustered. After a time, one of them said, a little tentatively, as if unsure that it was a fit topic for conversation, that the last twenty-five minutes of the half were our worst defensive performance of the season.

Bill Shankly, the great Liverpool manager, was famously quoted as saying, 'Football is not a matter of life and death, it's much more important than that.' The first time I heard this, it seemed to me as perfect an example of the stupidity and insularity of football-mad people as could be imagined. Nothing is more important than life and death, is it? Would you not call off a football game to save a life?

One's reflexive answer to this is, yes, of course you would, but if you kept on doing so you would end up with no football matches at all, without having solved the problem of death. People die, and sometimes they die at football grounds: most notably Jock Stein, who as manager of Scotland, had a fatal heart-attack at an international match. I presume he would have said it was a good way to go. I simply didn't know, as I stood about outside the men's toilets, what attitude to take to the death of the anonymous spectator, nor how much it had, or should have, diminished my engagement with the game. I wanted to discuss our defensive shortcomings, and felt vaguely ashamed. But the game hadn't been cancelled, and it was why I came. Could Bill Shankly have known, after all, what he was talking about? Or was I simply just another football-crazy fan who had lost all perspective? So what should I have done? Gone home? Is that what the anonymous spectator would have wished?

Whatever was wrong with the Coventry side (like whatever was wrong with me), wasn't put right at half-time. In their uninspired way, Sheffield United – without a moment of grace, a flash of inspiration, a single redeeming flicker of artistry about their play – began to take a grip on the game. They were fitter and keener, quicker to the ball. But most of the chances still went to Coventry, and when Moldovan missed a free header directly in front of goal, he put his head in his hands in disbelief. The crowd was begging Gordon to take him off, and bring that nice Mr Dublin up front, with Paul Williams coming into defence. The minutes drifted by excruciatingly, Sheffield United pressed forward, it was almost over. Newcastle in the semi-final – they're no good, we'd win that – and then it would be Wembley. What a great season!

I intended to insist to Gordon – well, to beg him, anyway – that I got to sit in the dugout during the Cup final. And then, when we won the Cup, I was going to get my hands on it, right in the middle of the pitch, and run about like crazy, doing South American dances.

In the final minute United won a corner, which was delivered to the far post. David Burrows' challenge in the air only deflected it on to Noel Whelan's shoulder, and across goal to David Holdsworth, who hooked a shot past Oggy and into the far corner. A keeper with the eyes of an owl and the reflexes of a cheetah wouldn't have got close. Bertie held his head in his hands. Max shook his head like a damp spaniel and announced 'We'll do them in extra time.' I resisted the tendency to say 'I knew it.'

Not much happened in the half-hour of extra time. Tired, and afraid of making a fatal mistake, the players got a little negative, and no good chances were created. The game was decided on penalties, which, according to the Sheffield police, had to be taken at the Sheffield end 'for reasons of public safety'. After a harrowing few minutes (to which I will return), Coventry lost, 3–1.

We had been ahead in both games, controlled most of the play, and made a lot of chances, but hadn't actually managed a goal from open play. Sheffield United did, twice, and perhaps they deserved to go through.

'It was a disgrace,' said Max, disconsolate, 'and the reason we lost was Gordon. Sheer bad management.' Strachan, aside from saying that he thought we ought to have won, that he was very disappointed, and that he wished Sheffield United the best of luck, was relatively unforthcoming after the match. So it was with great interest, and some trepidation, that I went early to Ryton the next week to ask if I could join him for his morning tea. 'Sure,' he said, 'no problem.'

OK. Out with it. 'There was a lot of feeling, Gordon, that Dion should have played up front. What was your thinking?'

'No thinking at all. I didn't have a choice. Shaw wasn't ready, Marcus was hurt and Williams was only on the bench in case of emergency – he hadn't played in ten games, and he wasn't really fit. So there was no choice at all. Actually, I thought Viorel played well in the first half, and he could have put away that free header, but he snatched at it. Just a little anxious. We had plenty of chances to win the match, and then we threw it away.'

So what had happened? 'We lost it due to a lack of professionalism. It had nothing to do with the corner – that's just bad luck. It came back across the goal from Noel's shoulder, and the lad knocked it in. But just before that we'd had a free kick on the left about ten yards from the halfway line. And we had five players waiting for the ball, all lined up down the left touchline, and Telfer sixty yards away, level with Whelan, who is taking the free kick. So when we lose the ball, all of a sudden we only have five men behind the ball instead of eight. Sometimes you have to lose a few in tight situations like that before you are ready to win one.'

He made it sound as if he anticipated that City would be in similar situations over the next few years. 'I lost in a couple of semis and a final myself before winning anything.' (After which, over the next four years – three at Aberdeen and the next at Manchester United – his team won the Cup each year.)

'You've got to learn. The lads,' he added, with a sour look on his face, 'won't make that sort of mistake again. If we had kept possession, kept it down their end for a bit, we'd have won it. Instead United get it and hoof it forward, and it goes under Roland's foot for the corner'– he made a gesture like a slow bowler delivering a ball – 'just like one of those ones that skids along the pitch. Not his fault, nothing you can do about those.'

'Did you think that was it, then? I thought they looked fresher than us at that point.'

He was shocked. 'Not at all. I thought we would win it in extra time. And when it went to penalties I thought we'd win it then. I never thought we were going to lose.'

I'd never been to a game that ended in penalties, and always wondered what approach the manager takes with the team as they flop about like exhausted fish on the pitch. Exhortation? Instructions about what order to take the penalties in? Advice on how to hit them?

'Not at all. I was just trying to relax them, have a little laugh, calm things down.' The players, in fact, had looked spent and shell-shocked: Whelan and Telfer were white with exhaustion, while Boateng simply dropped to the ground, having run himself to a standstill.

'Presumably you practise penalties in anticipation of an ending like this?'

'You talk about it, but you really can't practise penalties.'

I was rather surprised to hear this. In fact, I don't entirely understand professional footballers' attitude to practice. I don't mean training, which is done by the whole team, and involves skill and flexibility work together, five-a-side matches, perfecting set pieces and the like. I had watched a good deal of this at Ryton, and seen the beneficial consequences of it in later matches.

No, when I talk about practice, I mean something individual. If you look at professional golfers or tennis players, you will observe that practice forms the basis of their preparation for tournaments. Of course it does, since these are individual sports. Training is simply doing the physical work necessary to be sufficiently fit, but practice entails making an analysis of one's game, locating its weak points, and working to eradicate them. If your opponent keeps winning points by serving high to your backhand, there's no place to hide; you either have to rectify the weakness, or you'll keep losing to him. He'll exploit your weaknesses mercilessly.

Part of what is fascinating, and slightly repellent, about sport lies in that curious inversion of values whereby much that we admire in ordinary life – humility, compassion, unwillingness to take advantage of the weakness of others – is reversed on the field of play. Professional sport is all about winning. And, within reason, the more you practise (and the more you train), the better your chances of doing so.

In a team game like football, a weakness in a player's game can be camouflaged, if not from his team-mates, then at least from most of the crowd. The capacity to strike the ball well with either foot, head it with power and accuracy, hit accurate passes, time a tackle, take a soft first touch – players have (and need) these skills in varying degrees, and they are good at covering their own deficiencies. Richard Shaw is not a very good passer of the ball, so he hits short and safe passes out of defence; Huckerby is a bad header of the ball, so he doesn't make runs looking to get on the end of crosses. They were both having good seasons, but why shouldn't they try to improve these relative deficiencies? Although Gordon pointed out that Shaw had done some work on his long passing, and that he had given Huckerby extra training on heading the ball, I got the impression that these were marginal activities, not central ones. There is no real ethos of individual practice in the English game.

Yet even the finest skills need to be kept in good order, which is why as errant a spirit as George Best was well known for staying behind after training to practise on his own. I know that George Best did this because it was rare then, as it is now, for a player to work by himself with such dedication. Hence people noticed and reported it. Occasionally in the afternoons at Ryton one may find Gordon working with Huck or Dion, or Moldovan practising knocking balls in from the edge of the box, or Oggy or Magnus gathering crosses from one of the youngsters. These are by no means uncommon sights, but they take place on an ad hoc basis rather than according to a plan for each individual player.

Does it not seem odd – oddly unprofessional – in a game where each player is now given individual targets with regard to weight, diet and fitness, that a programme is not also designed specially for him to sharpen the areas of his game that are weakest? Why doesn't Paul Williams work more on improving his first touch? Why doesn't Huckerby practise going one-on-one with the goalkeeper, because he doesn't convert enough of the chances his astonishing runs provide? Why doesn't Oggy kick and distribute the ball more accurately? If Tom Watson, at the top of his game, could hit golf balls on the range until his hands bled, I can't see any good reason why a football player – even one of the excellence of some of the players I have mentioned – shouldn't strive for that extra 2 per cent improvement which might sometimes make the difference between winning and losing.

On the other hand, what do I know about it? So I asked Jim Blyth why players don't practise. 'I've never really thought of that,' he said, 'maybe you're right. It's just never done, or only rarely. Goalkeepers do it.' Meeting the chairman later in the day, I asked him what he thought. 'You've got a point there,' Richardson said. 'Cricketers practise a lot. It isn't done so much in football.'

Convinced I was on to something, I found Gordon, and put the same point to him. He didn't look very interested. 'Yeah,' he said, 'they do a lot of that sort of thing in Spain and Italy. Better climate. Here, in the winter, it's so cold that players would resent it.' Practising, the implication was, was a funny foreign habit. It's a good thing we have the old bulldog spirit with which to combat all those show-off skills.

I hardly knew what to make of Gordon's response. I took it to mean: 'Bugger off – what do you know about it?' But his comment helps to account for a difference that anyone can note between English players and those from, say, Spain or Italy: the foreigners have better ball skills. Germans, too, even though they have cold winters, same as us. Take all those awful Germans whose names I can't remember who mercilessly rifled penalties past helpless English keepers to knock England out of the World Cup in 1990 and Euro '96. And then think of poor old Stuart Pearce, Chris Waddle and Gareth Southgate, whose names we do remember, exactly because, in sport, nothing is remembered like failure. Could it have been that the Germans were better at penalties because they – perish the thought – actually practised and practised and practised until none of them missed? Because none did.

Most of the Coventry players, of course, will never have to take a penalty, because penalty shoot-outs are so uncommon. Oggy told me later that he thought the chips had been stacked against us in the replay against Sheffield United. 'First of all, in extra time United were playing for it to go to penalties. They were the underdogs, so getting that far was a triumph for them. But as soon as I got to the centre circle and joined the lads, just before the shoot-out, I knew we were in trouble. They looked shattered, and you could see in their eyes that the self-belief was gone. At that point, I thought we were going to lose.'

It didn't stop him saving the first United effort, after which up stepped Dion Dublin. He had scored from a penalty in the first game, which he had stroked (not pinged) lowish and to Kelly's left. In fact, in his run of five straight penalties he had always gone to the keeper's left. Presumably there is a sort of bluff and double-bluff element here – surely this time he has to go the other way? or does he? – but Kelly, a simple soul, had no doubt about it: Dublin hits them low and to his right, so I will go to my left. Given that keepers no longer have to wait until the ball is struck to make their move, Kelly had moved so quickly that by the time Dion hit the ball, he was sitting there in a deckchair drinking tea, and simply swatted it away like a fly. (The papers reported this, the next morning, as a great save.) Boateng, watching from midfield, kicked a plastic water bottle into the air, his shoulders hunched with dejection.

After United scored from their second attempt, David Burrows, a great pinger of a ball, who once held the record for the fastest dead ball struck by a Premiership player, came up to blast one. He didn't seem to catch it cleanly, Kelly got a hand to it, and it rolled along the goal-line and hit the inside of the post, which meant it ought to have gone in. It didn't. Boateng, from the centre, could barely watch. When the ball finally rolled slowly away from the goalposts, he stomped furiously on a red balloon that had drifted from the stands on to the field.

After Sheffield United scored again – could it be that they practise these things? – Paul Telfer knocked one in, though Kelly seemed to get a hand even to this one. Then United took a turn to miss, but still led 2–1. If Coventry missed again, and United didn't, that would be it. No cavorting in Wembley's green and pleasant land for me. We'd be out of the Cup.

So who stepped up to take this crucial penalty but Simon Haworth, who had come on for Moldovan in extra time. Though a regular scorer in the reserves, Simon hadn't yet got a goal in the League, and had looked keen but uncomfortable in many of his appearances. Though he has played for Wales, he hadn't the experience to match the occasion, and one feared the worst. The crowd, seeing him walking up to take the kick, were uniformly astonished. Bertie and Guy groaned; Max held his head in despair. The noisy fellow directly behind us put the general feeling most articulately and elegantly: 'What the fuck are you doing, Strachan?' he screamed.

Simon hardly looked full of confidence. George Boateng, still in the centre circle, turned his back as Simon ran up, scuffed the ball tamely and Kelly bent down gently to pick it up. You could imagine him tossing it back to Haworth, saying, 'You can hit them better than that – why not try again?' After which Kelly wandered away from the goal, Oggy trudged in, some United player or other slammed in the final penalty, and it was all over. Coventry had missed three out of four attempts. Boateng, a religious man, lay on his back looking up into the blackness of the sky, as if seeking the ultimate answer to the question, 'How could something as miserable and senseless as this have happened?'

'I guess if there's one thing I would do differently,' Gordon told me after the match, 'it would be to use Roland. Then Whelan was going to come next. It's easy to be wise after the event. But I used Simon because he'd been brilliant at Ryton during the week, and was striking the ball really well.'

In the silent dressing room afterwards, the mute and exhausted players slumped wearily. They had done enough to win in both games, and hadn't gone down through lack of effort. Whether they were that little bit complacent is hard to know. Gordon didn't think so, but it can sometimes be difficult not to underestimate teams that are inferior to one's own. That is what Alex Ferguson meant by 'these sorts of games' – games in which you think you are trying as hard as you can, but it's a tough job to produce that extra effort, because you know you are expected to win. Perhaps that is what Garry Pendrey had been worried about all along.

The Coventry spectators, following Haworth's miss

and the final goal, sat stunned for a while before slowly and silently rising to leave Bramall Lane. Behind me, a little girl with a snub nose and freckles, maybe six years old, rested her chin on the iron railing, and her tears, as they trickled down her cheeks, fell softly on to the curved metal, where they glowed like raindrops in the floodlit night. Her father, in his sky-blue shirt, put his arm round her, and looked out on to the pitch, his eyes glazed in mourning.

I wondered, as we left, what had happened to the body of the dead spectator – in what hospital or mortuary it now rested, and how his son was coping with the tragedy. In the brightly lit street outside the ground, as Coventry fans slumped off into the darkness towards their cars or coaches, ready to make the sad procession south, the Sheffield United supporters were singing a psalm of happiness:

> Che sera, sera
> Whatever will be, will be
> We're going to Wem-ber-ley
> Che sera, sera!

On Friday 27 March the funeral of Maurice Spencer, who died at Bramall Lane at the age of fifty-two, was held in Coventry. The cortège left from Highfield Road at 2.30, on its way to Canley Crematorium for the funeral service, which was followed by a reception back at the football ground.

A lifetime Coventry City supporter, who had been resident in Leeds, Maurice Spencer had been met at Bramall Lane by his son David, aged twenty-seven, who had travelled to the fixture from Coventry. According to his widow, Mary, 'He loved football and he went the way he lived.'

14

Clump 6

Coventry v. Derby, 28 March
Leicester v. Coventry, 4 April
Coventry v. Aston Villa, 11 April
Tottenham v. Coventry, 13 April
Coventry v. Liverpool, 19 April
Leeds v. Coventry, 25 April
Coventry v. Wimbledon, 29 April

'**O**K, let's calm down a little.' Bertie was counselling me with his usual exasperated wisdom, as Jonathan Strange and a lot of bemused Leicester fans watched me warily. I was leaning against a small garden wall, a few hundred yards from the ground at Filbert Street, hysterical with laughter, whooping and spluttering, holding myself, sides aching. If it went on much longer, it would have started to hurt, and I wouldn't be able to get my breath.

Above my head a sign announced the name of an Asian corner shop – 'Meat, Chickens, Grocers' and I had just cracked myself up by asking Bertie to go in and buy us a couple of grocers and chips. Or, I wondered, how about a grocer in a basket with mushy peas? Or two breaded breasts of grocer?

Each of these suggestions struck me as wittier than the one before, a view which neither Bertie nor Jonathan shared in the least. 'Look, stop it now,' said Bert, as I kept on spluttering. 'It isn't that funny, and everybody's looking at you like you're a loony.' It's curious what being safe from relegation, with eight games still left, can do to you – how that knowledge relaxes the entire system, and allows you to focus on otherwise unnoted possibilities of leisure or entertainment. On the way into Leicester we'd seen a big Edwardian bed and breakfast called 'Southfork', as in the ranch in the old soap opera *Dallas*, but the guys wouldn't let me go in and ask for Miss Ellie.

The previous week a 1–0 victory over Derby at Highfield Road had looked unspectacular, but it was a sign of how far the team had progressed. Gordon had worked on mental approach with the squad for the week before the match, and the result was an immensely satisfying, professional performance. I suspect that not many fans in the crowd were aware of how well Coventry had played.

But the winning streak had to end somewhere, and Leicester, still the only club to win at Coventry, was as good a place as any for the record to go. So I was reconciled to defeat, unlike the four blokes in front of us, who aimed an incessant barrage of criticism at Oggy for the first fifteen minutes, during which he found himself out of position once or twice. 'Get him the hell off!' screamed one of these cognoscenti of the goalkeeping arts. When Oggy proceeded to make three terrific saves, arcing like a salmon to parry shots headed towards the corners by the excellent Muzzy Izzet and Neil Lennon, and one point-blank bullet from Matt Elliott, the four responded rapturously and decided Oggy was a good old stick after all. The 0–0 half-time score was not reassuring.

In the second half, a lateish Leicester goal seemed to spell the end of things, but two minutes later Dion flicked an adroit pass across goal, and Whelan ghosted in to score crisply. And in the last ten minutes it was Coventry, if anyone, who was going to win it. On balance a draw was a bit lucky, but it was a gritty performance.

It was, Oggy said after the game, the hardest the team had had to fight all year to get a result. Gordon said that Oggy – 'the best uncapped goalkeeper I've ever seen' – had taken his knocks (largely from the brutish Emile Heskey) and had been 'magnificent'. But Coventry had, in fact, looked a little jaded: I hadn't seen the midfield so comprehensively outhustled all season. Perhaps it was the Bramall Lane result kicking in? Or might it be that City were experiencing for the first time in some years the feeling that the season was as good as over? On 43 points before the game, and with an extra one now tucked away, we were clearly going to stay up. And as for qualifying for Europe, it was almost certainly too late. To do that, we would have to continue in the form we'd shown since the defeat at Chelsea, and that wasn't going to happen. We weren't that good. Oggy put it realistically: 'This is a good team, with a lot of good players, but we still have to rely on heart, and fitness. There's still a way to go.'

Which is why Gordon was still going on about 46 points (a figure he puckishly admitted to have picked out of the air) as his safety target, and until that was achieved he would talk of nothing else. This was a bit funny, because at the same time Martin O'Neill (with Leicester 3 points behind Coventry) was scoffing at any mention of the possibility of relegation, and still thinking about Europe. All Leicester needed to find, O'Neill said wistfully, was someone who could score twenty goals a season.

Dion was momentarily stuck on nineteen, but he'd get there soon enough. There was still no indication that he was going to sign a new contract. But Martin O'Neill wasn't going to get him: Dion had his eyes on bigger things. And, it transpired, on an even bigger salary. During the previous week, Richardson and Strachan had made yet another attempt to get Dublin to sign. 'After all,'

Richardson told me, 'if he signs now, instead of waiting for another fourteen months, he'll go on to the new salary immediately, and that will produce a serious amount of extra money. So I told him, "We're not that far apart, let's sit down and talk."' At which point Dion informed the chairman that he now wanted £25,000 a week. 'I suppose his agent is winding the situation up,' said Richardson unhappily, 'but it is out of the question. The England call-up is brilliant for Dion, and the profile of the club, but perhaps not so good for us financially.'

It would, I presumed, ruin the wage structure? 'Look,' said Richardson, 'there's no such thing as a wage structure really. That makes it sound too formal. But your Bergkamps are always going to get more than your Ray Parlours, that's a fact. And my problem with Dion is that that is too much money, that's all, and we shouldn't pay it. I can't imagine who would. But if he wants to go and try to get it,' he added, sounding fed up, 'then good luck to him. He has every right to max-imise his earnings, but we must, for Gordon's sake, and the supporters', know if he's staying or not. If he won't sign a new contract, he will have to be sold this summer.'

It may be that Dion was as aware of his talismanic status at Coventry as the fans were, and was trying to profit from it. Why shouldn't he? If a team is demon-strably unable to win without its star player, that player has a right to be regarded, and paid, as someone special. Although Dublin had not missed a game since the coming of Moldovan, it was possible that, as Moldovan slowly settled in, Dion would not be as essential to the side as he had been. Certainly, three recent games had been won with Dion in defence. Had Richard Shaw been fit, and Dion unavailable, those games (like the ones at Southampton and at Palace) would surely have been won anyway. Or would they?

I suspect that what was going on was that Dion was actually worried that, having made an outrageous wage demand of £20,000 a week, Coventry, equally outrageously, were about to pay it. But – by this surmise – he didn't want them to pay it; he wanted to go, without actually asking to do so, hence the increased demand. However, since he wouldn't talk about it, nobody was quite sure what he was up to. I'd had an occasional chat with him, in passing at Ryton, or in a hotel lobby, but as soon as I tried to extend the time with a suggestion that we have a cup of tea, he would counter by saying that I should set up an interview at Ryton. Though outwardly amiable, Dion was, in fact, one of the least accessible of the players on an informal basis. He shared the general distrust of outsiders, and the dislike of journalists, but he also seemed aware of his growing celebrity, and didn't give himself away easily.

Gordon said he'd seen it coming for a few games – we'd been lucky to get a draw at Leicester – and, after all, we were never likely to beat the Villa twice in a row, so the 2–1 loss at Highfield Road didn't come as a surprise. Before the game, and still feeling the afterglow of the win at Villa Park in the Cup, I'd asked him if the players felt that there was something special about fixtures with the Villa. 'I don't think so,' he said. 'Most of them haven't been here long enough to care. That's for the fans. Anyway, it isn't a derby in the sense that same-city games are – Liverpool and Everton, or Man United against City – I played in some of those, and there was something special about them. Big ground, big atmosphere. But not Coventry and the Villa.' All the players I canvassed agreed, even Oggy, though he had been at the club so long, he admitted, that he did feel something special about the Villa matches, 'but only because I know so many people who care about it. I don't myself.'

Under new manager John Gregory, Villa had risen up the table and looked increasingly confident. Two sharply taken Dwight Yorke goals put them well in control, and the final score of 2–1 didn't flatter them. Though Gordon denied that City now had nothing to play for – the very idea made him professionally cross – and believed that a relaxed player would play better than an anxious one, City still looked a little flat.

It was even worse at our happy hunting ground, White Hart Lane. This time it was Spurs rather than City who feared relegation, and a dour fixture ended in a 1–1 draw when Dublin equalised late in the game from Coventry's only chance. Spurs, still without the right blend, looked apprehensive, but still should have won. City, becoming harder and harder to beat, managed to wangle the sort of point that, over the last few years, we would have found it impossible to come away with.

Some time after the game, Trond Soltvedt made an interesting observation. I had remarked to him that it was surprising that Spurs were struggling, given the quality of their squad, and, in particular, the tremendous form of David Ginola. But Soltvedt was unimpressed. 'They don't look a very good side to me. At Highfield Road they were very poor after we scored the first goal. And though they worked very hard in this game, they looked unhappy and without confidence.'

'Is this the fault of Christian Gross?' I wondered.

'Not exactly. I think the problem is Ginola.'

'I love David Ginola,' I said. It is yet another example of the perversity of the French that they think they have better players available to their international squad than Ginola, or, previously, Cantona: two of the outstanding players in the English Premiership over the past few years.

'A lot of the Spurs players don't like playing with him in midfield,' said Trond. 'He's selfish, and he keeps the ball too long. He only thinks of himself. If he plays a ball he wants it back immediately in a one-two, and he doesn't make the kinds of passes that the strikers want.'

'Is that what Klinsmann and Gross were arguing about?'
A couple of months earlier Jürgen Klinsmann had been
quoted as saying that Ginola should be playing on the
wing, as he had at Newcastle, and that he disagreed
with Gross's deployment of him in a free role in the
middle of the pitch. Klinsmann was disparaged in the
press for the remark, because journalists, like Spurs fans,
love watching Ginola, especially in his new free role.

'Yes. And the other players agreed with him.'

Soltvedt, whose form had improved over the previous
few games in an extended run due to Gary McAllister's
injury, had had a stressful, but satisfying, introduction to
English football. 'When I came from Rosenborg,' he said,
'I expected to be in the first team. I always have been, and
Rosenborg are a good side – they would come in the top
ten of the Premier League. So when the gaffer played me
for the first seven games I was grateful, but I thought
I deserved my place, and I thought I was playing well.
The major difference here is in the first twenty minutes
– everything happens so . . . fast.' He shook his head. 'I
don't know the word for it.'

'Frenzied?' I suggested.

'Maybe that's it,' he said, a little doubtfully, 'but very
fast. I wasn't used to it. But I was maybe a little tired,
too, because when I came here I had just finished the
season in Norway. When the results after the first games
weren't so good – we drew some home games, like
Bolton and West Ham, which we should have won – the
gaffer told me that he thought we needed to make some
changes, and I got dropped. That had never happened
to me before.' (Bryan Richardson, though not regretful
about signing Soltvedt, had agreed with the decision: 'We
thought him, perhaps, just a little short of Premiership
standard.')

'Was it devastating?' I asked Soltvedt.

'No,' he said thoughtfully, 'not that. But I was very
upset, and I thought to myself that I would have to work
even harder and show the gaffer that he was wrong. But

when you are not sure of your place, and you play sometimes as a substitute, it is harder to play your best, and keep up with the pace. Now I have had a regular place I feel I am playing much better.'

The recent £625,000 signing of Belgian international midfield player Philippe Clement, due to join the team in July, together with the likely return of McAllister, meant that Trond's future first-team appearances might be limited, and Soltvedt knew it. I hesitated to ask him about it, because it seemed insensitive: so, what do you think of this fellow who's just done you out of a job? I still hadn't adjusted – and I suppose I had no desire to do so – to the harshness of this world, its unrelenting insistence upon competition for places, its overvaluation of winning. I was brought up in the mushy world of university teaching, where, on the basis of an hour-long interview and a couple of references, one was given a job for life. Not only did we feel, in those days, that this was agreeable, we thought it was right. This may, in retrospect, seem naïve, but it certainly left me with a soft spot for the plight of people in tougher professions. I don't know how they can bear it. If I had known I could lose my job at any moment, because my professor had found a replacement who was that little bit sharper than me on Prosody, and had a wider perspective on Modernism, I wouldn't have worked harder to ensure my place, I would have folded with anxiety.

It's a very hard world, and uncongenial to me. I hated talking to Oggy after he was dropped. I loathed watching Salako after Gordon decided that he didn't fit into his plans. I couldn't bear seeing Martin Johansen mooching about, unable to get a game. I disliked having to ask Soltvedt about Clement. I wanted everybody to play all the time – as many as the pitch would take, like kids mucking about in the park – and I wanted them all to be happy.

'What do you know, Trond,' I asked, in a tone intended to mix gentle understanding with a tinge of bonhomie, like a cross between a psychotherapist and a *Blue Peter* presenter, 'about this fellow Clement?' Soltvedt was sufficiently experienced to deal with such questions, but a slight stiffening of his facial muscles, which affected his voice, betrayed the underlying feeling. 'I don't know much about him,' he said, a little woodenly. 'He came on for the last few minutes when I was playing for Norway against Belgium, but you couldn't tell much from that. They say he's a good player.'

At much the same time that Coventry were signing Clement, Soltvedt learned that he had been left out of the Norwegian squad for the forthcoming international match, a bad sign with the World Cup just round the corner. Had that come as a surprise?

'No, the boss called and told me he's trying some new players. Half the squad is different. He also told me that I won't be going to the World Cup.'

He said this so equably that it rather took me aback: Soltvedt was thirty-one, and though he had never had a regular place with Norway, he had won a handful of caps. This was, surely, his last chance to appear in a World Cup?

He paused to think for a second, and to adjust his English. 'I think I am . . . relieved, really,' he said. 'You see, my wife is having a baby in June. I've been playing football steadily – like non-stop, almost – for the last three years. I want to be at home, to see more of my family, and be there when the baby comes. It is hard when you come to a new country. Even when we came to England, which is quite like Norway in a lot of ways, it was still hard to settle down. We are lucky, we have nice neighbours, who have been very kind to us, but my son had to go to a new school when he was just five, and he didn't speak a word of English.'

His sensitive face creased with pain at the memory, and he looked, fleetingly, his full age. He put his hand on his heart, as if only that gesture could adequately articulate the feeling: 'And it hurt so much. I like to take him to school, and every day, for months, he would hold on to me and cry. And then one of the kids hit him in the face in the playground, and he couldn't even tell the teacher what had happened.'

'Didn't it help that you were a well-known football player?

He smiled. 'Maybe a little. When I went to pick him up some of the kids would raise their arms and go, "City! City!" and maybe that made it easier. But he is very shy, and he would lower his head' – Trond ducked his head into his chest, cowering slightly, by way of example – 'and say in a little voice, "Come now, Dad, please, let's go." It was very hard, and very hard for my wife.' He brightened up. 'But it's better now: his English is so good, perfect. We're very happy.'

A drawn home match with Liverpool followed, the 1–1 result a reasonable reflection of play, though Liverpool pressed hard in the last twenty minutes. Once again Michael Owen, who scored a neat goal, was given the headlines. He'd become the darling of the press for the moment, but I could see that Nilsson's assessment of him still carried some weight. The major thing he did during the afternoon, as far as I was concerned, was to try to get David Burrows sent off by falling to the ground after a challenge, rolling about histrionically and clutching his eye. Replays later showed that Burrows had made no contact, so presumably Owen must have got a fly in it.

In the corner by the puddings – you got a choice of fruit salad, chocolate mousse, cheesecake, and something obscure and nasty-looking with cream in it – Dion Dublin leaped into the air and feigned a jump shot. It looked good: he got up well, his back straight, neck arched slightly and his fingers poised elegantly as he released the invisible ball. He came down grinning. He is apparently an excellent basketball player, and was later to tell me that he would 'much rather' watch an NBA game on television than the FA Cup final.

Most of the rest of us were still finishing our dinners

at the Leeds Crown Plaza Holiday Inn, where, with the
benefit of a private dining room, we had the luxury of
a blaring television, showing Bruce Forsyth's *Play Your
Cards Right*. At the managerial table, where Gordon had
allowed Bertie to join us for the meal, Garry Pendrey
watched eagerly. 'Higher!' he cried. 'Two hundred!'
Gordon nodded in agreement as the card was turned.
Higher it was. 'I'd be three hundred ahead by now,'
said Pendrey happily.

To my left, physiotherapist George Dalton was eating his meal quietly, and I took the chance to ask him
if George Boateng's dead leg had been responding to
treatment.

'We'll have to see,' he said, without looking up.

'If he's not playing tomorrow, what are the chances for
Wednesday night against Wimbledon?'

He glared at me, his face puckering as if he'd just
sucked a lemon. 'You're starting to sound like a fuckin'
journalist,' he said tartly. 'I said we'll just have to see.'
His moods ranged from dour to hostile. I didn't think
he'd miss me the next year. From across the table Bertie
made his 'you'd better shut up' face, and, reflecting how
little trust I seemed to have gained over the course of the
season – what did George think I wanted to do, sell the
story to the *Sun*? – I decided to refresh myself with some
pudding.

I now had three excuses to make my move: (1) George
was being a pain in the arse; (2) I loathe Bruce Forsyth
almost as much – and for the same reasons – as I detest
Cilla Black, that other icon of the English love of the
common; and (3) Dion's practice jump shot had given
me an idea. Leaving the table quickly, I headed for the
desserts. Dublin, obligingly, shoved over, and the two of
us contemplated our choices.

'I don't think,' I said, with what I hoped would sound
like a kind of casual chumminess, as if we had met in a
sports bar, 'that the Bulls can do it again.' (The American
NBA Championships were just beginning.)

He looked up sharply. At last I'd said something that interested him. 'Sure they will. When it comes to it, Michael always comes through. They'll win it again.'

'Bet you a fiver they won't.'

He considered this carefully. 'Only if you name the team that will.'

'Utah Jazz,' I said, after some thought, 'though I don't really believe that it will be them. But somebody is going to beat the Bulls. Longley is hurt, Jordan hasn't been at his best and Rodman bottled the play-offs last year.'

Dion gave his best Jordan-like grin, a smile so infectious and immediate that you could see what he must have looked like as a little boy, friendly and direct. I suspect that he grew up surrounded by love. 'It's a bet, easy money,' he said, contentedly.

'Fancy a cup of tea and a chat after dinner?' I interjected quickly, taking advantage of the fleeting camaraderie.

The smile faded. 'Will it take long?'

'It'll be pretty painless,' I promised, 'like a visit to a good dentist.'

A few moments later my plan was almost disrupted when Dion's room-mate, Willo, showed up bearing large ice-cream sundaes with chocolate sauce and a lot of whipped cream, which Dion eyed longingly. 'Just hang on for a couple of minutes,' he said, 'and I'll be right back for mine. Don't let it melt.' Willo nodded uncertainly and looked apprehensively at the dishes, unclear as to how you stop ice-cream from melting, as Dion and I headed off for the bar.

'Let's sit over here,' he said, pointing to a corner, 'for the view.' Around us a number of self-consciously befrocked local ladies were having a drink before dinner.

'Do you remember those women up at Liverpool before Christmas?' I asked. 'The ones in all the party dresses? Did you see the one in the gold lamé gown with the great bum?'

He concentrated hard. 'No, can't say I do.'

'That's funny, it was pretty memorable. A lot of the

guys noticed her – you know, Telf, Snowy, Huck, sitting out in the lobby having a laugh . . .'

'I love that,' said Dion, 'I love all the banter, and the mickey-taking. There was a lot of it under Ron, he was a good laugh. And he was the best manager I've ever known at motivating a team – especially for a single game, but even over the season.'

'Is Gordon good at that?'

He reflected for a minute. 'In a different way. He's more of a player's manager – he's still a Premiership player himself, and he's a great coach, great in training. You see him running about passing the ball around and it's impossible not to have respect for him. All the guys do, every one, you won't hear a word said against him by anybody. He's been brilliant. He's got such a lot of passion for the club, it drives you on.'

'I wonder if that doesn't have some negative effects? It seemed to me that, when we were having a hard time in mid-season, Gordon's frantic shouting from the sidelines made the players jumpy, and maybe contributed to some of the bookings we were getting.'

He shrugged. 'Everything has a down side.'

'What was Gordon like,' I asked gingerly, knowing the topic to be dangerous, 'when you were having your contract negotiations with Bryan Richardson?'

'Brilliant. He just took me aside and said that as long as things were OK between me and him, that was all he asked. And I kept my mouth closed for that whole time, because I knew that whatever I said it was going to be taken the wrong way. So you just let your football do the talking for you, and I've been lucky, and had a great season.'

'I know you don't like to be asked, but what is the likelihood of you going?'

He hesitated, wondering how much to say. 'I th   '
he said, 'that it is likely. But it's too early to say
been very happy here. It's a great bunch of lad
when you've been at a big club, it's different, the

302 • STAYING UP

you so well. I loved the set-up at Manchester United, but I was right to go. There were all these strikers ahead of me, I was probably fifth in line: Eric, Hughes, McClair – even Scholes. I don't regret going, but a big club is something different . . . The thing is, people always say that there are like two leagues within the Premiership, but that's wrong. There are four or five big clubs, but that doesn't mean there are four or five big *teams*. The smaller teams can beat the big ones, it happens all the time. That's what's so interesting about English football.'

He had been on the bench for the England international against Portugal, having played the full previous match, and Glenn Hoddle was known to admire him as both a target man and a central defender. What did he think about his chances for the World Cup?

'I would love to go. When I first got picked, the whole week before the match everything was really new to me – going down to train with the team, and all the media coverage. One time I was being interviewed, and there were thirty or forty microphones being pushed at me, and I could hardly believe it. I've never experienced that – it was like they were talking to Michael Jordan. There was a lot of nerves at that point, but when I put on the England shirt, and ran out on to the pitch, and then I'm standing there belting out the anthem, I thought 'Let me at them!', and after that it was fine, brilliant. Loved every minute of it.'

He was sitting back comfortably now, his guard down for the moment. From the corner of the bar Willo came over, to inform him of the state of the ice-cream (gooey), and Dion got up to go. 'Any time you want a chat, mate, just let me know,' he said airily, but I thought sincerely, as he wandered away.

The conversation, in both tone and content, felt right to me as I sat back with my drink. It marked how far I'd come. I was not, of course, likely to have many more chats with Dion Dublin – after the close of the season I might never speak to him, or to most of the rest of the players, again. But I felt less anxious in their presence, less inclined to tiptoe around them. By now, either they liked me, and wished to talk to me, or they didn't. It was up to them. When I arrived at Ryton now, or at an hotel, the hellos felt genuine, the reception easygoing. 'How's it going, big man?' I would be asked (the other person called 'big man' is Dion), and I didn't feel shoulders hunched against me.

David Burrows noticed the difference as well. 'The lads have got used to your face. They don't know exactly what you're up to, but they are interested. You'll see a change after the book comes out. Most of them will look at it, some will read it. And if it's all right, then you'll see it when you come up to Ryton. People will know you and trust you, ask you to go for a drink, that sort of thing. I know I will. You'll be part of the set-up, because they'll know what you do. You'll be the guy who wrote the book.'

It was a helpful observation, because part of what had impeded me all year was that I didn't fit in, didn't have a role. Football is an immensely hierarchical game: from the class divisions enshrined in the seating of the spectators to the pecking order in the boardroom; from the kids at the lowest youth level, busily cleaning the boots of the senior players, through the youth and reserve teams, to (and even in) the first team; from the lower levels of youth-team managers up to Gordon Strachan; everyone knows his place, and defers, however sub-liminally, to those of higher rank. They are united, of course, by football, which, whether they are playing, managing or administrating it, provides the glue that holds them together. But I am neither an employee of the club, nor a journalist, nor, any longer, simply a fan. And so, not being able to fit me in, they hadn't known what to make of me. They weren't nervous, that would be putting it too strongly. Just a little unsure. And that, too, had passed.

Buoyed by this hard-won self-confidence, I decided to

press on and take on the Company. Outside the bar, overlooking the lobby, there they were, having their after-dinner tea. Whelan, Huckerby and Shaw were reclining on an oversized settee, and looked up at me as I approached, their eyelids hooded, like snakes basking on a rock. With Noel and Huck the look is endemic, a sign of some great inward lassitude, but with Shawsy it's more complex, the eyes clear and intelligent, but never quite meeting yours, radiating wary impenetrability. In a chair next to them, Telfer was pouring tea.

'I was wondering,' I said, 'if games like this one are hard to get motivated for?' It immediately felt the wrong sort of question. Rephrase. 'Nothing to play for sort of thing?'

The boys hooded their eyes extra hard, and sank further into the cushions. As often happens, Telf spoke on their behalf, and, as usual, he wasn't giving anything away. 'All games are important,' he said. 'You still have to try as hard as you can. If you're a player like me, and you have to work hard, then you never let up. But Huckerby,' he added with a straight face, 'sometimes he can't be bothered.'

Huck turned his head languidly to the side, in indication of the fact that he had heard this, but he didn't say anything.

'This your first full season, isn't it?' asked Telfer.

Huck nodded, allowing that, sure enough, so it was.

'So how many games have you played, then?'

Huck thought about this for a long time. 'Maybe forty.'

Whelan shook himself to life. 'Forty? Nah.'

'Will you have any problem getting yourself up for the game tomorrow?' I asked Huck, a little disingenuously.

Huck slid further down the cushion, making himself more comfortable. He didn't look like he'd be able to get himself up to have a pee.

'Me? No problem,' he said lazily.

In the previous season's fixture, Huckerby had terrorised the Leeds defence, making innumerable sinuous
runs, scoring one goal and creating a host of chances
as Coventry won 3–1, only our second-ever victory at
Elland Road. But this season was likely to be different: Leeds, placed fifth in the table and heading for
Europe, were in the process of becoming stingier and
more George Graham-like, and anyway, in testimony
to Huck's menace, he was to be individually marked
by the combative and adhesive Irish international Gary
Kelly.

In comparison to 1996–7, it kept Huck relatively quiet:
he made only four breathtaking solo runs, in each beating
his marker with that compelling combination of pace,
strength and fabulous close control. In each case he went
one-on-one against Nigel Martyn (who was named as
PFA goalkeeper of the season), provoking memories of
three similar efforts against David Seaman at Highfield
Road, all of which Seaman saved.

Either Martyn isn't as good as Seaman, or Huck had
improved. Three of them went in – Huckerby's first hat-
trick – while the other, a delicate chip over the keeper,
went just wide. Following the first goal, an equaliser
after Jimmy Floyd Hasselbaink had made both Breeny
and Oggy look a little silly, Huck raced over to the
Coventry end and executed a clumsy cartwheel, followed
by an aggressive series of arm thrusts, in perfect parody
of Hasselbaink's mode of celebration. (When the goal
was shown on television that evening the commentator,
unaware that Huckerby is a wit, simply thought him
ungraceful.) After his second goal, again to equalise one
by Hasselbaink (and again one that Oggy might have
saved), Huck returned to salute the crowd, his arms held
aloft, a look of beatific pleasure on his face, eyelids no
longer hooded, but positively aloft, aglow with feeling.
If that isn't better than sex, I'd like to get to know his
girlfriend. His third goal (his fifteenth of the season),
which followed a superb through ball from Soltvedt

early in the second half, looked to have won the game until Leeds equalised after Kewell got the better of Roland Nilsson.

Gary McAllister, already a month ahead of schedule in his recovery, had made the journey up to Leeds to watch the match. 'I love this club,' he told me. 'I was really happy here. But they give me a really hard time when I come back; call me "Judas," that sort of thing. But I never really wanted to leave. What happened was I found out there were three or four players making twice as much as me, so I went in to the chairman to see if we could sort it. I wanted to stay,' he said a little wistfully, 'it's a great club. I would have stayed if they'd offered me half of what Coventry were offering . . .'

After the game, the managers were united in their praise of Huckerby's display. 'That must be one of the best all-round attacking performances of the season,' said George Graham. 'He was sensational. He had everything – touch and finishing. He was direct, held the ball up, and his passing was good. If he plays like that every week there's no doubt that there should be a place for him in the World Cup.' To which one could only retort: if he played like that every week, George, they would name the World Cup after him.

Gordon had worked hard with Huck all season, and hadn't been slow to criticise him, even after good performances, but this time he was effusive: 'In all the games I've watched I have not seen anyone play like that. He is doing things I've never seen before. No one could have stopped him. In the World Cup things are very tight and England need someone like him, a player who can turn a game any time. He has individual brilliance and he is definitely now going about his job with more awareness about what he is doing. People like him can win cups.' Given that it was only three months before that Gordon had described him as 'nowhere near international level', Huckerby was quietly delighted: 'When you get praise like that from the gaffer, it means something.'

The following Wednesday's game, though, at home to Wimbledon, had all the hallmarks of tepid end-of-season fare. Needing a point to be sure of survival, and having drawn three of their last five games at Coventry 0–0, Wimbledon set out to spoil the game, as Chris Perry (who never gave Huckerby a sniff) later admitted. The City side looked jaded, and Dublin seemed to be having one of those I-don't-feel-like-playing evenings. Or perhaps he was never allowed to. But Magnus Hedman looked distinctly pleased to be back between the posts. Oggy, dropped for the second time this season, looked gloomy as he took his place in the dugout, though he perked up as the game went on.

Speaking some time later, Oggy was quietly philosophical. 'Look,' he said, 'the writing has been on the wall. I'm forty, and we've signed the Swedish goalkeeper. It hasn't been a bad season, all in all. I've played thirty games.' And he was not considering – as he had suggested to me after the Southampton game that he might – going elsewhere to get first-team football. 'I'll stick with it. This is a good club, and I'll just have to fight to get my place back.'

Gordon overreacted neither to the efforts at Leeds, nor to the boring draw with Wimbledon. He had never really believed that a European place was likely, and, having achieved the aim of staying up, was already ruminating about what might be done to make the side better the next year: 'We just lack a bit. We're one pass away from great moves and it's the difference between good teams and great teams.' That Coventry had become a good team was beyond doubt. By the end of the season, Dublin and Huckerby had scored thirty-six League goals between them (after Blackburn's Sutton and Gallacher, the best partnership in the Premiership), the midfield had pace, athleticism and quality, the defence was solid, both goalkeepers gave one confidence. As May began we had lost only one League game since 10 January, and only three teams in the Premiership (Arsenal, Manchester United, Liverpool) had lost fewer games during the season.

If we could keep the side – a youngish one, as Gordon kept saying – together, 1998–9 could be even better. But Jonathan Strange anxiously insisted that, without Dublin, it would all fall apart. He felt the same way about Cyrille Regis, and seems to have the impression that City need a pivotal figure through whom the play can flow, though I don't see why. Which is not to say that Huckerby and Moldovan would form a productive partnership – they make, as Soltvedt remarked, similar kinds of runs, and would require a different kind of service from that provided to Dublin. Dion has a lot of time for Viorel – 'He's good, but it always takes time for foreign players to get used to the pace. I can't think of anybody except Eric who slotted right in' – and believes that he will eventually make a big contribution. But then again, he would. He doesn't like to think of himself as about to abandon ship, just considering moving on.

Richardson, talking on the day of the Wimbledon game, appeared resigned to the loss of Dublin. 'Liverpool inquired about him last month,' he said, 'and we quoted them a price of £6 million. They didn't get back about it then, but I suspect they will over the summer. I don't think it matters that there's only a year left on his contract. If they want him now, they'll make a move. I think Paul Ince has been pushing hard for the signing – he and Dion were mates when Dion was at United – and they want him to play up front with Owen.'

'There are problems, aren't there, with Robbie Fowler?'

'I think that they may well let him go.'

'Would the money be available for Gordon to replace Dion?'

'All of it, certainly,' Richardson assured me. 'We are close to signing another young Dutch player, name of Boudewijn Zenden – George [Boateng] recommended him – who plays for PSV. Gordon's been over to watch him, and Ray Clarke has been tracking him. Plays on the wide left side of midfield. Strong and athletic like Clement, too. So when Gary Mac comes back we should have as strong a midfield as I can remember here, or anywhere, for that matter.'

'Where would that leave Noel Whelan?'

'He might go back up front. He likes it there, and with him and Viorel and Huck it isn't clear we would need another striker. We are looking to find a right back to replace Roland eventually, though he's been magnificent, and we might try to add an experienced, quality centre back. These days we need a strong squad to compete seriously. Nothing short will do – we'll have 45,000 seats to fill soon.'

There had been rumours during the past week, this time linking Huckerby to Liverpool. But Richardson was dismissive of them: 'Haven't heard a thing. Nobody's been in touch with me'.

'Anyway,' he added firmly, 'Huckerby isn't going any-where.'

15

A Relegation Battle and a Final Report

Coventry v. Blackburn, 2 May
Everton v. Coventry, 10 May

As we walked down Swan Lane towards Highfield Road, prior to the final home match of the season, against Blackburn, a group of four enormous nuns, one of them with a beard, passed us singing something about Burnley going down (presumably there is some rivalry between these northern B-places). As they caught sight of Anna, yet again in a short black skirt and looking distinctly more Chelsea than Coventry, they stopped in their tracks, gave a series of Oo!-Oo! grunts, and broke into applause. She tipped her head slightly at this theologically disgraceful display, blushing, as Barbara, Bertie and I giggled. We'd never been to a game as a family, and Mark Jones had kindly left us a couple of complimentary Vice-Presidents' tickets at the VIP window.

Outside the ground I picked them up with a studied casualness that Bertie spotted immediately. 'Makes you feel a bit of a snoot, doesn't it?' he said slyly as I clutched my free tickets in my hand. But, to tell the truth, I was already beginning to feel something of an ex-snoot. Though I hadn't yet assimilated what it had all meant, and its implications for the next year, I was very aware that my tenure behind the scenes was drawing to a close. I had an elegiac sense about the forthcoming match, and it was important to me that the family should be there together.

Barbara had only been to Highfield Road three times: once to see the 7–2 loss in that friendly with Benfica, once for a 6–1 defeat by Liverpool (during the second half of which she had leaned towards me conspiratorially and asked, 'How can you support these wankers?') and once to watch a dire goalless draw against QPR. So it was brave of her to come. I was hoping that she'd get to see a decent match: Blackburn were sixth in the table, with a good chance of getting into Europe, while we still had the slimmest hopes of doing so ourselves. And George Boateng was back after his dead leg; she'd go for George.

It turned out to be just the sort of game she likes: she was a great fan of John McEnroe, and is fond of a bit of the 'you cannot be serious' sort of thing. We were sitting just to the left of the Blackburn dugout, a few feet away from the disgruntled and bestubbled Tim Flowers, who'd been dropped in favour of the in-form (and ex-Coventry) keeper John Filan. After the usual niggly first twenty minutes, with George swooping and buzzing in midfield, as if unsure what species he belonged to (Gary McAllister, commenting on Boateng, once said to me: 'There's quite a lot to be said, sometimes, for just standing there. Then the ball can come to you'), referee Steve Lodge turned down an appeal for handball in the Blackburn area, and waved play on. Surrounded by City players, and feeling a tingling in his arm (which signals either the electric impulse triggered by a linesman, or the onset of a heart-attack), Lodge stopped play, went over to the sideline for a chat with his Mr Vosper, and gave the penalty.

At which point, we noticed, Tim Flowers jumped off his seat and raced, like a demented quiz-show contestant anxious to deliver the right answer, down the sideline towards the referee's assistant. Flowers' answer to the question 'Which part of the female anatomy does this linesman remind you of?' was repeated four times, so loudly that Lodge, after the game, saw no need to confirm which letter it began with. All he had to do, in fact, was to send Flowers off, thus reducing Blackburn, as I explained to Barbara, to eleven men. Lodge, who was called an 'absolute disgrace' by Gordon on his last visit to Highfield Road – for which Strachan had been warned as to his future behaviour by the FA – remarked after the game that, in twenty-eight years of refereeing, he'd never before sent off a substitute before he came on to the pitch, and that Highfield Road sure was an interesting place to work.

The incident didn't improve the morale of the Blackburn players. Up to this point, Colin Hendry had been winning his 'How many interesting things can you do with your elbows?' contest with Chris Sutton when Sutton decided to expand his repertoire by using his feet, and scythed down Noel Whelan so callously that a mêlée ensued, with players calling each other the names of bits of both men's and women's anatomies.

Hoots of derision had followed the England keeper on his walk to the dressing room, and Barbara watched with pleasure and keen interest: why hadn't I told her that a football match was like a good episode of *EastEnders*? And Dion had knocked in the penalty, she liked that too. She liked it even better towards the end of the first half when George Boateng, to whom she'd taken an immediate shine, latched on to a ball inside the area, and scored his first goal for the club.

George had been promising some sort of grand celebration when this event finally occurred, but in the event, he later explained, he didn't have the energy. 'I got a great touch and then, bang! – a lovely shot! It is difficult to describe the feeling. It's like being born again.' Rarely have religious and sporting fervour been so happily conjoined. 'But when it happened, I was so tired I couldn't celebrate properly. I have been out injured for a few weeks and didn't train until Thursday, so my legs were a bit weary.' I can't imagine what he'd had in mind: running a marathon round the pitch? He restrained himself, however, and instead danced about gleefully, throwing kisses to the crowd like a prima ballerina.

With Mexican waves rippling round the ground (some of the vice-presidents even stood up) the second half had a partyish atmosphere. At the end of the game, which finished 2–0, thanks in part to the excellence of Magnus Hedman, the players congregated at the centre of the pitch and did a lap of honour. The crowd stayed on to applaud – even the vice-presidents – and the players politely applauded back. It was lovely to end the season with a such a good performance. It was clear what we'd been missing, these last few weeks. We'd been missing George.

After the close of play, there was a buffet and some entertainment scheduled at the Vice-Presidents', and I thought that having the family there would mark the end of the season in a festive way. But, as we entered the dining room, none of us fancied it. I'd never felt comfortable there – probably my own fault; no one had been unfriendly to me – so we set off for the Ladbroke Club, to which I intend to return next year, and had a drink with Guy and Max.

After Sunday's away match with Everton – ironically yet another final-day relegation battle, only this time it was theirs, not ours – my season as fan-in-residence would have ended. The experience had, as my reader will be aware, been an uncomfortable and frustrating one, but with the compensating exhilaration of being close to the action, and (what's more) being able to tell my friends about it. But I had not supposed that being, as it were, a resident outsider would be so complex.

As I have said, I had been interested in how the staff and players would respond to a stranger in their midst, and in observing and charting their reactions. I intentionally made my status ambiguous by refusing to behave as if I were a journalist. I relied on what chance threw up, on my eyes and ears, and recorded what I remembered of the experience as it was passing.

What I had not counted on, and did not expect, were the effects of the experience on me. I had offered myself up as an observer and an outsider, and was duly, and rightly enough, treated as one. From the beginning Gordon, his staff and the players had dictated the ground rules: I was allowed (By Order of the Chairman) to be there, but this didn't give me any rights. For the first three or four months it was made clear that I was unwelcome and an object of suspicion, and what friendly counsel I did receive (from Oggy, John Salako and David Burrows, for instance) was to just sit tight until people got used to my presence.

Sitting tight meant just being there, and (largely) keeping mum. This is foreign to my nature. I'm friendly, curious about the world and interested in other people. But none of these qualities helped a bit: indeed, for many months, over dinner at the managerial table, I was implicitly forbidden even to initiate a topic of conversation. During the playing of the Ryder Cup, for example, I came in to dinner and asked Gordon (who loves golf) what he thought of the play. 'Good,' he said, and turned away to talk to Alex Miller.

I don't want to generalise unduly here, for I don't believe that this would necessarily have happened to me at any other football club. Just as stereotypes of players are misleading, so too are stereotypes of managers. I cannot imagine Barry Fry and Arsène Wenger having much in common. Some managers are presumably friendlier and less suspicious than others. But Gordon is not by nature easy with outsiders of any kind. He has learned to respond, articulately and thoughtfully, to questions, but he does not initiate much in the way of conversation with strangers. Whether this derives from a lack of interest, or of social self-confidence, I am, even now, unsure. Some combination of both, I imagine. But having watched him in a variety of social situations with fans, at supporters' club dinners and club functions, it is clear that he is never relaxed, has little time for small talk, and is only comfortable with people he knows well. I think he knows and rather regrets this about himself.

The effect of his initial coolness and formality set the tone of what followed, though, as the season progressed, he, like the players, warmed up somewhat. Gordon had told me, from the beginning, that when the lads started to take the piss out of me, I would have made some inroads. But it was he, interestingly, who first did so. As I stood up at Ryton watching practice one day over Christmas, still full of bronchitis, he came over and peered at me intently. 'Got a big red nose there,' he said. 'Where'd that come from?' I replied, in a dignified tone, that it came from the Spirit of Christmas. 'And a lot of it, by the look of things,' he said with a straight face as he walked away. This may not seem to amount to much, but it was one of those barely perceptible moments when things started to shift, and my life among the team became a little less anxiety-provoking.

Yet this experience was supposed to be fun, and it often wasn't. It was pretty lonely and miserable a lot of the time, though there were the compensations of learning, watching, overhearing, asking the odd question. And it got easier as it went on, and more enjoyable. But I would be kidding you, and myself, if I were to claim that I ever entirely relaxed, or was ever encouraged to do so. Not, it bears adding, that the players ever did so, either. The prevalent form of hanging out and casual piss-taking is not a form of relaxation, but a parody of it: players do not reveal their true natures to each other very much (as John Salako remarked), and certainly not in front of the others. Telfer seems to make a conscious point of never saying anything remotely serious in public; Breeny clearly has an inner life that he protects assiduously; Huckerby has a sensitive boyishness to his face that makes him look vulnerable, and I (still) harbour the belief that he plays the fool, rather than being one. The same is true, I suspect, of Noel Whelan, whose face in repose has a poignancy that he never reveals when he is up and about, and who looks like he has a store of painful memories that he keeps strictly to himself. In short – and why be surprised about it? – they have a private part of themselves that has nothing to do with football.

But unlike the players, who of necessity separate their public and private lives, I wanted mine to stay together. I didn't want a football self and a non-football self: that's stupid. I just wanted to walk on in and be me. And that's not what happened: they don't get to do that, so why should I? Gordon had, obscurely, warned me of this on my first meeting with him, when he said that he was only ever relaxed at his house, and that I should talk to him there.

So what I had not been allowed to be, or to reveal, during these long months with the team, was a self. I had been obliged to sit on the sidelines, watch and listen. This had partly been by choice, but if I had been more active, and invited players out for drinks and interviews, it would have made it easy for them to place and to dismiss me. So the problem, all year, had been one of perspective. Think of looking at a picture on a wall: first you have to get it straight, then find the proper distance. If you stand too far from it the details don't emerge; if you get too close you are in danger, as it were, of getting paint on your nose.

I had supposed, in some naïve way, that the players would be interested in me, once a little initial sniffing-out had occurred. 'I am, after all,' I said to Gary McAllister as we played golf one day, 'not the sort of person most of them have met before.' He nodded politely. 'So I assumed,' I added, 'that they might find me an interesting specimen.'

He laughed loudly. 'They couldn't give a fuck,' he said.

Surprised by the kind of passivity that was imposed

on me, I'd made a season-long effort at self-restraint.
I was beholden to Gordon. He was the gaffer, and he
made it reasonably clear to me that my job, if I was
to avoid conflict with him, was to shut up, keep the
right distance and draw my own conclusions. I have no
complaint to make with regard to this. He was under no
obligation to tutor me in the fine points of the game, and
my opinions about football were about as interesting to
him as his about James Joyce would have been to me.

So I was feeling more than slightly relieved as I drove
up the M6 to the Haydock Thistle Hotel with Bertie for the
final fixture against Everton. This was the end, and on balance I'd had enough. I no longer had to tiptoe about, keeping my own counsel, suppressing my impulses towards
conviviality, sitting back and observing from just the
right distance. The hell with it, I thought. I began as
an outsider, looking on, and I've ended as an outsider
observing my own outsiderness. There's something nar-
cissistic about the process. It had begun to feel like some
perverse form of masturbation: watching oneself in a
mirror, fiddling about surreptitiously, trying to get some
pleasure from watching the image.

I wanted to get back among the supporters, because
they, I had come to realise, are what Coventry City
actually is. Gordon Strachan and Darren Huckerby care
about Coventry City Football Club because they are
employed to do so. But in some years' time, Bertie
and I, who will still care, will talk of the Strachan
years, or of the time Huckerby was here, as we talk
now of John Sillett and the Cup side of 1987, and of
Coventry greats like Cyrille Regis, Tommy Hutchison
and Ian Wallace. In time Bryan Richardson will go too,
and we will remember him, and compare his reign with
those of previous chairmen. By that time, Highfield
Road will have been redeveloped into some nasty new
housing complex, and the Microprocessor Pentium II
Stadium, or whatever it is eventually called, will be
in operation. The only things that will stay the same

are the name 'Coventry City Football Club', and us, its supporters.

What is Coventry City Football Club, after all? Gordon and the players, Richardson and the directors and staff? It isn't. It's us: me and Bertie, Jonathan Strange, Max and Guy, the folks round the ground, the Ladbrokeans and even some, God bless them, of the vice-presidents. We are the club, we provide the continuity and the meaning. We have common memories, aspirations and desires, like a tribe or a nation. It is no wonder that the game means too much to us, and that we can behave so foolishly. We're in the hands of heavy archetypes. We no longer have real villages, churches or communities, and the idea of the nation, except at times of war or during the World Cup, fails to move us. So supporting our team focuses a lot of otherwise unallocated feeling, centres and intensifies it. At football matches thousands of otherwise emotionally inarticulate supporters bellow out, 'We Love You City, We Do!' when, I suspect, they would never overtly express that much love to their children or spouses. Certainly not with the same intensity.

So I was reconciled to my imminent removal from behind the scenes to in front of them. There would be a lot of compensations. But I was aware, as I was thinking this, that it had a little sour-grapeishness about it. The key question was this: if Bryan said 'Why not have another year?' would I say yes, or no? And the answer is that I would want to stay. I'd find a role. Perhaps I could help Gordon develop his tactical sense? Or organise proper practice sessions? Or help Huck with this novel?

I made some inarticulate attempt to explain these feelings, and my general sense of frustration, to Bertie as we drove towards Liverpool, and he was distinctly unsympathetic.

'You have had the experience that every fan dreams of,' he said. 'So what if you didn't get closer to the guys? What did you expect – to make friends? They aren't your sort of people, and they're half your age. They play football. Why should they be interested in you?'

This seemed to me fair, but failed to dispel something vinegary in my mood.

'Anyway,' he added, 'you have loved it. I've seen you talking with the fans, and with our friends all year. I've heard every one of your opinions a hundred times – and you have absolutely loved being in the know. It's been, "As Gordon was saying the other day . . ." and, "Actually, Bryan doesn't think that, the true story is . . ."'

'OK,' I said, anxious to cut him off, recognising the ring of truth when I heard it. 'OK, you're right. So why do I feel so low?'

'Because you wanted it to be easy, and fun, and some of it was hard work. And because you're sad that it's over.' He smiled, as much to himself as to me, adding: 'But I know you, and you loved it.'

So something of the ungraciousness of my mood was prompted by the pain of withdrawal. I wouldn't miss my silent dinners at the managerial table, or the uncomfortable rides on the team coach. I could do without hanging about at Ryton hoping to catch a chat with someone, or to overhear something of interest. But I would miss knowing, even from that certain distance, what was going on. I'd got to like a few of the players. I would miss being able to tell people about it all.

And then some surprising things happened.

After checking into the Haydock Thistle, as Bertie and I headed upstairs towards our room, Huckerby came up to me. He put his arm round my shoulders, and said, 'You're not going to disappear next year, are you?'

'Dunno, Huck,' I said. 'I guess so. This is it, really.'

He looked a little sad (I thought) to hear it. 'We've got used to you now,' he said. 'I hope you'll come up and see us next year.'

'I'm sure to see you once the book comes out. There will be some sort of launch up at the club, and I hope we can get together.'

We chatted for a few minutes about the book, and, as he ambled off amiably, up came David Burrows. He was a little concerned, he said, that there might be a riot after the game if Everton lost, and he hoped that Bertie and I would make plans to get away from the ground safely after the match. He gave us good advice on the safest place to park the car. I asked him if, as an ex-Evertonian, he had any feeling about sending them down.

'The chairman just reminded me,' he said, 'that we're on fifteen grand a man if we finish ninth, which we probably will if we win.' (The bonus, of course, would be the direct result of the incentive clause in the new contract that the players had signed at the beginning of the season.)

'Does that matter to you?'

He gave me an incredulous look. 'Would it matter to you?' he asked. 'Sure it matters to me.'

'Fifteen grand? Are we?' asked Dion Dublin, who had ghosted in from the sidelines and joined us. He nodded his head. 'That sounds good to me.' Turning to me, he asked if Bertie and I needed tickets for the game, it being his role as captain of the side to give out the complimentaries. I said I'd be happy to have a couple, but that I was hoping to get Gordon to let me sit in the dugout. Dion raised his eyebrows. 'Not a very good view from there,' he said, 'and it might be a little too close to the action.'

'I want to watch Howard Kendall's face as the game goes on,' I said. 'I still remember the agony of the last few minutes last year against Spurs, and I'd be interested to observe a manager going through the experience. I had spent some time, on the way to Liverpool, remembering the misery of the previous year's climax, that battle to stay up. Because, for Everton, tomorrow's game would be like a Cup final, or a match for the Championship. Oggy told me, for instance, that the delight he felt after the final whistle at White Hart Lane in 1996–7 was at least the equal of his joy at having won the Cup in 1987;

Gary McAllister said that he felt happier than when Leeds won the Championship. It is a mistake to suppose that winning a final relegation battle isn't winning a prize. It is a single game for the biggest prize of them all: continued membership of the Premiership.

But it's too hard on the nerves. 'All I can say,' Gordon observed, 'is that the thirty minutes of celebration when we survived was not worth the four months of hell that preceded them. If you compare the four months of sleepless nights I had last season with the kind of stuff we're getting this year, I'm more than happy.' He had decided, for the week leading up to the Everton match, to keep quiet about the horrors of the previous season. 'I have purposely not mentioned what I went through to try to avoid putting any pressure on Howard or Colin Todd for Sunday's games. Nobody in that position wants patronising, and they certainly don't want advice.'

He didn't seem keen on the idea of me watching from the dugout – it's the sort of thing that he might feel was disrespectful to the other manager, given the circumstances – but he said he'd think it over. He had, however, brought quite a full squad up to Everton, and he wanted all of them in the dugout with him (rather than having those not selected as substitutes sitting up in the stands), 'in case anything goes wrong after the game'. As David Burrows had intimated, there was much concern in Liverpool that, if Everton went down, a riot might ensue. There were five times the normal number of police at the ground, local pubs were to be closed and chairman Peter Johnson was to be given police protection throughout the day. Everton fans, dissatisfied with his perceived unwillingness to sign top-quality players, had already been chanting 'We want your skin!' and the police were concerned that, following relegation, they might try to take it off him.

There was a distinctly different feeling about the Coventry squad, though, an end-of-termish relaxation: faces were brighter, voices louder, postures more relaxed.

All they were playing for, after all, was £15,000 a man: not *that* big a deal. They would not roll over, but they knew that, for this season, the work was really done. There was more smiling, more teasing: some indication of how much pressure they had been under, and for how long a time. At Torquay they had been relatively easy and approachable; as the season progressed the shutters came down; now that the League programme was almost over you could sense the feeling of sheer relief. The vaguely partyish feel in the air was enhanced by the fact that, unusually, Richardson and a number of the directors and their wives were staying in the hotel overnight before the match. Bertie and I ran into them in the bar before dinner.

I had intended for the two of us to eat alone, because I thought I ought to let the players have dinner by themselves on their last night, and, anyway, I wanted to have a good time and a decent meal. Richardson, though, who was in an extremely warm and upbeat mood, insisted that Bertie and I join the directors for dinner. It didn't seem possible, because Bert hadn't brought a suitable jacket. Bryan eyed him carefully. 'About my size, aren't you? Try this on.' He took off his sports jacket and handed it to Bertie, who put it on.

'He looks better than you in it,' remarked deputy chairman Mike McGinnity. 'You ought to give it to him.'

'That's settled, then,' said Richardson, satisfied. 'See you for drinks at about seven.'

It was a thoroughly relaxed set of Coventry folks over dinner: directors McGinnity and John Reason and their wives Diane and Joan, Peter Richardson and his wife Shirley, stadium architect Geoff Mann and his wife Meg, and the chairman himself, dressed in a different jacket. Bertie, always easy in company, looked particularly smart in his other jacket, and Bryan and I jokingly negotiated a price for it. The tone was familiar and cordial, and as I sat laughing, telling them all about the progress of the book, and the difficulties of the early months, I had the sudden, sharp realisation that I was speaking in my own voice.

I'd got my self back. It had never strayed as far in my dealings with Richardson as it had with Strachan, but I recognised it immediately. I didn't feel tense. I wasn't on my best behaviour. I was talking, a little flamboyantly and probably too much, as if I were among friends. I had heard a lot over the year, from Bryan, Gordon and the players, about the fraternity of football, the warmth and conviviality shared by the insiders in the game. I had witnessed examples of it, in directors' boxes, dressing rooms and training grounds, enviously taking mental notes, but always (and irrevocably, I supposed) excluded. Yet now I was, in some odd way, one of them. Much of what was said, as the evening wore on, and a nice amount of drink was consumed, was anecdotal, personal and totally uncensored. No one asked me to keep it off the record, because no one felt the need to. They trusted me.

'Can you imagine,' Bryan was at one point heard to reflect, 'that there are still boardrooms round the League where you get offered a drink but there is no warmth or friendship or fun? Coventry is always warm and friendly, and has been rated the most hospitable club in the Premiership.' It was easy to see why. Talk drifted to the recollections of the night, almost exactly a year ago, before the Spurs game, and the tension of not knowing what was going to happen the next afternoon. 'It's terrible, awful,' said Richardson, 'and Gordon has been quite right to keep mum this week. Nobody who's in that position wants your opinion.'

'Tell them the story about Doug Ellis,' said McGinnity as he poured the red wine.

'It was,' said Richardson, 'a couple of years ago, up at Highfield Road – you'll remember the game, Villa scored in the last minutes to win. Steve Staunton hit one from outside the box, and it took a deflection and shot in. Nothing to be done about it. And at the final whistle [Villa chairman] Doug Ellis comes over to me and says,

"Bad luck, but you'll be all right. You're much too good to go down."'

Drinking from my newly filled wineglass – sitting next to the liberal-handed McGinnity, its contents magically never seemed to diminish – I reflected that that was a pleasant and reassuring thing to say, and that this Doug Ellis person wasn't as bad as he was sometimes said to be. Not a bit of it.

'I was livid,' Richardson retorted, 'and I turned to him and said, "Doug, don't you fucking patronise me!" I must have said it loudly, because the whole room went quiet, and Ellis went white. He didn't say a word for the rest of the time, just went over to a corner and sat there, looking furious.'

The anecdote located an essential difference between amateur and professional sport, and recalled Gordon's similar use of the word 'patronise' with regard to Howard Kendall, which had puzzled me at the time. The point is that Strachan and Kendall, like Richardson and Ellis, are not colleagues: they do not offer each other advice and encouragement, at least not when things are tough. They keep a respectful distance.

My sympathy in the matter, I must admit, lay a little bit with Ellis. Presumably his intention, however crudely expressed, was to be encouraging, but perhaps it isn't part of the remit of the chairman of one football club to encourage another? I was relaxed enough to ask, and Richardson's answer was revealing.

'Not just after the whistle has blown. That's a bad time. It was wrong to say what he said when he said it, and I think he knew what he was doing. I usually know when a person is being sincere. You're feeling rotten: we've just lost a couple of vital points, and you don't want to hear that sort of thing . . . A day or two later, though, I did send Doug a handwritten note, not exactly apologising, but trying to explain this.'

As the story ended, a waiter entered with a good-sized humidor offering cigars. Richardson picked one out, ruefully noting that it was his second of the week; a moment later, having perused the choice of Havanas – Montecristos, Bolivars and Cohibas – I picked one too, cheerfully announcing that it was my twelfth. Lighting up, we departed for the bar, which was still, some time past midnight, open and busy. I settled down for a chat with stadium architect Geoff Mann.

'I've done some big projects,' he said, 'bigger than this, but this is my favourite.' The stadium, of futuristic design with a retractable roof and pitch, and a planned capacity of 45,000, has received a lot of favourable publicity. Indeed, João Havelange, the president of FIFA, had recently said that the building of the new stadium at Coventry was one reason that England might be given the World Cup in 2006.

'It's a very Richardson thing to do,' I said. 'He always says, "We're having a punt."'

'Having a punt doesn't begin to describe it,' said Geoff. 'What it is is an act of faith. And he'll pull it off. It's the best thing to happen to Coventry since the new cathedral was built.'

As we talked, Richardson, sitting across the bar, stood up, and with a cry of 'Motty!' rose to greet a smallish, dapper man who had just entered the room. They embraced warmly, and came over to join us. As they talked, the stranger's voice, as recognisable as Muhammad Ali's, struck me immediately. Fancy him having a body as well. 'Rick,' said Bryan, 'meet John Motson. You must tell him about your book.' Motson listened to my story attentively, and said, 'It's a great club to do a book about. You know,' he added, looking at Richardson as he spoke, 'I deal with all of the Premiership managers all the time. They're all right, all of them. But the best, in terms of returning calls and being straight with you, is Gordon Strachan. He's been superb.'

Coventry fans historically have no particular animus against Everton, save that which the poor often hold towards the rich, but I've never much liked them. They were late in beginning to sign black players, and they still don't seem to have many, and, a bit like Spurs, they often give the impression that they have some sort of divine right to success. But my major reason for wanting them to be relegated was that, if Everton went down, Coventry would become the third longest-serving member of the top flight after Arsenal and Liverpool. Further, if Everton went down, Bolton would stay up, which made at least one team I was confident we could finish ahead of the next year. You don't give up a training in dread so easily. But as we approached Goodison, watching gangs of wan Everton supporters, hanging round the ground silently, their faces creased with anxiety, it was impossible not to feel sympathy. I remembered the feeling too well.

We had got a ride down to the ground with Gary McAllister, who had just returned from South America, where he'd been helping with the English television commentary for a Brazil–Argentina fixture. 'It's easy,' he said. 'They ask you what you think, and you tell them.' He had been astonished, though, by the sheer volume of the Maracana Stadium (which holds 130,000) and the way in which it rocked on its foundations when the fans were cheering and stomping their feet. 'You'd be sitting there, and the whole stadium was moving. You could feel the concrete swaying.'

As we pulled into the directors' car park, the attendant leaned towards McAllister, and asked, in a plaintive voice, 'Tell your lads to go easy, would you, Gary?' He meant it. Reflecting that it was a funny world in which Evertonians begged for mercy from Coventrians, and an agreeable one, Bertie and I headed off to find our seats, Gordon having predictably decided against having me in the dugout.

Before the match, the usual hostilities prevailed. The Coventry fans chanted: 'Going down! Going down! Going down!', and the Everton fans foolishly responded with, 'Who the fucking hell are you?', which only prompted the inevitable answer: 'We are Premier League! Yes, we are Premier League!' Reflecting that, in a couple of hours they might well not be, the Evertonians subsided and, clutching their transistor radios (in order to follow the Bolton match at Chelsea), glumly waited for the game to begin.

They gave their side fabulous support, though. I'd never heard sound like it. Magnus Hedman, from the Coventry goal, was mightily impressed. 'You couldn't hear a word out there,' he reported afterwards. 'Couldn't hear yourself think.' Huckerby, who was carrying an injury throughout, didn't seem to care, though. 'Noisy?' he said. 'I guess so.' Maybe strikers run about such a lot that they don't realise they are in the middle of a cauldron of screaming people, or perhaps Huck simply never noticed.

Everton sat back protecting an early goal, and the loudest cheer came during the second half, when Chelsea went 1–0 up against Bolton. 'Vialli! Vialli!' screamed the crowd in delight, their anxieties assuaged until, late in the game, Everton missed a penalty, and then Dublin scored with a header to make it 1–1. It was his eighteenth Premiership goal of the season, which was to tie him for the Golden Boot Award with Chris Sutton and Michael Owen. If Coventry were to score again, or Bolton to equalise, Everton would be relegated. The Everton fans sat mute, heads in hands, until, after four minutes of extra time, the referee's whistle signalled the start of a massive pitch invasion of delirious supporters. Most of us in the Coventry end stayed to applaud them, and a phalanx of blue-shirted Evertonians stood in front of the Coventry stand, applauding back.

'We are Premier League!' they sang; 'We are Premier League!' we answered. 'Blue Army!' they chanted; 'Blue Army!' we responded. 'We want Johnson out!' they screamed; 'We want Johnson out!' we echoed, many of us unsure who this Johnson fellow was, but if our Evertonian pals wanted him out, then we wanted him out as well.

It isn't often that football supporters experience this kind of fellowship, and it was a perfect end to the season. Better, almost, than if we had won, and finished higher up the table, but been obliged to watch the despair of a bunch of people who were, after all, like ourselves. That the Bolton supporters would be mourning their loss of status a couple of hundred miles south was more tolerable: misery is always easier to accept when you don't have to see it. Anyway, they were a northern B-town. Certainly Gordon, with whom I had a quick word shortly afterwards, looked happy enough with the result. He declined, though, to go to the customary post-match press conference. 'It's Howard's day,' he said quietly. 'Let's leave him to it.'

A couple of days later I dropped in to see him at his house – my first visit there since the beginning of the season. Relaxed and, for him, expansive, he felt that it had been a pretty reasonable year. 'After all,' he said, 'only Arsenal, Man United and Liverpool lost fewer games than us, and if we hadn't drawn so many when we were ahead, we'd have qualified for Europe. And we had a couple of decent Cup runs. But what really pleased me is that everyone in the squad improved this year. I can't think of anyone who hasn't.'

For the first time, too, he had the time and emotional space to ask how the book was going, and whether I'd enjoyed the experience. I tried to explain, a little, how difficult it had been to break the ice with many of the players. 'Of course,' he said. 'I warned you about that. And I had to keep a certain distance, too. I hate those sort of managers – the celebrity managers – who are always on the telly. In private I can be unpleasant sometimes, or morbid, depressed, maybe funny, but it's between ourselves. Doesn't have anything to do with anyone else.

'The other factor was you. You forget we've never met anybody like you before. You're not only a large person, but a very big personality, and sometimes at dinner you'd talk so forcefully and intelligently about things, and have so many opinions, that we all felt a little intimidated. So if you thought we were being rude, or silent, perhaps you should have talked to me about it, and I could have told you the reason.'

I was distinctly surprised to hear this, though it must have some truth in it. Bertie, after all, says the same sort of thing about me. But in my memory of those dinners I hardly said a word, much less a torrent of them. My first experience of a meal with the team, at Torquay, had been one in which I had been nervously inarticulate and largely silent amid the general silence. Nor, in my memory at least, was I much more forthcoming in later dining-room encounters. I suppose I should be pleased, in retrospect, that the intimidation operated in both directions – that I had an effect on them as well as them on me – but I'm not. It should have been sorted out. But my relations with Gordon early in the season weren't such that the topic was likely to have come up.

However, things were easier now, and I felt I could talk with him more frankly. I wanted to ask him about his future. Gordon had been linked, during the season, with various managerial vacancies or possibilities: at Benfica, early in the season, and later with the job at Liverpool. There was talk that he might become Alex Ferguson's successor at Old Trafford, but that sounded unlikely. In fact, the strongest interest in him, which was never made public, had been from Celtic. But did he anticipate, I wondered, seeing out the new five-and-a-half-year contract that he had recently signed?

Gordon has a history of staying five or six years at clubs, and hadn't given any indication of unhappiness at Coventry. But, these days, you don't have to be unhappy to contemplate a change. Graham Hover told me, at the start of the season, that though the club was fully committed to Strachan – 'We'd keep him even if we go down this year' – in the normal course of things managers 'rarely last more than two or three years'. But even in the short time he had been in charge at Highfield

Road, Gordon had come, somehow, to exemplify the spirit of the club: it was now incontrovertibly Strachan's team. He had imprinted himself upon it, the players almost without exception admired and responded to him and the crowd adored him. Surely the good work had only just begun?

But he's a realist. 'Only two managers in the Premiership,' he said quietly, 'have stayed that long: Ferguson and Kinnear. It would be a minor miracle if I stayed on. Things can change so quickly in football: Bryan could leave, there could be a flotation and a change at boardroom level, like at Newcastle, and all of a sudden the situation is completely different. But while I'm here,' he added, 'all I want to do is for us to keep improving. We'll need to sign a couple of new players, and if we can get a good start next year I hope we can finish in the top eight.'

In 1998–9 he would have a whole new set of problems, particularly up front, though to my surprise he was still hopeful that Dion would stay. 'After all,' he said, 'there's nobody in for him at the moment, and I think we'll do some sort of a deal.' If we were to lose Dion, he believed, we might well need to make another signing (both he and the chairman had an interest in Chelsea's Tore André Flo), though he would consider playing Noel Whelan up front. The option of playing him with Moldovan, however, and moving Huckerby to right wing (where he has played in the past), had no appeal: 'We've spent all season teaching him to play up front. I don't want to start teaching him a whole new position.'

Moldovan, who missed the Everton game because he was training with the Romanian World Cup squad, was himself becoming increasingly problematic. He had been quoted a couple of days before in a Bucharest newspaper expressing dissatisfaction with his experience at Coventry. 'My team-mates,' he remarked, 'are very happy when they see me as a substitute. At one training session when Gordon Strachan announced the squad, Darren

Huckerby was looking at me like I'd just killed his mother. The British style of play is very different from on the continent. Strachan is a typical British manager who doesn't like the skill, the fantasies. Kick and run is their way.'

I wouldn't have been very happy, in Gordon's place, to hear this, but he was remarkably unfazed. 'I got a fax from Viorel the next day,' he told me, 'and he says that he didn't even talk to that journalist, and that the story was completely untrue. In fact, he thanked me for a good season, and said he's looking forward to next year.'

I put it to Richardson, later that day, that nonetheless the story had a ring of truth about it. What journalist would make up a story about Huck glaring at Viorel up at Ryton? Surely this would tax even the most developed Romanian powers of invention? 'Who gives a fuck?' said Richardson. 'What's the difference? In fact, I can tell you when it happened. It was just before the Tottenham game, and Gordon decided to leave Huck out because he wanted to teach him a little lesson. He didn't want him to think he was some sort of celebrity striker.' (The term 'celebrity' raises Gordon's hackles: he had used it disparagingly about David Elleray after the Derby game, and again earlier that afternoon about certain other managers. For him it describes people who are more interested in their image than in their work.)

I relayed Gordon's comment that it would be 'a minor miracle' if he saw out his contract, and thought I saw a flicker of unease cross Richardson's face. 'I think,' he said carefully, 'that it will depend on a number of factors. And one of them is whether I'm still here – I think Gordon feels comfortable working with someone who was a sportsman himself, and we have a good working relationship. Very honest. I always make it perfectly clear to him what our situation is, what money is going to be available. I think he respects that.' As he had no intention of leaving Coventry, Richardson was hopeful that Gordon would see us into the new stadium, which is due to open in July 2001.

That Strachan has led the club in the right direction,

he had no doubt. 'He's done a superb job,' he said, 'and I've just rewritten his contract – he didn't ask me to – to include a very substantial bonus if he stays another four years.' He said the words 'Very Substantial Bonus' in a Winnie the Pooh-ish kind of way, with Extra Emphasis, which suggested that archetypal figure that has seven digits in it, though he wouldn't say so. We have clearly moved into the age of celebrity managers, and Gordon, whether he likes it or not, is one of them. They get big salaries now, commensurate with those of the best players. George Graham's contract with Leeds, for instance, pegs his salary on a par with that of their highest-paid player.

'But Gordon,' Richardson conceded, 'has no real interest in money. It isn't what motivates him, and he has simple tastes. He and the family are flying out to Arizona next month and I've seen the tickets. They're flying economy class. He doesn't like the children to get spoiled.'

Though the season had just ended, Richardson had been busy, once again, trying to get Dion Dublin to sign a new contract. He agreed when I observed that Dion's importance to the team exceeded even his abilities as a player, and said that he felt that he might have an answer to a problem that had, so far, proved intractable. 'I think,' he said, 'that what we should do is put a longer-term deal on the table: maybe five or six years. Then Dion could play, say, two or three more years up front, and then move to the back. Central defenders, if they've got the legs, can go on for a long time: think of Steve Bruce or Steve Bould. If we can get him to sign, it would send a message to the city that we're really serious – and it helps me that he's the last in the queue to sign a new contract. If he were first it might be more difficult. Anyway, I think most of the players accept that Dion is a special case, and that he should get special treatment.'

A couple of further signings, he thought, would also have to be made: Zenden was still a possibility, though no decision would be forthcoming until after the World Cup.

(He was increasingly being compared, in Holland, to Marc Overmars.) We needed cover, too, Richardson believed, at both left and right back, though he felt that Nilsson had been our player of the season: 'He's been superb. He sees danger so quickly that he can react before it happens. I think he has another couple of years in him, but we need specialist cover.'

His goal, like Gordon's, was simple. 'We want to keep improving. I want another ten to fifteen per cent next year. It doesn't happen in a day. But I want us to believe that we are a good side. I'd love us to be arrogant, and believe that we can beat anybody. I'd love it.'

The Coventry season ends with a club golf day, held this year at my home course, the Warwickshire. Bertie, Guy and I had entered a team and had asked for – and been given – Gary McAllister as our celebrity (if you will pardon the term) partner. Almost all the players turned out, except Dion and George, who had already left on holiday, and Gary Breen, who is notoriously reluctant to attend such functions, though not all of them actually played. Huck and Willo got themselves a motorised cart and had fun zipping about the course as if they were playing dodgems, visiting the various foursomes. When they got to us, Bertie hit his best drive of the day. 'Fuckin' show-off,' said Huck. Bertie smiled modestly.

McAllister is not only a superb golfer (he played off plus 1 at sixteen) but turned out to be a remarkably congenial and interesting partner. Now that the season had ended, he was more relaxed, and consequently revealed more of himself. We talked a little about football, and a lot about other topics. He was surprised to hear that Coventry had spent some time, earlier in the season, trying to sign Monaco's Trezeguet together (possibly) with McAllister's Scottish team-mate John Collins. 'First I've heard about it,' he said, 'but then again, you know a lot more about it than I do.'

I was gratified to think so. But why, I wonder, didn't he know about it? It seemed odd that Richardson had told me, but not him. Gary McAllister is a diligent student of the game, a seasoned international, and will one day make a good manager. He knows John Collins very well, and has played with him a lot. But neither Richardson nor Strachan had talked to him about the possible transfer. This was, presumably, a direct result of that strict hierarchy in which everyone's roles are kept separate. So players are rarely consulted about possible deals, even though they are often knowledgeable, and have the only available on-pitch experience of other players, at least of Premiership ones. It seems curious management practice not to utilise their input.

Though he had previously described himself to me as 'knowing nothing about anything besides football', McAllister and I spent most of our time talking about travelling, food and wine. He has a substantial wine cellar, and seemed to know a lot about Burgundy. 'You'll have to come up to the house' (a fifteenth-century nunnery in Loughborough, with Georgian additions, set in fifteen pheasant-stocked acres) 'and drink some wine with me,' he suggested.

This may or may not happen, just as David Burrows' invitation to come up to his club for some golf over the summer, or Paul Williams' desire to get together for a meal, may or may not eventually pan out. But in a way it doesn't matter, because it was the offers themselves that were important. The players were telling me, in their various ways, that I was accepted now. Still, I suppose, an outsider, but their outsider. I couldn't have hoped for more.

Just before dinner, Huckerby loped over for a close-quarters whiff of my cigar. 'That's the greatest smell in the world,' he said, sniffing greedily, his head almost resting on my shoulder. 'I love that.'

'Huck,' I said, 'I haven't said anything like this to any of the guys, but I did want to say something to you.' He inclined his head with interest. 'I just wanted to say that watching you play football is thrilling, and that it has been one of the major pleasures of my year.'

He smiled modestly. 'You don't have to say that.'

'I know I don't, but I just wanted to thank you.'

'Thanks a lot,' he said, as he began to move away towards the dining room. After he'd taken a couple of steps, he turned back, looked around to see if anyone was listening, and said: 'Will you put that in the book?'

'Sure, Huck, you bet I will.'

After dinner, before the cabaret acts came on, there was an auction of various donated bits and pieces in aid of a children's charity. Seated at the table next to ours, the Company, fuelled by a few drinks, were in good and generous spirits. Noel Whelan bought two tickets to Silverstone for £550, with Huckerby the underbidder. Huck was having a great time, and bid for everything, though cannily enough in such a way that he didn't actually end up buying anything. But, lifting his finger in the air – at last, a useful gesture – he bid for a signed Coventry shirt, and then a Manchester United one. If the auctioneer, comedian Roger de Courcey, had offered a year's supply of tampons, Huck would have had a go.

It was no surprise, then, when he opened the bidding on a signed picture of the England and Australia cricket teams for the 1997 Ashes series. He was thinking of dropping out at about £200, when I heard Telfer lean over to him and say, 'Let's buy it for Oggy.' (Oggy used to open the bowling for Shropshire.) Whelan, Willo and Shawsy nodded their agreement, and raised their hands, so that, for a moment, they were hiking up the price by bidding against each other. Eventually they decided to let Huck keep his finger up, and the picture was knocked down to him at £450. When it was brought over to them a few moments later, Huckerby gestured towards Oggy, who was sitting at the next table, unaware of what was going on, chatting amiably with a couple of supporters, and said 'Give it to him.'

The picture was duly presented to the surprised Ogrizovic. A round of applause, led, I noticed, by Bryan Richardson, rang through the room. 'That's the nicest thing, the *nicest* thing,' said Oggy, with tears in his eyes. The five donors bounded over like inebriated puppies, and hugged him in a little scrum of fellow feeling. As I watched with pleasure from the next table, Huckerby caught my eye and gave a little smile.

When the function ended, an hour later, Oggy had a quick word with Bryan Richardson. 'That was,' he said to the chairman, 'the nicest thing that's ever happened to me in football. As soon as I get home I'm going to hang it on the wall right away.'

Richardson observed that, given Oggy's state of merriment, it would end up crooked. 'Maybe you ought to wait till the morning,' he advised.

'You're right,' said Oggy, 'I'll do that.'

The Final Table

	Total				Goals		Home				Goals		Away				Goals		
	P	W	D	L	F	A	P	W	D	L	F	A	P	W	D	L	F	A	Pts
1 Arsenal	38	23	9	6	68	33	19	15	2	2	43	10	19	8	7	4	25	23	78
2 Manchester United	38	23	8	7	73	26	19	13	4	2	42	9	19	10	4	5	31	17	77
3 Liverpool	38	18	11	9	68	42	19	13	2	4	42	16	19	5	9	5	26	26	65
4 Chelsea	38	20	3	15	71	43	19	13	2	4	37	14	19	7	1	11	34	29	63
5 Leeds	38	17	8	13	57	46	19	9	5	5	31	21	19	8	3	8	26	25	59
6 Blackburn	38	16	10	12	57	52	19	11	4	4	40	26	19	5	6	8	17	26	58
7 Aston Villa	38	17	6	15	49	48	19	9	3	7	26	24	19	8	3	8	23	24	57
8 West Ham	38	16	8	14	56	57	19	13	4	2	40	18	19	3	4	12	16	39	56
9 Derby	38	16	7	15	52	49	19	12	3	4	33	18	19	4	4	11	19	31	55
10 Leicester	38	13	14	11	51	41	19	6	10	3	21	15	19	7	4	8	30	26	53
11 Coventry	38	12	16	10	46	44	19	8	9	2	26	17	19	4	7	8	20	27	52
12 Southampton	38	14	6	18	50	55	19	10	1	8	28	23	19	4	5	10	22	32	48
13 Newcastle	38	11	11	16	35	44	19	8	5	6	22	20	19	3	6	10	13	24	44
14 Tottenham Hotspur	38	11	11	16	44	56	19	7	8	4	23	22	19	4	3	12	21	34	44
15 Wimbledon	38	10	14	14	34	46	19	5	6	8	18	25	19	5	8	6	16	21	44
16 Sheffield Weds	38	12	8	18	52	67	19	9	5	5	30	26	19	3	3	13	22	41	44
17 Everton	38	9	13	16	41	56	19	7	5	7	25	27	19	2	8	9	16	29	40
18 Bolton	38	9	13	16	41	61	19	7	8	4	25	22	19	2	5	12	16	39	40
19 Barnsley	38	10	5	23	37	82	19	7	4	8	25	35	19	3	1	15	12	47	35
20 Crystal Palace	38	8	9	21	37	71	19	2	5	12	15	39	19	6	4	9	22	32	33

Warner Books now offers an exciting range of quality titles by both established and new authors. All of the books in this series are available from:

Little, Brown and Company (UK),
P.O. Box 11,
Falmouth,
Cornwall TR10 9EN.

Fax No: 01326 317444.
Telephone No: 01326 372400
E-mail: books@barni.avel.co.uk

Payments can be made as follows: cheque, postal order (payable to Little, Brown and Company) or by credit cards, Visa/Access. Do not send cash or currency. UK customers and B.F.P.O. please allow £1.00 for postage and packing for the first book, plus 50p for the second book, plus 30p for each additional book up to a maximum charge of £3.00 (7 books plus).

Overseas customers including Ireland, please allow £2.00 for the first book plus £1.00 for the second book, plus 50p for each additional book.

NAME (Block Letters) ....

....

ADDRESS ....

....

....

☐ I enclose my remittance for ....

☐ I wish to pay by Access/Visa Card

Number ⬚⬚⬚⬚⬚⬚⬚⬚⬚⬚⬚⬚⬚⬚⬚⬚

Card Expiry Date ⬚⬚⬚⬚